IN SEARCH OF TRUTH AND HONOR

Reflections of an undercover Journey through the dark side of the badge

⟡

Joanne Takasato

introduction by Stephen R. Band, PhD

CONTENTS

FOREWORD

I would like to light a match
To start a fire that would set the world on fire
In realizations of Truth, Love, and Honor
This is an old world, but oh so immature
That man should still be so blind to Apathy, Prejudice, and Hate
If words can kill, then let my pen be my sword
Against all these unnecessary conditions
Let me begin to write of TRUTH.

Journal entry: 1970

In 1980, my journey into the world of narcotics trafficking as the first female Narcotics undercover police officer began, without any training, guidelines, or rules of conduct. I was literally plucked out of the comfortable routine of my life and dropped off on a dark street corner in an unfamiliar world with no badge, no gun, and no identification.

In order to accomplish the assignment, I became everything I did not want to be and lived a lifestyle contrary to the commandments of truth and honor. I was forced to sever all familial ties and friendships and then figure out how to create a new identity and lifestyle that would grant me acceptance and keep me undetected as an undercover officer. New friendships were sanctioned only for the purpose of betraying them with arrest and prosecution.

My undercover assignment eventually led me to investigations against those officers who dishonored their oath to protect and serve and misused their authority for personal profit, power, or recognition at the expense and efforts of others. I began to distrust cops before I learned to be one and learned the difficult lessons of truth and honor, loyalty and betrayal.

During my passage into purgatory, my journal was my only friend and confidant. I had hoped that someday it might help me understand what had happened to me by documenting my transitions. But the changes would be more than superficial, and the internal conflict between my new identity and my former self would almost destroy me. Everything in the life I knew would come to an end, except my spiritual faith.

My experiences are summarized in the journal entries.

PREFACE

In 1975, gender discrimination barring women from entering the Honolulu Police Department as sworn police officers had finally been destroyed. Doors were opened for the first time, allowing females to enter what was previously considered a career exclusively for men.

By 1979, the minimum height requirement of five foot eight had been eliminated. Many voiced doubts of whether women's rights had gone too far. The belief that police officers had to be tall, strong, powerful men in order to overcome and arrest the criminal element of society was still the opinion of the majority. It was outrageous that a five foot Asian female weighing only one hundred and five pounds would even consider doing what a "real" policeman could do. But I took the police entrance exam in spite of the ridicule.

Many male police officers verbalized their offense at the intrusion of unwanted females into their profession. Facilities for females had to be made, and the men were forced to give up more than just their locker room space to accommodate the women. All badges and badge numbers, a means of personal identification that carried sentimental attachments much like a name, were forfeited. New badge numbers and badges were reissued to say "Police Officer" instead of "Policeman."

Change was on the horizon, and for the men it came with the bitter knowledge that they had no voice or choice in the matter. The very foundation of the way things had always been for decades was now slowly crumbling. The realization that things would never be the same was met with defiance and resistance, but civil rights and gender equality were, after all, the law.

In 1980, during this time of evolution and uncertainty, I became the first female undercover Narcotics police officer in the Honolulu Police Department.

There were those who saw the main theme of this story being my difficulties as an Asian female. I did not. Although being an Asian female often played a part in how I was judged, I believe the true reason for my difficulty was the choice I made to place honor above loyalty.

I did not write this book to be judged a hero or to be an advocate for Asian females or women's rights. Perhaps it's because I grew up in Hawaii where it is true that we are a melting pot of blended ethnicities, ancestries, and cultures. Most of us who grew up in this state have already learned to see beyond the façade of the color of one's hair, skin, and eyes, which are too often not a reliable way to identify the true roots of one's origins. Many of us have already learned that a better way to identify a person is by the truth in their heart and the honor of their conduct.

This work chronicles my search to find the essence of truth and honor during my undercover assignment in the field of justice. I kept a journal to document my difficulties and turmoil in hopes I would one day understand what had happened to me and then maybe help myself and other undercover officers to survive and overcome the extreme distress and alienation of the assignment. And that is truly what this story is about.

All the names in this book have been changed, except those recognized in the epilogue.

⚭

ACKNOWLEDGMENTS

The writing of this book began thirty years ago. I am not an author or a poet and after much difficulty and disappointment, I finally found the right persons and path to help me complete my task to thank those who taught me the meaning of truth and honor.

There was no one more qualified to introduce this book than Dr. Stephen R. Band, not because he has a PhD. in psychology but because of his in-depth insight and understanding of undercover stressors and his personal experience as a law officer.

Dr. Band entered on duty as a Special Agent of the FBI December 1983. His twenty-two-year career with the Bureau focused on counterintelligence, counterterrorism, and undercover and behavioral science operations. "'Doc Band'" is credited with developing the FBI's Undercover (UC) Safeguard Unit, a program that has been modeled nationally and internationally for selecting, assessing, and monitoring the readiness and wellness of undercover operatives. During his last seven years in the FBI, he served as Chief of the Bureau's 'famous' Behavioral Science Unit and has appeared and been portrayed on television in this capacity. 'Steve' retired from the FBI in 2005. He is presently an executive consultant serving the U.S. Intelligence Community; and, Federal, State, and Local Law Enforcement Agencies. 'Doc Band' presently owns and operates Behavioral Intelligence Specialists, LLC, a company positioned to perform applied behavioral science training, research, and consultative services. 'Steve' is a graduate of the New Jersey State Police Academy, - 140th municipal class, and served his local community a Police Officer during the seventies. He earned his PhD at Fordham University, New York City, in counseling psychology, and was a post-doctoral Fellow of forensic psychology at Indiana University -School of Medicine. 'Steve' is a Fellow of the American Psychological Association; former faculty member, University of Virginia at the FBI Academy,- National Academy, Quantico, Virginia; and, author of articles, analytical reports, and book chapters reflecting his professional expertise. For his continuous guidance, contributions and support of my efforts to finish this project I am deeply honored and grateful.

To my parents, who always stood by me and allowed me to do what I felt compelled to do in spite of their fears; and to my daughter who gave purpose to my life and who stayed up around the clock to work on the aged photos I had collected for the photo gallery, I dedicate this book with eternal love and gratitude.

To the exemplary law officers mentioned and also those not mentioned, who helped me survive throughout my years of service, I acknowledge my deepest appreciation for their inspiration, support and friendship.

My heartfelt thanks and appreciation to BookSurge Publishing Company, for their excellent editorial services, outstanding assistance and guidance through each phase of preparation for this publication, and for providing the means to fulfill my promise to validate the courage and sacrifices of the intrepid undercover officers all over the world who continue a battle against unrelenting odds.

⚜

INTRODUCTION

It was a day like any other in the history of the FBI when a letter arrived on the Chief's desk at the Behavioral Science Unit (BSU) in Quantico, Virginia. My desk. But I'm getting ahead of myself.

Detective Joanne "Jo Jo" Takasato's story is a journey of extreme courage, undercover survival, and honor. It's a story that actually begins many years ago, when law enforcement was less informed of the grave risks and danger associated with the undercover (UC) investigative technique and the life-altering impact it can have on those who dare to work undercover.

As legend has it, J. Edgar Hoover was not a proponent of undercover operations. It's certainly true that before his death in 1972, the Bureau did not engage in the widespread use of this complex investigative technique. Perhaps Director Hoover had a premonition that UC work would cause embarrassment to his beloved Bureau and the agents who would fall prey to its stress. Nonetheless, police agencies began to use the technique, with varying degrees of success. Common applications in the early days of the seventies included vice decoy operations and police-run pawnshops that caught unsuspecting burglars. Short- and long-term counter drug operations evolved over time, and more sophisticated operations emerged against organized crime targets, including biker gangs and domestic terrorists. The selection and training of undercover officers was primitive at best. In most instances, those selected and operating in undercover assignments were at risk of grave personal and professional consequences—some more horrific than others.

An Important Frame of Reference

UC work is truly a sacred trust between law enforcement and the citizens of a free and democratic society. When the police pretend to be something they are not, in extremely hostile environments, unimaginably horrible things can happen. I know this from firsthand experience. To this day, some countries' laws prohibit their police from assuming undercover identities. Perhaps they fear a return of the secret police, who abused the sacred trust bestowed on them. Imagine the terrible consequences if those who supervise undercover employees (UCE) betray them. Detective Takasato didn't have to imagine this—she lived it.

Undercover operations (UCO) by definition are about developing relationships and lawfully betraying them: through a ruse, being at the right place and time to observe and interact with people while they break the law—something bad guys are going to do anyway, whether law enforcement is discreetly in their presence or not (the no entrapment zone). History has proved that some officers, deputies, and agents survive this well and some don't.

Truth or Consequences?

During the mid- to late seventies, a series of tragedies rocked the FBI; by "tragedies" I mean very uncharacteristic behaviors on the part of some agents who worked undercover—for example, unlawful activities, inappropriate relations with targets, and extreme personal stress. As if J. Edgar Hoover's ghost were saying, "I told you so," there almost seemed to be a cause-and-effect relationship between working undercover and going to the "dark side." Episodes of criminal activity, illicit drug use, and inappropriate relationships with criminals emerged from living the life undercover. And then there was a violation of the sixty-minute rule: never get on the TV show *60 Minutes*.

A Turning Point

A *60 Minutes* segment aired the following story: An FBI agent appears to be doing well in a deep cover investigation against organized crime figures. The operation winds down:; bad guys are indicted:, bad guys go to jail. After the operation, the agent is transferred to another FBI field office, and ends up in a department store one day. As he leaves, store security officers stop him, because there, tucked in his bag, are items he did not pay for. The agent is arrested for shoplifting, and he has a problem with being honest about the theft. Because of his inability to act truthfully, his previous testimony against organized crime targets becomes suspect. The bad guys are released from jail, and the agent is fired. The segment ended ambiguously: "The FBI 'sucks' for shooting it's wounded ... but did they?" It was left for the viewing audience to decide.

This happened when Judge William Webster was director of the FBI. It's easy to imagine that some in the Bureau were thinking, "Was Hoover right about avoiding UC operations?" Well, I'm here to tell you, though there were a number of unpleasant consequences to this publicity, the baby was not thrown out with the bath water.

At the time of this incident, a BSU Supervisory Special Agent (SSA), Howard "Bud" Teten—also known as the FBI's father of profiling serial killers—had already begun to investigate what happens to the FBI agent in UCOs. SSA Teten's benchmark research established the foundation for a program that would safeguard the wellness and readiness of UCEs, nationally and internationally, over the next quarter century.

On a day like any other in the history of the FBI, the phone rang at the desk of a duty agent at the New York office—my desk. It was SSA John Vasquez, who envisioned and initiated a new FBI program, based in part on SSA Teten's research that would begin 'safeguarding' UCEs. SSA Vasquez, an action-oriented warrior of honor and dignity, was searching for a candidate to replace his former partner at Quantico, someone who would inherit and fully develop this 'safeguard' process. I had a doctoral degree in psychology and had worked undercover, and SSA Vasquez. thought I might be the right candidate for this challenge.

I was selected by an FBI Career Board, was promoted from Special Agent (SA) to SSA, and left New York City for Quantico, Virginia, in 1988. Over the next ten years, I was deeply immersed, behind the scenes, in all of the FBI's UCOs; my mission was to assess, monitor, protect, and advocate the wellness and readiness of the bravest men and women I have ever met—those who volunteered to work undercover for the FBI. My fortunate journey partnered me for a time with Joe Pistone, the famous "Donnie Brasco," who in large part was instrumental in convincing Director Louie Freeh to commit the substantial personnel and funding resources required to bring the undercover 'safeguard' vision to life. The Director's vision statement was fully realized: "No investigation takes precedence over the wellness and readiness of personnel who work undercover." And undercover work became, by policy, strictly voluntary.

So who is capable of working undercover? Someone who is streetwise, without anxiety? Should it be a manipulative person and convincing liar? Perhaps someone with ice water in their veins? Or a psychopath, incapable of remorse about putting up a front and lying to others? Well, no—those just won't work! The most successful UCEs are those who first develop a close bond and successful working relationship with their law enforcement agency. This foundation is critical before a UCE develops any relationship with criminal targets. The Hollywood notion that recruits from a police training academy should be sent undercover because they're a new face in town is just that, a Hollywood notion. In the real world, UCEs must be experienced in their profession and have the moral, ethical, and spiritual values that enable them to operate undercover. They must not be running away from traditional assignments or volunteering based on what they've seen in the movies. The cinematic "lone wolf" undercover agent is only half the story. A successful UCE must be able to operate independently but must also be able to revert immediately to being a team player.

The Stressors

So what is so stressful about working undercover and how do modern law enforcement agencies defeat these aspects of working undercover?

Someone who is not in law enforcement might think the most stressful thing about working undercover is the risk of being revealed as a cop. While this is a grave concern, UCEs believe the *most* stressful part of operating UC is when their managers and supervisors lack commitment, support, and sensitivity to the UCE's undercover mission. This lack of commitment (a real or perceived betrayal committed purposefully or unwittingly by the UCE's supervisor) can cause UCEs to feel abandoned and betrayed by the agency and citizens they serve—alone, unsupported, and left to fend for themselves. In effect, on a high wire without a net. Other undercover stressors reported by UCEs include, in descending order:

- Maintaining the undercover role or assumed identity in a hostile environment

- Maintaining relationships with targets while anticipating their inevitable betrayal

- The lack of any break from the mental preparation and role rehearsal

- The physical and cultural distances from "home base," safe and familiar surroundings

- Preparing for prosecution

- Working with other agencies

- Distance from family and friends

- Working wired, because of the risk of discovery

- Returning to traditional, overt professional assignments

The symptoms and responses associated with these specific stressors have ranged from minor emotional and/or physical discomfort to suicide.

In February of 1999, I had the privilege of coauthoring an article for the FBI's *Law Enforcement Bulletin* (LEB) called "Managing Undercover Stress: The Supervisor's Role." This article revisited the stress associated with undercover assignments and offered strategies to defeat the identified complex and stressful issues. I won't belabor this introduction by revisiting this article word for word (available to the interested reader at http://www.fbi.gov/publications/leb/1999/feb99leb.pdf), but it is important because of the impact it had on Detective Takasato's lonely and courageous undercover journey—in effect, it caused our paths to cross.

Past as Prologue

Recently the FBI turned one hundred years old. More than a quarter of that century was given to the hard work of understanding the human dynamics associated with undercover work and figuring out the best methods for sustaining a human life in that hostile environment. To be deployed undercover without a caring infrastructure is extremely dangerous. To be deployed undercover and betrayed on all sides can be deadly. Going undercover, losing and finding oneself in the process, is the incredible journey you are about to take with Detective Takasato. Alone on a high wire without a net is very alone indeed. This was her life. Her nightmarish journey, guided only by her own sense of honor and duty, could not lead to inner peace until she knew that net would be there for others. Yes, undercover work is a sacred trust between those who dare to operate in this arena and the citizens they serve. Detective Takasato reminds us that this trust begins with those who supervise and lead UCEs in this endeavor.

And so … it was a day like any other in the history of the FBI when Detective Takasato's life crossed paths with mine. Her letter arrived at the FBI's Behavioral Science Unit, dated April 2001.

Dear Sirs,

I first read your article, "Managing Undercover Stress," in 1999 and broke into a silent sob for about an hour. I was so hurt that I felt empty for a few days following.

I pondered then about sending you the enclosed materials, but the overwhelming hurt and emptiness I felt kept me from doing so. My emotions were again trying to slip through, and I did not wish to deal with them.

I also felt that I would be betraying a "code of silence," or opening up my own wounds and scars. I put your article away with my "writings."

Today, 4-13-01, I found your article again. I am sitting here at my computer in an empty state after I swallowed back the hurt, the silent tears, and the anger.

In 1980, I was the first female undercover Narcotics officer in the Honolulu Police Department. I kept a journal because I felt my "self" dying and felt the journal would help me to find my way back "home" if I could document my own changes and experiences.

If you look into what has happened to me throughout my career, you will find incredible support for your work.

I have always hoped that my "writings" would someday be used to help others ... I truly hope that my decision to open my files will not cause you to label me as "affected," "crazy," or "mentally defective" as I have been labeled before. I am now a Detective in Narcotics Vice and have managed to survive on my own for twenty-one years. I was afraid that when I sent these materials, I would again be hurt by their contents. I don't talk to anyone about my UC difficulties or my personal feelings.

I am trusting you with very private pages of my undercover life because I truly believe in what you're doing. I hope maybe you can truly understand the pain and loneliness without the negative judgments.

I'm still very alone.

Respectfully submitted,

Joanne Takasato, 4-13-01

The letter moved me to tears; I could literally feel her painful burden. I shared this letter with my brother FBI agent, heroic Steven E. Rayfield, who at that time and by good fortune was in residence and working at Quantico. He too was moved; he too knew Detective Takasato's pain very well. We reached the same conclusion instantly. Detective Takasato had to be brought in from the cold immediately; we were, by luck or fate, positioned to do this. Detective Takasato had never traveled to our nation's capital before, but she was about to. The timing of a major law enforcement conference, in which her insights could be shared, could and would serve as the vehicle to bring her face-to-face with the ghosts that haunted her and the path that would eventually bring closure to her undercover journey.

We walked the great monuments at night in the shadows of Washington DC, as her true story unfolded and the healing began. Join Detective Takasato now on this walk through the shadows—and back to Hawaii.

❦

Chapter 1
The Journey Begins

Standing at the threshold of destiny
The time will come when all that is will become a memory
And all that will be shall come to pass in the moment . . . now

Today . . . is yesterday's . . . tomorrow
And what shall be my last journal entry?
Perhaps the answer is and always will be now
For there is really no future, except in expectancy
And no time, except in concept
I alone shape my future
But then not really, for I contend with Destiny
In the acceptance or non-acceptance
There then is the reality or illusion of fate
Change is the only constant

Journal entry: July 24, 1979

The Police Entrance Exams

It was summer in 1979, seven thirty in the morning, and the sun, hanging unobstructed by clouds in the clear blue sky, radiated blinding beams of light that bounced off the long rows of dusty glass windows. The grounds of the schoolyard were void of grass except for the sparse patches of parched green grass that still thrived in spite of the incessant trampling of feet. An occasional light breeze created tiny swirls of fine dust that disappeared as quickly as they had appeared. Lolly was the only female I saw amongst the gathering of police applicants waiting to take the Honolulu Police Department entrance exam. She was waiting for me near the swinging entry doors that led into the dull brown concrete cafeteria building of Kalakaua Intermediate School. From where I stood, I could see her looking anxiously at the huge crowd of young men of all ethnicities, shapes, and sizes.

The night before had been difficult at work, waiting tables in the popular nightclub at the hotel. My shift had ended at four thirty in the morning, just a few hours before, and the sounds of the blaring music and loud crowds were still ringing in my ears. Working nights and trying to carry too many credits at college had drained my energy, but I finally made my way through the thick crowd of males towards my best friend.

Lolly had always wanted to be a cop. She was Filipino, Spanish, and Korean in ancestry, five foot eight, and very athletic. She had an unquenchable thirst for excitement and never slowed her pace, and her heart was as big as the sun. I could see her pacing back and forth with nervous energy and excitement, waiting for my arrival.

The police department had dropped the minimum height requirement of five foot eight and opened its doors to female applicants. I was only five feet tall and weighed only one hundred and five pounds, but I promised Lolly that I would accompany her to take the police entrance exam.

I had thought about becoming a criminal prosecutor, but too many of my friends had passed the bar exam and were still working at retail stores while waiting for a break into the system. "It's who you know, not what you can do," they explained with frustration.

I was already beginning to learn about the ironies in the criminal justice system from my Criminal Law college courses. The case laws I had studied seemed to document that the suspects had more rights than the victims. The Constitution and Bill of Rights, originally created to protect the innocent, were so often interpreted, twisted, and manipulated by shrewd defense attorneys to find technicalities and loopholes so that the bad guy ended up being set free. It made no difference, it seemed, that the bad guy was guilty. The defense attorneys would often use theatrics and eloquent rhetoric to distort the facts of a case to distract those who sat in judgment from the truth. The victims and their families were often doubly injured, first by the bad guy and then by the justice system that had failed them.

I had already seen too many instances of favoritism in the "politics of justice." You could get off easy if you knew the right people. I was stubborn and idealistic to a fault and way too serious and sensitive about everything. I wondered if I could be part of a judicial system that I had already begun to doubt.

Lolly and I were unlikely best friends. Our personalities were so dissimilar. Lolly was as bright as the day, tanned, strong, always laughing, and mischievously playful, while I was small, pale, and definitely not athletic. Lolly came alive with the sun and I with the moon.

We both knew that even with great time or distance between us, we would always be there for each other. We were both Capricorns, born four days apart, and shared a fiercely independent nature. We did almost everything together, but we also knew when to give each other some privacy, and I needed my solitude like the earth needed its sun.

I had already grown distant from my other high school friends, who all talked, acted, and dressed alike. They looked forward to a college degree, marriage, and a house. But today, Lolly and I ventured together towards an uncertain future, breaking the accepted rules and stereotypical behavior expected of females by attempting to enter a career deemed suitable only for men.

Lolly gasped a sigh of relief when I finally approached her. "Wake up, wake up. I thought you weren't going to make it!" she exhaled all in one breath. She looked sympathetically at my bloodshot eyes. "Just got off work?"

I nodded and made a quick visual assessment of the crowd. "I promised I would be here, but I'm not too sure about this," I said doubtfully. Some of the huge, buff-bodied men stared at me in shock. Some laughed, and some shook their heads in disbelief at the possibility that we were there to take the test.

"I knew you wouldn't let me down!" Lolly whispered as she too glanced around at the stares of reproach and contempt.

"What is this, a joke? Go home; cook rice!" one of the alpha males yelled from the crowd. It was as if our female presence at the event had offended their manhood.

"Are we the only two females?"

"I think so," Lolly said. "I think they all hate us!"

"Yup," I agreed. "But I think they're staring at me more than at you."

Lolly spontaneously burst into a loud laugh. "Yup," she agreed, and with a twinkle of mischief in her eye, she announced loudly, "That's okay, girl, you show 'em! Bust out your gung fu and take all these guys down!"

"Lolly!" I whispered in reproach and prayed to become invisible. Some of the guys turned around to scrutinize me while others tried to puff up their chests and stood a little taller in a challenging posture. Lolly laughed with delight at the curious expressions of the men and my total embarrassment.

"Dynamite comes in small packages!" she yelled out loud and then whispered to me, "Let's get out of here!" She suddenly pulled me through the swinging doors of the cafeteria, which closed behind us.

We had escaped from the stares and glares outside only to find that we had stumbled into a room full of more guys, sitting very quietly, waiting for the written test to begin. They had all turned to see who had burst into the room. I knew they had heard the commotion outside.

"Good grief!" Lolly whispered in utter despair.

We both stood frozen at the door, realizing that the judgmental stares of disapproval from the crowd of guys outside were nothing compared to the stares of hostility from the guys already seated in the room.

"Let's sit down—quick!" Lolly whispered, and we both moved immediately—and very quietly—to the first two available seats we could find on opposite sides of the room from each other.

The tension mounted as the young men outside began to file into the stifling, overcrowded cafeteria. I watched the guys check each other out silently as they pushed their way onto the bench tables of the cafeteria. Some wore shirts that were a size too small to make their bodies look more buff. Some were dressed in coats and ties, and some had splashed on a little too much cologne. When the last man had finally found a seat, the examiner began with an announcement.

"This is the Honolulu Police Department's written entrance examination. If you do not belong here, leave now." He looked directly at me, paused, and then continued in a lackluster voice, identifying the locations of the restrooms in the area. He paused again, glanced at me and then at Lolly, and asked an assistant if the women's restroom had also been opened. The silence of the audience was broken by the sound of snickering.

The test began, and I shrugged off the doubts. I finished the test and walked out of the room without looking back. Outside, I lit a cigarette and inhaled deeply, feeling the fatigue of the previous night and the hostility of the morning. *What am I getting myself into?* I wondered, but before I could pursue the thought, Lolly exited the swinging doors and we walked silently to the parking lot.

"Think you passed?" I asked.

"Don't know," she shrugged. "How about you?"

"Don't know. I know I need some sleep."

A moment passed as we stood silently in the shade of a pink shower tree. Tiny pink and white blossoms floated around us in the occasional light breeze.

"Thanks," Lolly said very seriously.

"What for?" I asked, curious at Lolly's uncommon seriousness.

"For coming out," she said. "I know you weren't too sure about this."

"No problem. Let's just see what happens next."

A strange feeling of anticipation began to creep up my spine.

"Oh no!" Lolly said in alarm. "You got that look on your face—like something's going to happen. What's up? Tell me!"

"Don't know. It's like something really heavy is waiting in the distance, like I'm going to be tested. I feel very sad all of a sudden and I don't know why—like something's waiting for me out there but I can't pinpoint it."

"Sometimes you're spooky, girl!" Lolly said as she looked searchingly into my eyes. She was familiar with my off-the–wall moods.

"I don't know; maybe I'm just tired," I offered. I searched the horizon anyway, just in case a hurricane or something was coming our way.

"Go home and get some sleep!" Lolly scolded with a sympathetic smile. "Call me later!"

I watched as she drove off in her beige Volkswagen bug. I tried to quell the sense of deep sadness and foreboding but couldn't. I knew that I was about to begin a journey that would change my life forever and probably challenge every philosophy I believed in about truth, honor, and justice. Or I could choose to live a passive life of acceptance and live within the parameters acceptable for Asian females, who were expected to be conservative, subservient, and silent.

A female trying to become police officer was still perceived as an objectionable endeavor. I had often overheard discussions that women entering the police force were presumed to be lesbians in the male role or groupies who were attracted to policemen. When I first learned that the barriers of gender and height requirements were dissolved and deemed unconstitutional, I too had wondered if females could live up to the challenge and become successful in a law enforcement field. The only thing I was sure of was that I had to choose between a life of passive acceptance or a life of challenge and change.

Something was definitely in the wind. I could feel it approaching. Perhaps this feeling would make sense one day.

I went home and did what I had done so many times before: wrote the experience down in my journal. Sometimes the entries I wrote would have meaning years later.

Each of us has two paths from which to choose
Acceptance and passivity, or discontent and search
Either one can be a good path but it can also be destructive
When acceptance becomes apathy and discontent becomes violence

Should the rule of confrontation be force against force?
Or shall I rise above hostility and violence and turn the other cheek?
Would I be called low of standard if I meet him on his level?
Or wise and versatile?

Perhaps we must always play two roles
Be true to ourselves, but still adapt and respond
But what is the universal law of response?

Man is not created equal, yet his soul creates that equality

Journal entry: 1970

Months had gone by and still I could not calm the growing feeling of anxiety and anticipation of what lay ahead. It was as if there was something I had to do, something waiting for me, something I had to face. Once again, I found myself looking through the journal I kept, which documented my own philosophies and the lessons I had learned during my search for the meaning of truth and honor as a child. I had often forgotten what I had written and sometimes did not understand the true meaning of the lessons until they helped me deal with a difficulty I would face years later.

I had begun my journal in my elementary school years, writing down philosophies and resolutions to conflicts I had sometimes not yet faced except in dreams. But I had learned not to talk about what I wrote to friends and even a few teachers I had approached, who responded by saying, "You're different, you're weird, and you're thinking too deeply about things that no one wants to think about."

I often learned through my dreams, from teachers who first appeared when I was five years old and afraid of the dark. The unfamiliar beings spoke without speaking, but I heard their teachings and followed their guidance. They had come out of the shadows and had stayed with me for years, forcing me to face my fears and to search for the truth in all matters. Slowly, as I completed and learned the lessons each had taught me, the spiritual guides began to disappear.

No matter how hard I tried not to see them, they appeared through the years to disturb my sleep and force me to study religious teachings and philosophies about truth, honor, harmony, justice, and loyalty. In my search to discover who and what they were, those I approached said they were guardian angels or ancestral spiritual guides. A few said they were past-life memories, and some advised me that they and their teachings should be disregarded as childish dreams. But the lessons I studied under their guidance forced me to see into the heart and soul of mankind.

They were not male or female, and each being carried symbols. It was only when I gave up trying to figure out where they came from and what gender or race they were that I finally learned it didn't matter. What was important was what they each represented and the lesson they taught me.

"It's your choice" the spiritual being said unexpectedly appearing in a dream.

Who are you and why have you come back after all this time? You're just a childhood dream that disappeared a long time ago!"

"You can face what's out there and learn, or you can sit back and stay as you are."

"I feel like it's my destiny waiting for me out there. How can you say I have a choice?" I argued.

"Everything is as you choose it to be."

"Doesn't make sense," I argued again. "Are you trying to tell me that everything that happens in our lives are the result of the choices we make?"

"Yes."

"But what about sickness, injuries, or difficulties," I argued in my sleep.

"All of these things are caused by physical, emotional, or spiritual imbalance. It is how you react or respond to influences in your life. The choices each one of us makes affect everything and everyone around us, causing distress or peace in others or ourselves. We are all connected to each other."

"So what's the answer?" I demanded. "What about destiny?

"Everything is your choice, even your destiny. You can accept what I teach you or let it go. Every choice you make will have a ripple effect through time and affect everyone around you."

I felt like I was being compelled to enter the police department, but a sense of foreboding and great sadness was there, waiting in the future.

"You always have a choice. If you choose that path, you will learn, but you will be alone."

I watched the figure dressed in white ride away and disappear and then woke, disturbed and restless, to write it all down.

A letter did arrive the next day. I had passed the written entrance exams and would move to phase two of the testing, which was the physical agility test. Lolly would not be with me to continue the journey as the dream had revealed. She would instead find and choose a career with the federal government and marry her childhood sweetheart.

I turned back to my journals again, to write and to find an old lesson to help me with my decision. It would be a few years later, when I learned the true meaning of his warning that I would be alone.

Fear is the enemy of wisdom
Ignorance is the enemy of enlightenment
Attachment is the enemy of truth

I break away from expectations
And do what I am compelled to do
I follow my destiny to wherever it leads
I am lonely. But then again ... I am not

Journal entry: July 27, 1979

Mind Over Matter

> *True Strength is conjured from the mind*
> *Reality is elusive . . . it is not universal or absolute*
> *What Reality is, like beauty, is in the eyes of the beholder*
> *There is strength and energy in all things*
> *Only through humility can we perceive and then acknowledge*
> *Our co-existence with all things in the universe*
> *The mind is the key that opens the doors to all things possible*
> *And creativity is born of discontent and pain*

Journal entry: 1977

Phase two of the entrance exams was the physical agility test. It didn't matter if you were five feet tall or six feet tall or how old you were. Male or female, the obstacle course and the time constraints were the same.

I declined to participate in the agility test several times, explaining that I wasn't interested in the position anymore. Each time the date of the test had passed, I was notified again of another upcoming test date. I finally called the personnel department of the Honolulu Police Department to request that they take me off the contact list.

"You're being considered for a certain position," a female voice in charge of the recruitment schedule explained. "It's the first time that they're considering a female for the position, and that's why the department keeps sending you the notices, even if you've declined. Why don't you try it out, and if you don't like it, you can quit?" she suggested. Curious and more uncertain than ever, I agreed to perform the agility test.

On the day of the test, I sat doubtfully in my blue Toyota Corolla, watching the other applicants arrive. Keehi Lagoon Park was near the Honolulu International Airport, on the beach side of Nimitz Highway. The sun burned hot in a clear blue sky, and the grass had begun to turn white and brown in the heat. An occasional airplane flew by in the near distance. I watched their ascent to the heavens and descent to the runways of the nearby Honolulu International Airport as they flew unknown passengers to and from unknown destinations.

Some of the young men had already gathered in the testing area. I listened as they announced confidently, as they stretched and flexed, that they had been training for months and would breeze through the test. I, on the other hand, had not prepared and had not been able to eat or sleep the night before.

"Just go for it, girl," Lolly had said on the phone last night, and I had finally fallen asleep with a prayer: *"If this is what you want me to do, God, then I will follow my destiny."*

Again the young male candidates stared at me in shock, laughed, and shook their heads in disapproval when my name was called in a roll call. They didn't know until then that I was another candidate.

"No shit!" one of the males exclaimed. "I thought she was somebody's girlfriend!"

"If you fail the test, you have thirty minutes to recuperate at the site and try again. If you cannot pass the agility test today, you have to start over with the written exam," the examiner announced, interrupting the comments from the guys.

It was finally my turn, and I began running towards the first obstacle in the course looming ominously in the distance: getting over a six-foot wooden wall; running up two flights of stairs, back down one flight and back up again and jumping off; dragging a one-hundred-and-fifty-pound fire hose for a measured distance; getting over a chain-link fence; and then pushing a sled made of galvanized steel used for football training over the uneven grass.

I failed by five seconds on the first try, and the world around me began spinning. My head ached, and my stomach began to heave and belch empty air as I slumped over under the shade of a nearby tree. It was worse than the worst ever hangover!

Lolly was suddenly standing over me, rubbing my back soothingly as one of the Johnny Big Bodies strutted past us.

"This is a piece of cake!" he boasted. "*I've* been training for this. Let me show you all how it's done."

He began his run with grace and ease, smiling arrogantly as his muscled, dark-skinned legs flew through the beginning of the obstacle course. He sprinted towards the six-foot chain-link fence like a black stallion and began to sail over the top. He jumped, grabbed the ragged top of the fence with both hands, and flung one foot easily over the top. But somehow his second foot didn't follow through, and he came down hard, straddling the protruding metal links. His eyes rolled back, and he moaned and whimpered and slid slowly to the ground in a heap. He tried to focus his tearing eyes and, for a moment, glanced at me. There was no arrogance or confidence anymore, only delirious pain. All the guys gasped and moaned in empathetic pain.

"Don't you give up, girl! I know you can do it! Try again!" Lolly coached.

"I can't do this!" I moaned, hardly able to get any words out.

"Yes, you can! I know you can! Just do that thing you do and psych yourself out. Don't let these guys see you fail!" she pleaded.

Lolly glared at the guys, who were shaking their heads in disgust as they turned away. Others stared at me with doubt and pity.

The training officer approached us with sympathy. "Thirty minutes to rest and you can try again. Are you going to try again?" he asked doubtfully.

"Yes!" Lolly answered confidently for me.

If this is what you want me to do, God, I prayed silently and began to psych myself out until my rest time was up. This time, I pretended that my mother was at the end of each obstacle and needed my help.

It worked! I passed with time to spare, and Lolly was jumping up and down, screaming and cheering while the other candidates stared in disbelief.

"You did it!" the timekeeper said in disbelief. "Thirty seconds left!" He stared at me and then back at his watch to check it again. "Why didn't you do that the first time?" he asked, bewildered.

"Let's eat!" Lolly screamed in delight. "My treat!"

"You better wait a while," the training officer cautioned.

In a delirious glance at him from my fast deteriorating state, I suddenly realized how incredibly handsome this police officer was. His name was Walter, and he was a perfect blend of different ethnicities. He was tall, tanned, and buff, with striking features. He looked at me with concern and sympathy as I desperately tried to compose myself but could only remain slumped over on my knees in exhaustion. "You okay?" he asked again, staring at me with genuine concern that embarrassed me.

I knew I was turning green, and my stomach begged to heave. "Drag me to my car, Lolly!" I gasped as I tried to erase the bright tiny bits of lights darting in front of my eyes like little asteroids.

Lolly pulled me to my feet and half dragged me to the parking lot. Hiding behind her car and dropping to my knees again, my entire body heaved and belched air and bitter bile several times, turning my empty stomach inside out.

"Get it out," Lolly soothed as she rubbed my back again, but my stomach was empty. "You went too fast!"

Stars still danced in front of my eyes, and my head felt like it was exploding as I struggled for composure. "Felt like I was going to barf but I just couldn't in front of that guy!" I practically burped the words out.

Lolly nodded and smiled in agreement. "What a hunk!"

But the hunk was walking over to us in spite of our efforts to be unseen.

"She okay?" he asked. "Probably heat stroke. When did she eat last? Should I call an ambulance?"

I belched again in spite of myself and wanted to die from embarrassment. I absolutely couldn't straighten out my crumpled body!

"She'll be okay. I'll take care of her," Lolly said reassuringly as she shoved me, her tragic-looking friend, into the passenger seat of her VW bug.

The hunk looked doubtful but finally left at Lolly's insistence.

Lolly drove quickly out of the parking lot as I groaned from both cramps and embarrassment. I felt like a cat heaving up fur balls … or a dog throwing up grass … and I knew without a doubt, that's exactly what I looked like.

Lolly suddenly burst into laughter at my pathetic state. "That's okay, you did great!" she beamed proudly.

"Promise me something," I begged. "Don't take me back to my car until the hunk leaves, okay?"

Lolly laughed and nodded reassuringly.

The Interview

The willow bows its head
Not in sorrow, but in homage to God
All things in harmony
Are reflections of enlightenment.
In a bamboo forest, I wait ... silently

Journal entry: June 28, 1979

A few months later, it was time for the oral interview that would take place at the main police station on Young Street. I checked in and waited for my turn in my home-sewn three-piece suit. The old Sears Roebuck and Company building had been turned into the police station, and the squeaking old escalators transported me up to the third floor, where others waited in the quiet corridors.

The bare cement walls of the building were painted beige on the top half and dark brown on the lower half, splitting the wall in a straight line running parallel to the floor. There were no pictures or embellishments on any of the walls, which made the place look like and feel like a sterile and cold-hearted institution. My footsteps echoed on the bare, tiled floors as I found my way to the interview room. A few folding metal chairs had been placed outside of the interview room for the candidates.

I was the only female once again, and a few of the applicants shook their heads and smirked. Others were oblivious to my approach, pacing back and forth, trembling and sweating in spite of the cool temperature inside the building. A few would stop pacing for a few seconds only to study the face of a candidate who exited the room after completing the interview. It was finally my turn.

The interview room was actually a large library. Six uniformed male officers sat at one end of a long conference table. Each one looked through his small stack of manila folders in front of him, shuffling the order of the folders and the papers they contained until he was satisfied. One of the men glanced up and pointed silently to a large wooden chair at the other end of the polished wood table. Old but polished hard wood bookshelves that seemed to touch the ceiling lined the walls of the room. Each shelf had been filled with books that smelled of aged paper. One of the interviewers scrutinized me for a moment, looked back down at the papers while shaking his head, and said in a loud voice to no one in particular, "What are we becoming!"

The interview began, and the seasoned officers each took their turn asking me questions. They watched every move I made, studied my facial expressions, and listened to every word I said in answer to each question, pausing only to scribble on their papers.

- Why do you want to be a police officer?

- Do you know any police officers?

- What would you do if you had to arrest a family member or a friend?

- Would you give your mother a ticket?

- What would you do if you found a dirty policeman?

- What do you have to say on your behalf?

The interview finally ending with one last question: Why do you want to be a police officer?

"I believe in the ideals of justice," I answered without hesitation.

All the interviewing officers put their writing instruments down and stared at me in response to my answer. A deafening silence filled the large room for what seemed to be an eternity as I sat and stared back at them, not knowing what else to do. I had nothing else to say.

"We'll let you know," one of the officers finally said as the others wrote and scribbled in their folders again. The interrogation was finally over, and I was allowed to leave.

Stepping Into Darkness

A few weeks after the interview, I received a strange telephone call during my evening shift as cashier at the hotel in the popular Japanese restaurant. The anonymous male caller identified himself as a police detective and informed me that I was being considered for a special assignment. He wanted to meet with me at a drive-in restaurant located a block away when I finished working. I remembered what the woman in the police department's Personnel Division had said and agreed to meet with him out of curiosity.

"Don't tell anyone about this call or where you're going. Come alone," he instructed in an authoritative voice. "Just buy something at the window and sit down at a table. I'll come up to you." He hung up.

Give me a sign, God, if this is the path you want me to take, I prayed.

The weather was clear that night. Wisps of clouds dotted the dark skies, their silhouettes illuminated by the moon. The busy daytime traffic on Keeaumoku Street had dwindled down to just a few cars. Businesses were closed, and the area was dark except for the dim streetlights, moonlight, and a few stars sparkling in the sky. The drive-in restaurant was still serving hot meals and sandwiches for several late-night customers.

I followed directions. I had told no one where I was going or what I was doing. I bought a soda and waited alone at a cold cement table and bench, looking out into the night. For half an hour I studied the face of each person who walked up to the window, trying to match the voice on the phone by listening to them ordering their food.

There was an old man with puffy circles under his eyes who had arrived alone, and a small group of young guys, loud and drunk, ending the night out with a hot bowl of saimin noodles. People straggled in, but no one approached me or acknowledged my eye contact.

I began to feel uneasy. *This is all wrong—this is someone's joke. Why did I come here?* I thought.

A cool breeze drifted through the dining veranda, bringing the smell of burgers on the grill and a shiver through my soul. *Leave now. Just get up and leave!* Something was in the air that night, something that I knew would change my destiny if I stayed.

Just as I was about to leave, I noticed a man sitting at a corner table, staring at me and motioning for me to join him. He was about six feet, stocky and burly, with no waist, a full beard, and short brown hair. He was wearing a baseball cap that shaded his eyes, a faded T-shirt with Mickey Mouse on the front, long jeans, and rubber slippers.

I cautiously ignored him, but he walked over and stood looming over my table.

"Are you by yourself?" he asked.

"No, I'm waiting for somebody," I answered honestly.

"Yup, that's me," he said and sat down across me without asking.

This is really wrong! I need to leave! He definitely did not look like what I thought a police detective would look like.

"I'm the detective you're supposed to meet," the man explained.

Yeah, right! I thought. I quickly glanced around to see which way I should run to escape, but he whipped out his badge. I had never seen a real police badge up close before so I wouldn't have known if it was real or not, but I remained seated.

"You don't look like a detective," I said cautiously, still thinking he was either a psycho or that I was on *Candid Camera* and this was all a joke.

For the next half hour, the man who introduced himself as Detective Stanley convinced me that he really was a police officer by telling me everything he had read in my personnel jacket and finally explaining why he had called me. The Honolulu Police Department was considering me for an assignment as the first female Narcotics undercover police officer.

"You'll be opening the doors for other females," he said. "It's an opportunity that's unprecedented—no one had ever used a female before. This opportunity is a unique, once-in-a-lifetime experience," he coaxed, sounding like a salesman on a TV commercial. "You can make a difference," he continued. "Take the drugs and the drug dealers off the streets. You can help make the community a better place for the children. But if you do this, I will own you. I will tell you who to talk to, what to eat, what to drink, who to hang around with, where to go," he added.

Detective Stanley continued for the next several minutes, telling me that I was to trust no one, especially my family, friends, or any other policemen, because they would place me in jeopardy and expose my undercover identity. He alone would be responsible for my safety, my life, and my success.

I said nothing the whole time he talked but listened carefully to every word he said. He finally stopped talking and searched my eyes for a response.

"You will do what no one else has done before," he said finally and then pressed, "I need an answer now."

"Okay," I said, watching his eyes trying to read my thoughts.

Detective Stanley sat back in surprise. "I thought I lost you, girl! Here I was talking this whole time, and you said nothing. What did I say to make you say yes?"

"Before I came here," I explained, "I said a prayer for some kind of sign that this is what I'm supposed to do. You said that I could make a difference, help the children—and you're wearing a Mickey Mouse T-shirt."

He looked down at the face on his T-shirt. "What?" he asked incredulously.

"I have a drawer full of Mickey Mouse T-shirts and tank tops," I said. "I wear them all the time. And for me it was a sign that I should follow you." I suddenly felt embarrassed at this off-the-wall explanation.

"You mean all this time I sat here spinning my wheels for nothing?" he asked.

"No," I answered honestly. "Everything you said was important. I guess I was waiting for this. I knew it was coming." I didn't explain further. I had said too much already.

"You're spooky, girl!" he said, staring at me.

"So what do I do now?" I asked.

"Start hanging around in bars," he said. "Hang around with dopers, listen to how they talk, learn to talk and act like them. Start making friends with them. Start cutting the ties with all of your other friends, but don't do anything else until I tell you; just wait for my call."

He left first and told me to wait until he was out of the area before I left. It was dangerous if we were seen leaving together, he warned, but he didn't explain why. I drove around for a few hours till the early morning sun began to encroach on the dark sky. As instructed, I said nothing to anyone.

Oath of Office

I solemnly swear to faithfully support the Constitution and laws of the United States of America, and the Constitution and laws of the State of Hawaii. And that I will conscientiously and impartially discharge my duties as a police officer in the Police Department of the City and County of Honolulu, State of Hawaii, and any and all other duties devolving upon me in connection with such office ... so help me God.
Honolulu Police Department Oath of Office, 1980

One day in February of 1980, in the early evening hours, I walked into a vacant, chalky-gray cement building, still under construction, that would later be known as the Iolani Court Plaza condominiums. I had followed the detective's instructions to meet him at this location, but when I asked why, he didn't explain.

"Just be there. Don't make me wait. Wear nice clothes, no shorts or jeans."

I arrived fifteen minutes early and waited for a half hour by the only entrance I could see. No one was in sight. *This must be a joke*, I thought again, but everything in the past few months had been very covert, almost like a spy movie. Perhaps I should have left, but instead I decided to walk through the building to double-check for another entrance. I stepped carefully around bags of cement, lumber, and buckets of building materials that lay everywhere. I apprehensively made my way through the echoing structure until I finally saw the detective standing in the shadows in one of the corridors.

He motioned me to follow him and another male, who stared at me with piercing eyes. Sheets of plastic covered unfinished windows and doors in the area, and I scrambled to follow the two men into a working elevator that transported us in silence to one of the upper floors. As I followed their quick steps down a hallway, they spoke together in hushed voices, totally ignoring me.

I should just turn around and leave! I don't even know what I'm doing here! But the two men finally stopped their brisk pace and led me into a beautiful room, unfurnished but clean, carpeted, and painted.

I peeked into the room and was happy to recognize Mrs. Jones from Personnel, a short Japanese woman with white hair and gentle, smiling eyes. She greeted me with a warm smile: "Come in. You finally made it!"

I explained that I had been waiting outside of the building for a half hour at the only entrance I could find, thinking that I was at the wrong place. "I didn't see any cars," I explained. "I thought no one was here. What am I doing here?"

The detective and the other man had moved to a corner of the room and continued to talk to quietly. Mrs. Jones had prepared some papers and placed them out on the spotless new countertop. She and I waited silently for several minutes until the detective walked over and introduced me to the man who stood aloof a few step behind him. "This is Lieutenant Lee," he said, and I responded with a smile and said hi.

Lieutenant Lee was a well-groomed cosmopolitan man and looked like a real policeman. He was dressed in an Aloha shirt, knit trousers, and dress shoes, and responded to my greeting with a snicker and shook his head. I had obviously offended him but I didn't know how.

"That's all you have to say?" he snapped, but the detective intervened with a whispered explanation that I couldn't hear. "Let's get on with it then!" Lieutenant Lee said sharply.

The detective gave me a look that told me I had done something terribly wrong, but then he winked, as if to say it would be okay.

"Hold up your right hand and repeat after me," Mrs. Jones instructed in a soothing voice, and I complied even though I was confused about what I was doing.

I suddenly realized that I was repeating the words of the Honolulu Police Department's Oath of Office. I had never heard the words before and took its pledge of service to heart. Years later, that same Oath of Office would be deemed unconstitutional, offensive, and politically incorrect.

"Congratulations; you're a police officer," Mrs. Jones smiled. "Just sign here."

I signed several papers after a quick explanation about each of the documents. The turn of events had been a shock. I had no idea I was going to be swearing an oath. I didn't even know there was an oath.

"You're a police officer, but don't tell anyone, not even your family and friends if you don't want to get hurt," warned the detective.

Lieutenant Lee shook his head. "I don't know," he said doubtfully. "I've got a real bad feeling about this." He studied me briefly and then turned away, shaking his head again. Lieutenant Lee and Mrs. Jones left together immediately, but the detective said I couldn't leave until everyone else had left the area.

"What's wrong with that guy?" I asked the detective. "Looks like he really hates me or I did something really wrong."

"First of all, you showed up late and made him wait," the detective explained with a patronizing look. His tone suggested I should have known better, but how could I have? I tried to explain again but stopped when it was obvious by his impatient look that he didn't want to hear anything I had to say.

"And like I said," he continued, "you're the first female. Everybody is hinky about this, especially him! He's my boss. He's your lieutenant."

That meant almost nothing to me. I had no idea of what the titles and ranks meant. I didn't know anything about the chain of command he was talking about. I had no experience, no training, no badge, and no gun, but I was now supposed to be a real police officer?

"Then why are we doing this if no one wants it?" I asked, totally frustrated and angry. "Let's stop the whole thing now. I can just walk away. It wasn't my idea to be an undercover cop. I didn't ask for this; you asked me! You said that the police department wanted this!"

"You're the first female, and everything depends on you. If you can make this successful, it will open doors for other females. It's up to you. If you fail, this will never happen again!" the detective said angrily. Without any further discussion on the matter, he started to walk away, only pausing to give me his last instructions for the day. "Wait ten minutes before you leave. We can't be seen leaving together. I'll call you." He was gone in a minute, and I was left alone in the vacant building.

It was dark outside when I finally left the building. I didn't know what to do, so I drove around for a couple of hours thinking to myself, *I'm a cop?* But I listened to instructions and told no one what had happened. I wasn't really sure what had just happened, either. Nothing seemed real.

The weeks that followed were difficult. I stopped seeing or calling my friends.

"Any news?" Lolly always asked with genuine interest.

"Nope, not yet," I lied and felt like I had betrayed my best friend.

"Don't be seen with your friends. You'll get them hurt," the detective had warned. "Start cutting all your ties. Make new friends. Start being seen around town by yourself."

Lolly called to go nightclubbing. She knew something was different when I kept making polite, lame excuses. I wanted to tell her what was happening, but I was warned that it was critical, for their safety as well as mine, that I separate myself from my friends, my family, and from everything in my former life.

Instead of going out with Lolly, I went out to nightclubs and bars alone, which was very difficult at first. I had naively believed that any female who went to bars and nightclubs alone were usually prostitutes, easy prey, or women looking for a date or trying to score a free drink. I hated the feeling that people might think that of me, but the transition slowly took place and I was beginning to get comfortable with being alone.

My previous experience with nightlife had always begun and ended in the company of trusted friends just going out to have a good time. Now I was only going out to find a way into the drug scene, and I began to meet the "good time" people who lived their lives freely and without inhibitions.

The good time people didn't really care about tomorrow. They looked for the highest high and the lowest mellow. Excitement and getting totally wasted was the name of the game, and safety was irrelevant.

I started dropping college courses one by one, and the change in my lifestyle was becoming obvious. I slept during the day and stayed out till sunrise.

"What's going on with you?" Lolly finally asked about the changes she had noticed in me, but I couldn't answer. She was working at a good federal job and would be getting married soon. She had found her happiness and was concerned for me.

"What's wrong with you?" my parents asked. "What are you going to do with your life?" It crushed me to not answer.

I had always been kind of a rebel and challenged things I thought were wrong, such as believing that all guys who wore long hair and leather clothing were bad. Another thing I couldn't accept were people who were able to get away from being accountable for what they did with money, power, or connections. I had always done things my own way instead of listening to my parents, and all too often I had learned the hard way that their guidance had been right.

"Honor thy father and thy mother." The commandment of the Bible echoed in my mind, but in my attempt to honor them, I was hurting them. I saw the disappointment in their eyes and felt the hurt I was causing them.

"Don't trust anyone but me," the detective kept pounding into my head, over and over and over. "Don't trust your parents or even your closest friends. They might expose you and hurt you. Only I will protect you," he insisted.

One day when the time is right, I will tell them, I thought, trying to justify the great disappointment I was causing my family and closest friend. *One day when this is over, I hope I will make them proud.*

⚜

Chapter 2
Across the Threshold

The Narc

"Meet me tonight," the detective said ambiguously in the tone of a command instead of a request.

I was never given any information ahead of time and never knew what to expect. I swallowed back uncomfortable feelings of anxiety that burned like acid in the pit of my stomach. Night came quickly, and the smell of spring rain and flowers drifted through the night air.

March 1980, I thought, making note of the moment in time as I waited alone in the shadows of the unfamiliar street corner as instructed. I somehow knew it marked the beginning of a journey that would affect me for the rest of my life. The detective finally arrived on foot, scanned the area, and looked over his shoulder as usual.

"Go to the condominium across the street, use the entry phone, call this number, and ask for Julio." He paused and scanned the area again before he continued, "Buy some cocaine."

"What do I say?" I asked, dumbfounded by his instructions.

"He's going to be hinky, but answer his questions the best you can. Don't say too much. You've got to learn how to out-scam the scammer," he said without really answering my question.

The detective led me across the street towards the brightly lit multi-level condominium building that looked like a hotel in Waikiki, and pointed to the entry phone in the lobby.

"I'll wait here," he said, leaning up against the marble facade of the lobby walls. "Go call the man."

I walked purposefully towards the entry phones attached to a pillar in the middle of the lobby, trying to pretend that I knew what I was doing. I had heard about entry phones being a new type of security feature in the apartment and condominium buildings recently built, but had never used one. I had never bought cocaine, either, or even seen it except in magazine articles and in the movies. Nervous fear welled up and got stuck in my throat, and my hands began to tremble as I tried to follow the directions printed on the phone.

A few people walked past me in the lobby as I tried to call the number unsuccessfully. I prayed that no one would answer, but the phone was busy so I waited a bit before trying again, feeling totally conspicuous. A strange feeling of guilt crept into my soul—guilt about what I was about to do, guilt about buying dope—and I suddenly felt that everyone in the lobby was staring at me and knew I was doing something wrong.

A well-dressed elderly couple walked past me as I leaned against the pillars, waiting to try the number again. I felt my face flush red when they glanced curiously at me, and I suppressed an overwhelming need to justify my presence to the nice-looking good citizens.

"Look," I imagined myself explaining, "I'm just here to buy some cocaine, and I'm hanging around in your lobby because it's just my job. Honest! But I never did this before, and I'm really not what I can see in your eyes that you think I am!"

I shoved my feelings aside when I saw the impatient look on the detective's face and psyched myself out instead. *I am not who I am. I am who they need me to be. Everyone will understand later.*

I couldn't understand the anxiety and felt stupid for being afraid to dial a phone number. I tried the number again and nodded to the detective when the phone began to ring. He looked so out of place, hovering in the dark against the gold-speckled white marble walls in his old jeans and faded T-shirt. He actually looked like he was going to mug the first person who came around the corner.

"Who's this?" was the unexpected abrupt greeting from the confrontational male voice answering the call.

"Jo," I answered, and wondered if I should have given him a fake name. "I'm looking for Julio."

"What you want?" the deep, irritated voice demanded.

"I just wanted to pick up some cocaine," I whispered, feeling guilty for asking.

The unseen man belonging to the voice began to yell, "Who gave you this number? Who told you to come here? Who gave you my name?" He pounded me with questions, and I gave him answers as I created them.

"Meet me across the street at the bus stop, and you better be alone! I'll be watching you cross the street from up here so I'll know if someone is with you!" Julio said threateningly and hung up the phone.

I was shaken and walked towards the detective, who began to follow my steps. "Don't follow me. He's watching me from somewhere!" I said. "I'm going across the street."

"I'll cover you from up there. I'll be watching you," Stanley said, pointing to the parking structure of the building. "I'll be on the top floor. When you're finished, just wait for me to pick you up at the bus stop. I can see everything from up there."

The bus stop was a half block away from the parking structure and across a four-lane, two-way street. *I'm going to get killed!* I thought. *It takes one second to pull a trigger or stab somebody and I know Stanley can't run that fast!*

Detective Stanley handed me $120. "Don't pay more than that!" he said, and left to move to his cover position.

I was relieved to know that I wasn't expected to pay for the cocaine myself, but it still felt awkward to take money from someone to buy drugs.

My legs carried me steadily even though my mind had already melted with fear. I waited alone at the dark, deserted bus stop, which was furnished with a cement bench covered with graffiti under a small wooden roof.

The man crossing the street towards me in a slow sprint looked strong and mean, just as I had imagined from the sound of his voice. It had to be Julio. I watched him dart across the street towards me dressed in a faded T-shirt, shorts, and running shoes. He scanned the area with every few steps, just like the detective always did, constantly looking over his shoulder and into the distance. I knew this guy could kill me in an instant, and there was no one around to stop him if he tried.

I waited silently. Total fear had cut off my voice. *Can't even scream if I wanted to*, I thought. *And no one would hear me, anyway ... not even the detective!*

Julio had piercing eyes that scrutinized me from head to toe as he kept moving around nervously within the tiny structure of the bus stop, constantly looking around. He had dark curly hair that passed his shoulders, a mustache, and a goatee.

"You Jo?" he demanded gruffly.

"Yup," I squeaked, even though I was trying to be cool and calm. My throat was suddenly dry, and I could feel my whole body trembling.

"I got a gram for $125. I'm only doing you a favor cause I wanted to see what you looked like. You better not be the heat or I'll find you and kill you. I always get even!" he threatened.

"I don't have $125." I tried to use an even-toned voice, but I failed and it sounded like a plea.

Julio was silent and paced back and forth angrily. "Don't fuckin burn me, girl!" he said after pacing a bit more and looking around. "I'll do you a favor. $100. That's what I give my regular customers. You a cop?" he demanded all in one breath.

"Yeah right!" I managed a slightly cocky tone and stared back into Julio's piercing eyes.

Julio stared back and then threatened again, "I'm vindictive! If you fuckin burn me, I'll find you, girl. I'll kill you! I'll kill you and your family. You'll be sorry!"

"Don't threaten me!" I said with unexpected spontaneous anger. "Forget it. Don't do me any favors!" I was surprised at what I had said, but it had worked. I had even stopped trembling!

"Okay! Okay!" he said. "I gotta be careful. I don't know you. I gotta quiz you!"

Julio placed his foot onto the cold cement bench, pulled a small packet from the cuff of his athletic sock, and placed it on the bench. "Hundred," he said and glanced around nervously.

I picked up the packet and looked at it like they did in the movies, pretending that I knew what I was looking for. I gave him a hundred dollar bill even though it looked like a packet of baking soda.

Julio grabbed the money and ran across the street and out of sight after uttering one last threat, "Don't ever come here again!"

"Meet me at the graveyard," the detective called out when he drove up to me at the bus stop. It had seemed like hours had passed, and I hadn't known where to go or what to do. I wondered if he even knew that I had bought the cocaine. I had no way to contact him, and there was no pay phone in the bus stop, which didn't really matter since I had no number to call.

I went to my car parked a block away and numbly drove in circles before I got my bearings and found my way to the graveyard. The detective was already there, waiting in the dark. There was a thick numbness all over my body, and I was slightly nauseated. It was too easy. I didn't feel evil. I was not struck by lightning and I was able to buy illegal drugs no matter what I thought and felt. It was actually as easy as buying a pack of cigarettes from a stranger over the counter, and the white powder did not burn in my hand. I was okay, except I was suddenly feeling very ill.

"You did good, girl. Go straight home. Talk to no one. Tell no one what you did," he said when I turned over the packet of powder and the extra $20.

I had never bought Cocaine, didn't know what it was supposed to look like or how much it should have cost.

"Write a report on what happened," he said.

"What format?" I asked what I believed to be a reasonable question.

"Just write down what happened!" he answered, looking at me like I had asked a ridiculous question.

I went home and wrote an essay about what had happened, describing how I felt and what I did. Sleep came quickly, and in the early morning hours, I suddenly woke, wondering if it was only a dream. Detective Stanley met me at a graveyard in Kaneohe on the following day and refused to accept my report.

"What is this?" he asked me, dumbfounded at the story I had written. "Don't write a story. Use headings and just put down the facts, not the feelings."

I had remembered the look in Julio's eyes but not what color they were, and I could remember my nervous fear, not the color of the clothes he wore. Instead of paying attention to the physical attributes of the drug dealer, I only remembered and documented my feelings of guilt and fear. I had tried to get through the ordeal without really looking at Julio.

Detective Stanley gave me several books to study on police report writing.

"Go hang at bars, study the books, study the crooks. I'll call you every day. I have to know exactly where you are, who you're with, and what you doing. Do nothing without my approval," he ordered.

I gave up college all together and dropped out. It would be very suspicious if someone found out I was taking criminal law, philosophy, and religion courses. It had become so contradictory to be going to college when I was living this life. This life was drawing me in to a new world I had never seen before, and there was no time to study.

My parents were upset. Dropping out of college and going to nightclubs every night had never been what they had hoped for and expected from me.

I am caught now in the transition from myself to an undercover police officer.
I go now into the darkness.
I feel it is my destiny to search for truth. I feel I have been guided to this my entire life.
I have learned peace, harmony, and wisdom by studying philosophy and religion.
Now I go to the streets to experience and to learn the lessons of truth and honor.

Journal entry: February 26, 1980

Severing Ties

I belonged to a social club in high school, but before graduation arrived, I had already begun to stop identifying with the girls. They all played cards in the high school cafeteria and had straight long hair, false eyelashes, and giggled. The girls all enjoyed the latest fashions and socializing with boy clubs from other schools. Social status, academics, and going to college were the most important goal they had set for themselves, which was great, but it was not enough for me. They lived happily and with levity on the surface of things. I always dug beneath the surface of everything, often times too deeply.

"You're so weird" they would say, but I had met too many people who bragged at having straight As or a college degree but who failed at being compassionate human beings. "You're not one of us," they finally said. "You're different and don't belong with us," and by the time high school had ended, the distance between us had grown too great. I learned later it would never be bridged.

Most of the girls were now attending the university. Lisa, a friend since elementary school had called out of the blue one day and invited me to a fraternity party and explained further that she needed a ride and I had a car.

"You gotta meet these guys!" she said. "They know how to treat girls, not like the local boys."

Detective Stanley had allowed me to go. "Check it out," he said. "See if you can pick up something from somebody at the party." There had been many complaints about drug use among the university and college students, he explained, and there was sure to be drugs at a fraternity party. "Call me if you can score, and I'll come down."

I hadn't seen the girls for several years, and I looked forward to seeing what was happening in their lives. I was offended at what the detective had said, and I was certain that at least the girls I knew from high school would never mess around with drugs.

I was happy to see Lisa, and on the drive down to the party, she told me that she was going to marry a mainland Haole guy, because local boys had no class and were beneath her. She was trying on a mainland accent, occasionally enjoyed getting high, and insisted that wearing no panties was a turn-on for the mainland boys. My heart sank and my stomach had begun to turn.

The party was at someone's beach house. There were drinks on the counter and drugs openly displayed on a coffee table in the middle of the living room. Almost all of the guys were Caucasian and from the mainland. They stood scattered around the room with a GQ presence, and the local Asian girls giggled at their side. The guys seemed to know that they were Godlike to the local girls.

Some of the party guests were already getting high, and everyone looked like they could afford whatever high they wanted.

I left within the hour after securing a ride home for Lisa. I had no ties to cut here. My friends and I had become worlds apart, and I didn't stay to score drugs, even if I knew I could. I was outraged that I had committed my life and was willing to place myself in jeopardy to stop narcotics abuse and distribution, when those I had thought were my friends were part of the problem.

Detective Stanley was surprised that I had checked in so soon and that I was calling from home. "Did you score something?" he asked.

"No."

"Why not!" he demanded.

"They used to be my friends!".

"Make a choice, girl!" he snapped. "Do your job or protect your friends. Drugs are drugs. Are you going to take care of your friends or are you going to be fair? That's what this is all about. You're probably going to face this again. This island is too small, so you better start thinking about that right now!"

Detective Stanley was upset that I had walked away from an opportunity. If I had made a call that I had scored, a waiting team would have raided the party. I never saw the girls again, and Lisa refused to answer my calls to see if she got home safely.

I went back into my journals to document the incident. I knew there was nothing to hold on to. I could not identify with them anymore. I was changing and could talk to no one, and now I was monitored, owned, and controlled. I had, in error, tried to identify with friendships that had dissolved long ago. The girls had chosen their paths, and I had chosen a different one. They still had the comfort of their group, but I had embarked on my journey alone. I would never know if Lisa had called me just because she knew I had a car and needed a ride, or if she had really wanted to share the happiness she had believed she found with her new lifestyle.

I had to erase my past and become everything I did not want to be. Drugs were everywhere, but I had to hold on to who I was and why I was doing this. There were no rules of this game or training books. Ironically, I had to pretend to be what Lisa and the girls had already become.

I didn't know if I could win this game. I only knew was what I was losing to be a player. Looking back at journal entries I had written several years ago, I found the philosophy I had written for myself, and I knew I needed to train my mind.

There should be a harmony, never conflict
Between the mind, the heart, and the spirit
Therefore in life, every step, every path must be total or nothing at all
And a purpose must be recognized

Blowing like the wind
Its strength is in its surprise and versatility
But like the river
Constant and always in motion
Towards one destiny

Journal entry: 1975

Night Life

I'm tired, totally exhausted, but less frustrated and confused
The answer is not in the separation of the game ... but rather in the expansion
I do not need to separate myself from the game I play
But encompass it and expand myself into it
Stepping in and out of the game . . . watch the timing!

It's a sad world . . . ugly, frightening, sickening, nauseating ... darkness and hopelessness
I struggle with myself ... from time to time I run the gamut of emotions
The extremes of fear and loneliness, frustrations and hurt
But this is my learning, making me strong

I've been to graveyards, bars, empty schools, and back streets at midnight
I have no relationships. I guess it seems easier that way
But I still feel guilty at what I see, and dirty from the streets
I'm tired but I haven't even begun.

Journal entry: March 14, 1980

"Infiltrate the world of drug trafficking. Be seen around ... make friends with the dealers. Watch how they act when they're on the stuff. Drink only hard liquor, straight or on the rocks—no mixed drinks—or drink beer from bottles and never in a glass from the tap," Stanley instructed, but he never explained how to get accepted, how to answer questions, or how to explain who I was to avoid their suspicions. That part was left up to me.

My assignment every night was to go to different bars and nightclubs, hang around, drink, and get to know who was selling, what they were selling, and how much it cost. I had lost control of my life and was alienated from everything and everyone I knew. The only persons I was allowed to have contact with were drug dealers. The only places I was allowed to hang out at were places selling drugs. I was not even allowed near any police station or to talk to any cops.

It was interesting that both cops and crooks talked in cryptic codes. Both cops and crooks had deep issues regarding loyalty. Both cops and crooks were always looking over their shoulders. Normal everyday people don't act like that.

It was almost as if both cops and crooks lived in a different world than the norm, and yet they shared the same realm of existence. They were at opposite extremes but connected to each other and attached by the conflict they shared: good and evil, yin and yang, two sides of the same coin.

I had to learn the Ten-Code abbreviated communication of the uniformed cops, the cryptic codes of the covert cops, and the street slang of the drug dealers, which were different, and dependant on the group you were dealing with.

Snow, whiff, soda, coke, candy, blow, bang, powder. It depended on who you were talking to and where they had come from. From Waianae to Waikiki, the street vernacular for cocaine was different, but to call the drug by its real name, cocaine, was universally a big mistake.

I silently observed the frenzy to get high. Men and women, young and old, there was no distinction of race, status, or profession. Everyone seemed to be eating a pill or dabbing their noses for the quick but fleeting moments of energy and happiness, or the freedom from inhibitions the drugs had brought. But the real world eventually came back and sometimes with it, came the desperation, the begging, the prostitution for more of what real life had not provided.

I cannot control myself and get back to normal
I must get a hold of my real identity
I have no identity
GOD, help me please!

Journal entry: March, 1980

University Cues

March 17, 1980. The assignment came in the afternoon. "Go to University Cues near the university tonight and see if you can pick up some drugs." There had been several complaints about drug dealers selling Quaalude tablets and all kinds of drugs to kids and patrons.

The popular game room with huge glass walls facing the street was like a beacon of light in the distance. It was the only place still open for business in the cluster of shops and offices in the small business center. It seemed to offer a port of warmth as I walked towards it in the darkness of night and pouring rain. The game room was on the second floor of the two-story tile building, with iron guardrails dripping with rain. The detective always told me what to do, but he never told me how to do it, what to say, or how to make the approach.

"I am not me. I belong on the street. I am not afraid. I am not a cop. I am not lonely." I tried to psych myself out with each step, dragging my feet on the slippery wet cement walkway so that I wouldn't slip in the high-heeled sandals I had ignorantly worn.

Tiny bells attached to the large glass front doors rang softly when I pushed the heavy doors of the game room open. Everyone inside the game room paused to see who had just entered the place when I stepped over the threshold into the bright lights of the room, soaking wet from the rain. After a few uncomfortable moments of quiet, the game room patrons turned their interest back to their efforts at the noisy game machines and pool tables. I was obviously not worthy of further interest.

The shelter of the game room had offered no warmth, and my intent to slip in unnoticed had failed miserably. I scanned the room for anyone I thought I could talk to but found no one I felt comfortable enough to approach. Everyone was busy with the machines and clustered in separate groups of friends. I suddenly realized that most of them were teenagers, and I was the only adult female in the room. The restroom offered a quick escape to regroup as I inhaled deeply on a cigarette to end the chill of the air-conditioned room and stop trembling. Again, I psyched myself out: "I am not me. I am not a cop."

I finally mustered up some resolve and left the safe haven of restroom. I scanned the room again, hoping that I might have missed seeing another adult, but still failed to find anyone I felt I could approach for drugs. Alone and out of place, I sat at a game table near the doors and pretended to be waiting for a friend, constantly looking at my watch and gazing expectantly out into the rain. I was actually trying to figure out what I was going to do next. A young adult male I didn't notice finally approached my table.

"You waiting for someone?" he asked, and I nodded, pretending to be upset.

"Didn't show up yet? What a guy!" he sympathized.

"You work here?" I asked.

"Yup," he smiled. "I'm Leo. I work behind the desk. Who're you waiting for? Maybe I know him."

Leo was a Filipino male in his late twenties, slim, with shoulder-length black, straight hair and a goatee. He was the cashier and night manager at the game room. I grasped frantically for a name to give to Leo but for the moment, could not think of a single male name. "Johnny," I said suddenly with surprising ease.

Leo shook his head and shrugged. "Lots of Johnnies around." He sat down and looked curiously at me from across the table. "Your boyfriend?" he asked.

"No. I was just supposed to pick up something and head out to Waikiki to meet some friends," I answered calmly as I frantically began to create a story.

"What you looking for?" Leo asked helpfully.

"Ludes," I answered, feeling guilty again for asking for drugs and hoping he wouldn't get offended at my answer and despise me.

Leo looked around the game room for a few minutes, searching the patrons for a recognizable face. "The guy that's dealing the ludes is not here yet. I'll let you know when I see him," he offered.

Leo left the table, and I played the video game machines waiting for him to let me know when the Quaalude dealer had arrived. An hour later, I figured it was about time for me to appear impatient and leave. I motioned that I was leaving, and Leo smiled from behind the cashier's counter, shrugging an apology that the dealer had not shown up at the place yet.

Outside, the rain had turned to a light mist, and tiny rivers of water washed the dusty streets clean. I stood silently in the rain, looking out into the darkness. There was a rhythm pulsing in the night air. It surrounded and moved through my soul.

April 11, 1980. "Go back to the game room."

It was raining again that evening, but the rain felt good. I had called ahead this time and talked to Leo, who was working at the desk again.

"I don't want to talk on the phone! Just come down," Leo said abruptly and hung up on me.

Detective Stanley had asked if I had noticed the closed room behind the cashier's counter, but he didn't explain why. He said it was dangerous for me at the game room, but again, he didn't explain why. I hadn't notice the back room when I was there. I had only noticed that I was the only female in the place.

Leo was busy behind the counter when I entered the front glass doors. He was wearing a faded T-shirt, faded jeans, and rubber slippers. The game room was known as a drug store. "Anything you want. You've come to the right place!" was the report on the complaint.

This time, I made a mental note of the closed room behind the cashier's counter and scanned the room for any danger that the detective might have been referring to, but I had no clue what I should be wary of. I looked for anyone who might recognize me, too. It would be difficult if someone knew me and started asking questions.

There were a few females in the room this evening, but it offered no comfort. They were young girls, maybe in their early teens, and everyone was wearing T-shirts, jeans, and slippers. I made another mental note of how to dress the next time. Leo noticed me and walked over with a smile.

"How's it, Jo? What you looking for?" he asked helpfully.

Leo was a nice sort of guy, and my mind raced ahead to a time when the dealers and distributors would eventually be arrested. If he sold me anything, he would go down, too. He seemed to be the nicest person around and hardworking too, so I cast the thought aside. He wouldn't be involved, I reasoned. He just worked in the place.

"Just some ludes," I answered easily this time.

"Don't have that," he said, "The guy comes in at about ten o'clock … sometimes midnight. His name is Joon if you want to wait."

I glanced at my watch. "I gotta pick somebody up." It was only seven thirty, and the detective told me not to stay in the place for more than an hour. "I can't wait that long. You got anything else?" I asked, expecting him to introduce me to someone else.

"You want some weed?"

"Yeah, okay, I guess. How much?"

"Twenty cents for you," Leo smiled. "Anybody else, its twenty-five cents."

"Okay, give me two bags." My voice did not reveal the regret I felt when I realized that he was the source of the marijuana.

Leo got the bags out from under the cashier's counter without any hesitation.

"You leave your stash right there?" I asked, quite amazed that it was in the cashier's booth instead of locked up in some dark secret hiding place.

"Don't worry," he said. "Everybody's safe in here. We got protection. See that back room?" Leo pointed to the room the detective had asked me about. "All the heavies go in there. We got some cops taking care of us, too!"

As Leo spoke I tried to memorize the faces of the two men who had just entered the game room, unlocked the door behind Leo with a key, and disappeared into the back room.

Leo smiled reassuringly. "Don't use the phone, though. It's hot!" he warned.

"Who was that?" I asked and nodded towards the back room.

"You don't want to know!" he cautioned. "Stay away from those guys. The less you know, the better!" Leo paused to observe me curiously. "Twenty cents a bag. You want two?"

I nodded in response.

"All buds!" he said proudly.

I gave Leo $40 for the smoker's delight. He smiled at the money in his hands, winked, and returned to the counter to get change for a game room customer.

I stood in the brightly lit room for a while, looking out into the night through the huge glass walls and watched the rain pouring down in sheets just outside. There was a bit of sadness and guilt. One day he was going to be busted, and it was going to be because of me. I had always thought that all dope dealers were mean, vicious bad guys, but I was wrong. Leo was an everyday sort of guy, down to earth and very mellow. He had even tried to keep me safe from the heavies and honestly explained who they were and how to stay away from danger on the phone. It was Leo who was trying to keep me safe, not Detective Stanley. I glanced back at Leo, who had finished giving change to a customer and was busy shining the countertop.

I walked back into the cleansing rain, trying to shove back the thoughts of what lay ahead. I was shivering when I debriefed the deal, but not only from the rain. I was feeling dizzy again and felt like I was burning with fever. It was as if the whole thing was just a dream and I was acting in a movie.

Detective Stanley asked me about the back room again, and I told him about the two men, the heavies, and the cops that Leo told me about. He listened silently and then told me to be careful when I was in there. I realized he was going to send me back into the place even if he too thought it was dangerous.

The Lovers

It was Saturday night, April 12, 1980, and the Lanai Restaurant's lounge on Kapiolani Boulevard was crowded with patrons who had come to listen to the popular Hawaiian music band. There was only one seat open at the bar, and I grabbed it. I felt conspicuous being alone when everyone else was with a friend or a date.

"Scotch on the rocks, please," I requested while visually scanning the crowd. Marijuana cigarettes were being lit and passed between tables like pupu appetizers, bonding everyone in the entire place into one big party of uninhibited guests. Some passed small vials as each took their turn hunching low beneath the tabletop and then reappearing a few seconds later, dabbling at their dribbling noses. Everyone was being addressed as Brah (brother) or Tita (sister) instead of by name, and the few remaining dinner guests finished their desserts quickly and left quietly.

A group of girls sat in celebration at the bar next to me, laughing, gossiping, dropping pills, and drinking.

"What you got?" I asked the female sitting closest to me.

"Lemmons, five a piece," she responded with a smile and without hesitation.

Delia was Hawaiian, Filipino, and Spanish and was making jokes about her ancestry.

She was tanned, slim, in her early twenties, and definitely out to have a good time. It was her belated birthday party, and she was going to make a night of it, she yelled, as if competing with the noise of the crowd. Delia was with Sarah, who was Hapa-Haole—half Asian, half Caucasian—shy, and had a pretty face. She was more reserved in demeanor and giggled softly at Delia's jokes.

"How many you want?" Delia asked, turning her attention back to me again.

"Five," I answered and passed $25 under the counter to Delia's open, waiting hand. Delia whispered to Sarah, and the two girls switched seats.

Sarah was holding the stash in her purse. Carefully and silently, she slipped five white tablets into a bar napkin, folded it neatly, placed it on the countertop, and slid it gently over to me. Sarah had written a phone number on the napkin and said very comfortably, "Call me when you need," and smiled.

An hour had passed, and I began to enjoy the company of the girls. I had taken an aspirin instead of the drug I had bought, and the decoy seemed to satisfy any doubt and put everyone at ease.

"Let's go bar hopping!" they invited, but I declined, making an excuse that I had to meet a jealous boyfriend.

The girls were on their way to the lounge at the hotel where I had worked, and I knew the employees would recognize me.

I remained alone at the bar for one more drink, waiting until I was certain that the girls had left the area. I liked Delia, Sarah, and the girls, and had enjoyed their company. They were wild and free-spirited. Again I felt I had betrayed the girls but remembered the detective's words: "Don't get close. Be fair. It's your job!"

It was months later that I had learned from Detective Stanley that Delia and Sarah were lovers.

I'm going schizoid; I'm a dual personality
I cannot control myself and get back to normal
I live, think, talk, and act like someone else
I must get hold of my direction ... my identity
But I have no identity. GOD, help me please!

Journal entry: April-1980

❧

Chapter 3
Waikiki Whiff

Christy

April 14, 1980. The phone rang at 8:00 a.m. "Meet me in Kalihi," Stanley said. All the meeting locations had been prearranged in covert codes so I knew exactly where I had to be as soon as possible.

"You can wait for me, but don't ever make me wait for you!" he had told me many times, emphasizing that *he* was the man.

The restaurant was busy with the breakfast crowd, and the detective was not alone. He motioned me over to join him at the table in spite of saying that I was to meet no one.

"This is Christy. She's a footman." Detective Stanley introduced me to the tall, slim, natural blond female sitting next to him at the table. "She'll be working with you during the days. I'll be working with you at night." I nodded my greeting and sat across from them at the breakfast table.

In the ranking system of the Honolulu Police Department, a new officer's first rank was a footman. A footman was authorized to drive blue and white fleet vehicles. Five years later, officers were promoted to motorized positions and authorized to drive privately owned subsidized vehicles from the department's "Approved Vehicles" list.

"Eat something, girl." He looked at me curiously. But I was too sick to eat. My stomach burned acid, and my head felt light. The iced water on the table tasted sweet as it quenched the fire on the way down.

Christy and the detective talked as I sat silently at the table. They spoke in a language almost of their own, using codes, slang, and nicknames that only they understood.

"Talk to me, girl," Stanley finally said to me, but I just shrugged. I had nothing to say, nothing I understood, and I felt nothing except emptiness.

The Swan

Christy and I started off towards Waikiki in the undercover car that Christy had been given to use. Conversation was light as we got to know each other, since, after all, we would be pretending to be close friends. It was a hot afternoon, and the ocean beckoned, clear, cool, and blue. It eased the tension of what unknown events lay ahead.

Christy parked the car in a tiny back alley between two huge dumpsters overflowing with garbage from the nearby hotels.

"Were going to check out the King," she said, and pointed to a small two-story apartment building wedged like a architect's error between tall, beautiful hotels. As I glanced towards the rundown apartment building, a chill ran through my body.

"Wait, something's wrong!" I said softly and turned towards the source of the feeling. From the corner of my eye, a dark shadow swooped down from the top of the beautiful high-rise hotel. The shadow moved almost in slow motion as it dived like a graceful swan in silence and then disappeared from view with a loud explosive boom.

"What was that?" I asked, looking at Christy, who had followed my glance. Christy and I ran to the second floor of the King's apartment building to look towards the sound of the explosion.

A two-story parking deck stood directly across the alley. On the bare cement floor of the roof of the parking deck lay the swan. He was crumpled in a heap, next to a Cadillac with a smashed roof and shattered windows. "It's a body!" Christy gasped. "Look! There's one of his shoes!"

I stared in disbelief as the swan suddenly moved. It was a leg that was unfolding itself in one final gesture. A man ran towards the lifeless clump and hunched over it for a second. A few seconds later, he ran from the swan, yelling and screaming hysterically back into the building as others emerged and approached to have a look at the indistinguishable heap that only a minute ago was a living being.

"What made you turn around and look up?" Christy asked curiously.

"I don't know," I answered as we watched the flurry of activity in the parking deck as more and more spectators gathered. When the uniformed police officers arrived and the paramedics covered the swan, we made our way to the King's apartment.

Later that evening, I heard the story of the graceful swan.

He was a prominent businessman from Japan. He had brought his family to Honolulu for a vacation and fun and then received a phone call informing him that his business had collapsed. He had dressed in his best silk suit, gathered his family around him in his penthouse suite, and explained his failure calmly to his wife, mother, and two-year-old son. He knelt before them, asked for forgiveness, and then abruptly touched his head to the floor. He stood up and took a flying leap over the balcony toward his death waiting below. "It was the honorable thing to do," his wife had explained to police.

The family he left behind had bowed graciously and humbly when police made notification of his death. There were no hysterics or sobs, just a polite apology for the inconvenience.

The King

The King was sitting in a tattered Lazy Boy chair in his tiny one-bedroom apartment with the front door wedged open. He sat back with his legs spread open, wearing dark glasses and very short cut-off jeans with obviously no underwear.

The King was a large black man, clearly over six-feet feet tall, large-framed but almost skeletal, with a beer belly. A thick scar ran down the center of his chest to his navel, and he heaved as he breathed deep in slumber. A sculpted goatee framed his face beneath dark glasses and a clean-shaven head. Sunlight sparkled and danced on his gold earring in his left ear.

The King woke in a spasm and gathered himself together. "Bang or whiff?" he asked after a brief conversation, and I shrugged in indecision.

He had seen me around Waikiki, so it wasn't a problem. The King went to make a call on the phone, and Christy whispered that whiff is to snort and bang was crystal to shoot up, knowing that I had no idea what the difference was.

"Got a car?" the King asked after a whispered phone conversation, and I nodded. "Marvin's holding, but we got to trip for it."

King jumped into the front seat of the undercover Chevy Camaro. He didn't know Marvin's address but gave us directions. "Go up this street, turn right here, go left up there," until we finally arrived at a rundown, single-story row of apartments in the Makiki district. The wood support beams were rotting, paint had peeled almost entirely off the walls, and exposed plumbing pipes were covered in rust.

"Park on the road. I might be a while, but no matter what, don't follow me or come looking for me!" he cautioned, "or Marvin's going to be pissed off."

King left us waiting in the car, and as soon as he was out of sight, Christy got out of the car and peeped through an overgrown mock-orange hedge to see which apartment he had gone to.

Half an hour had passed and the King had still not returned with the cocaine. There was obviously a supply of heroin in the place, too.

Customers scurried back and forth in long-sleeved attire and hunched postures. The pain of their sickness and their desperate need for their drug were etched in the features of their faces.

Christy finally sent me to try to look for the King. "Go to the Mauka apartment on the Kokohead side of the building facing Makai."

I had never heard anyone talk like that and was confused at the directions.

"What! Do I have to draw you a picture?" Christy said sarcastically at my confused expression. She laughed a moment later when she realized that I was totally ignorant of police jargon and the universal code-10 series used by law officers. She did end up drawing a quick picture, and I finally set out on foot, feeling totally stupid.

I called out for King near but not in front of the apartment he entered, remembering King's warning and pretending to not know exactly which apartment he was in. There was no answer and no sound from inside the unit he had entered. I began to panic, thinking that the King had left with the money, but called out again. Several pairs of eyes peeped out at me from behind drawn curtains in some of the other apartments, so I knew I was being heard.

King finally answered from inside the apartment that he would be out in a minute. "Go wait in the car! We're still cutting the stuff!"

King returned an hour later with a gram of cocaine. He was buzzing big time, which was probably the only reason he didn't get on my case about looking for him and causing a scene at Marvin's apartment.

Tricks

April 16, 1980, 10:00 am. It was a picture-perfect day; clear skies, warm sun, and a light tropical breeze stirred the air. It was the kind of day that you would find on a postcard from Hawaii.

Christy and I tripped around in Chinatown on Hotel Street. Today, the assigned target was Black Willie, and no one seemed to know who or where he was. No one I approached on the streets even answered when I asked where I could find him. They just walked away. But we hung around anyway, hoping that someone would let him know that we were looking for him. Instead of drugs, we bought tidbits of delicious foods and treats from the Asian markets in the hustle and bustle of daytime Chinatown.

"What you looking for, some blow?" a voice behind me asked, and I nodded. A young male wearing worn-out gray sweats and sneakers had been following us and finally approached us, introducing himself as Tricks. He knew Willy and would go look for him. I watched Tricks go from bar to bar along Hotel Street as Christy and I waited on the corner at Smith Street. Tricks was a wiry black male who was missing a finger and had a large space between his front teeth when he smiled.

Chinatown had a certain scent. During the day, the smell of fresh fish, Chinese foods, and baked goods mingled with the smell of herbs and fresh flowers leis for sale. During the night, the smell of urine and garbage hung stagnant in the air.

"Black Willy ain't around," Tricks said when he finally returned. "But *I* could score you the drug if you take me to see *the Man* on Kapiolani Boulevard." Moments later, we were on our way with Tricks to see the Man.

Tricks directed us to a single-story apartment complex painted a pale green on the far west end of Kapiolani Boulevard. He jumped out of the car and disappeared inside the street-level apartment. I caught a quick glimpse of a very large shadow, opening the door to let him in. The voices inside were hushed, and I got out of the car to look for the numbers on the unit and sneak a peek inside the window.

Tricks told us not to get out of the car, so I pretended to stretch my legs a bit as I tried to memorize the address. A moment later, Tricks opened the door to leave and caught me standing outside the front door.

The Man was just behind him at the door, and both looked at me apprehensively.

"That's the customer," Tricks explained, but the Man made no comment and shut the door quickly.

"Sorry, Tricks," I apologized "I was just stretching."

"That's okay," " he said. "You thought it was a rip?" and I shrugged at the excuse he had made on my behalf.

Tricks directed us back to his apartment in Waikiki instead of returning to Chinatown. He liked us, he said, and wrote his name and number on a piece of paper. "You can come find me if you need any more," he said, jumping out of the car and disappearing around the corner.

April 18, 1980. "Go back to Tricks. See if you pick up a gram," he directed. "Go alone. You're going to meet Christy tonight," he said.

I gave Tricks a call on the number he had left me and asked if I could pick up a gram of the same thing. "Just pick me up at my place," he said, and I agreed.

I had no undercover car, no backup, no badge or gun, and no way to place an emergency call if I needed help. I drove to Tricks' apartment in my silver Ford Mustang, praying for divine protection, as I had nothing else to depend on.

Tricks was waiting outside when I arrived at his apartment, and he jumped anxiously into my car. "Go to Ernest's place," he instructed.

"Who's Ernest?"

"Same place as before," he said.

"I don't remember where it is," I said honestly.

Tricks directed me back to the one-story apartment building on Kapiolani Boulevard and explained that he'd be making $25 off the deal so the cost would be $125 instead of $100 for the small packet of powder.

Tricks was in and out of the place quickly, but this time, he introduced me to the Man. Ernest was a large black male with big, gentle eyes. He was very calm in nature and moved about very slowly, as if in a trance.

Ernest just smiled his greeting and never said a word. "Take me back to my pad," Tricks directed.

When we got back to his place, Tricks kept begging for a taste of the powder I had just bought, and I refused. "That's for me and Christy later tonight!" I argued. "You already made $25 off the run!"

Tricks was outraged that I had refused his invitation to join him in his apartment for a share of the whiff and some fun. He jumped out of my car and slammed the door shut behind him. I drove home feeling sick and dizzy. I could still smell Tricks' heavy cologne in my car.

Detective Stanley knew that Tricks and I would have to trip for the dope. "You have a problem?" he had asked when I asked why I had to use my own car. "You got insurance?" he asked sarcastically in response.

I didn't think it was safe to drive Tricks around in my personal car, but then again, as Stanley had emphasized so many times, "You're nothing. You're just the UC. I'm the detective. I own you!"

It was two thirty in the afternoon, a muggy, sticky day that matched my feelings. A hot soapy shower didn't help to scrub off the anger I had for Tricks or for Detective Stanley.

Rex

April 19, 1980. I met Christy that evening and told her of the events of the day.

"He sent you out by yourself?" she asked incredulously. "You had to use your own car? What about gas? You getting any overtime?"

"Yup," I answered her first question. "I've been using my own car all this time."

I didn't know anything about overtime and gas money, but Detective Stanley had me sign a whole lot of blank expense vouchers even though I was never reimbursed for the money I spent on my own, for gas or when hanging around game rooms and buying drinks at bars while waiting to meet the drug dealers.

"Was anybody watching you?" She looked at me with concern.

"No," I shrugged. "I just go out on my own and call him if I score any drugs. Then I meet him and turn the drugs over and tell him what happened."

Christy shook her head in disapproval. "That's not right!"

The Waikiki Disco on Kuhio Avenue was packed with people, and the music seemed to be bouncing off the walls. It was an older crowd, who looked like they were independently wealthy or successful professional businessmen and women.

The women were dressed in sequined, velvet, or silk designer dresses adorned with jewelry and high-heeled shoes that complimented their attire. They clustered together in small groups, some standing holding a cocktail in one hand and a cigarette or a clutch bag in the other; others sat with their legs crossed at their knees on the plush velvet sofas in the sunken areas of the carpeted room.

The men were well groomed with styled hair and sculpted facial hair. Some were dressed in silk suits while others wore knit slacks and long-sleeved shirts tucked in at the waist and neckties.

I had become comfortable with the people who wore T-shirts or disco clothes and was uncomfortable with this new crowd. I headed straight for the bar.

Christy sipped her drink, and I gulped mine down, still trying to erase the day with Tricks and the revulsion I felt for Stanley. I was very tired and void of energy as the trials of the day replayed in my mind like a movie. I knew nothing of procedure in an undercover operation, but one thing was certain: my dislike of Stanley as a person was beginning to increase. "Time to erase myself and focus on what's happening!" I disciplined myself.

I forced out my thoughts and personal feelings and began studying the crowd in the discotheque. I noted the great contrast with the people in this place compared to the people I was meeting in the downtown local bars and Chinatown. There was obviously cocaine floating around, a few Quaaludes and some capsules too. There was an air of arrogance in the place, and conversations seemed to be rehearsed with the intent of being impressive. Even the smiles seemed to be a presentation and not genuine.

"I know you," a gentle male voice offered, distracting me from my thoughts with a light tap on my shoulder.

I smiled in response and shrugged in non-recognition of the man standing behind me. He was dressed in a silk suit, had light brown, curly hair, and blue sparkling eyes. He had a nice face and seemed genuine and not like he was putting on a façade. I would have remembered if I had met him before.

"I don't think so," I said after a moment, but he insisted that we had met before.

Rex introduced himself and told me that he owned the nightclub. The conversation began to shift to getting high, and he asked if I wanted some cocaine. He offered the drug as if it was part of the service he offered at his club to make sure everyone had a good time.

In a moment, he had visually scanned the room, motioned someone over, and introduced me to Robert. I bought a half-gram from Robert and said I would keep it for later.

Christy and Robert began to talk, and Rex was very attentive for the next few minutes until he was called away to attend to other business.

I was uneasy at being too comfortable with Rex, but I liked his energy. He floated around the room for the rest of the evening, making sure everyone was having a good time, and would occasionally return to make sure I was okay, too. The patrons were mostly professional people, Rex explained, lawyers and business executives that came in to escape the day.

Rex and Robert seemed to be nice guys. They were intelligent, clean, and well groomed, too. I thought all dope dealers were unclean and uneducated, but I was wrong. The stereotypes I had believed all this time were all wrong.

Chapter 4
Trust

Drive-Through Drugs

April 21, 1980, 1:55 p.m. Monday. Christy and I had to look for a Japanese guy named Kenji. According to a complaint, he was a source for marijuana and Quaaludes. Kenji worked in a tollbooth of the parking lot of a bank and did his business like a drive-through fast food restaurant.

Kenji was in his early twenties, about five foot eight, very skinny, and had stringy, straight, long black hair. He was pale white, as if he had not been out in the sun for years. He spoke in a slur and slumped over like a puppet dangling on a string.

Christy drove up in the undercover car and, within a minute, had bought a bag of marijuana. No questions asked.

"How about some ludes?" I asked.

"Come back after eight o'clock tonight," Kenji answered and explained that his source was delivering a quantity of Quaaludes.

"Go back tonight, too, and get the ludes by yourself," Detective Stanley ordered in his authoritative tone.

It didn't matter if I was tired or if everyone else was going home. It didn't matter if I would be alone or that he was forcing me to stay in my undercover role twenty-four hours a day.

Before every assignment, I erased my identity and psyched myself out in order to play the role I had been assigned. Detective Stanley gave commands but never instructions on how to accomplish the assignment. The events of the day always turned to nightmares at night, and when I went out day and night, I felt like the real me was being destroyed. Detective Stanley was either ignorant of what was happening or he didn't care.

"They call him the Ayatollah," Christy had told me sympathetically when she heard Stanley was sending me out that night again without backup, an undercover car, or support. "You need your rest. Can't you go tomorrow night?"

I went back to meet Kenji alone at about eight thirty that evening. Kenji was still in the parking tollbooth, closing the cashier's drawer for the day. He was on the phone when I arrived but motioned for me to park in the loading zone. He staggered to my car after hanging up the phone, to tell me that he was just talking to Allen, who was on his way. We were to wait in the lounge at Bob's Restaurant, on the ground floor of the bank building, and Allen would meet us there in a half hour.

Kenji and I sat in the empty lounge while the manager glared at us. Kenji explained that the manager hated him and Allen and had tried to get them both fired from their parking lot attendant jobs.

From what Kenji had said, I had guessed that it was probably the manager who had called in the complaint about Kenji. I felt an urge to tell the manager why I was there but endured his hateful, judgmental stares while we waited for Allen to arrive. Allen finally arrived an hour later, explaining that he had girlfriend problems.

I refused to buy the Quaaludes in front of the manager and insisted we go outside to the parking lot to do the deal. Allen had already been upset when he entered the lounge and returned the manager's hateful stare with loud insults and threats. Allen made it very clear that he hated the manager, too.

I felt it was stupid to feel ashamed about letting the manager see me buy the drugs but realized it was the real me, in conflict with what I was doing.

Allen was about five foot four and Japanese with a medium build. He had a baby face and a wild temper. He was totally upset at his girlfriend and was going to Waikiki without her to have a good time. He was taking a bag full of Quaalude tablets, neatly wrapped in foil, packaged and ready for sale in quantities of ten. It looked like rolls of Life Savers candies, except without the colorful paper wrappers. Allen had already eaten two but stated he could eat up to five tablets and still handle. The carload of guys he had brought with him waited quietly near his car until he was ready to leave. Allen was obviously the main man in this circle of friends, and even Kenji shrank back at his angry outburst about the manager and his girlfriend.

April 22, 1980, 1:20 p.m. The next afternoon, Christy and I picked up a half-gram of cocaine from Kenji at his house on Oahu Avenue. He had given me his phone number, and a quick call had locked in the deal. Kenji lived with his parents in a nice neighborhood in the lush Manoa Valley. I was relieved to learn his parents would not be home and that I would escape their scrutiny.

Stanley sent me out alone again that night at ten. "Pick up more Quaaludes" he ordered. "Just go down to the parking booth and see who's there."

I did a quick purchase of twelve Quaaludes from Allen that night and finally went home to sleep. I was being forced to stay in my undercover identity around the clock. There was no escape from Stanley, my undercover identity, or the conflicts about pretending to be a friend to my suspects. I had no down time to be normal and no one to talk to. More important, I was beginning to feel more comfortable with my suspects than I was with Stanley, who was always playing a macho mind game.

Detective Stanley was heartless and selfish. Either that or he had no clue of the emotional and psychological trauma he was forcing me through. All he cared about was using me to get his job done. I reminded myself everyday why I had made the choice to do this, and I knew I had to finish what I started—not for Stanley, but because of what I believed in: the ideals of justice.

"Do you get overtime?" Christy asked again after learning I was still going out alone at night.

"What's overtime? I even have to wait until he makes the time to meet at the graveyard to get a paycheck!"

Detective Stanley liked to hang on to my check for a few days, and when he finally gave it to me, he gloated at his control over my life. I began to hate him and his constant gloating about his control.

Song Joon

April 23, 1980, I took Christy to meet Leo at the University Cues game room. It was 11:00 a.m. on Wednesday, and I was amazed to see so many children in the place, knowing that they must have cut out of school to be there. Leo greeted me with a smile and asked what I wanted.

"Grass?" he offered.

"Ludes?" I replied.

Leo nodded and pointed to a group of Asian males at the pinball machine in the middle of the large game room.

I walked over to the group of males as Leo watched. Just as I was about to tap one of the guys on the shoulder, Leo called out, "No, not that one; the other one!"

I pointed to another male, and Leo nodded. "Song Joon," he said.

Song Joon was Korean, in his twenties, short, and stocky. He turned and smiled. "What you want?" he asked with a Korean accent.

"Lemmons," I answered easily and surprised myself at the absence of any nervousness, fear, or guilt.

"How much you want?" Song Joon asked without looking at me. I ordered ten Quaaludes at $5 apiece.

Song Joon pulled out ten tablets from his pocket as he continued to watch the on-going pinball game. He glanced at me and then at the money I gave him, and shoved it into his wallet.

Christy came up and asked if he had some cocaine, and he pulled out a packet from his wallet without a second glance.

"Any good?" Christy asked.

"Try it first if you want to," he said, and stared at Christy as if he was insulted at her doubt.

Song Joon was agitated, walked to the front desk, and grabbed a key from behind the counter. "Ladies' room," he said coldly, handing Christy the key.

Christy and I went into the restroom, and Christy examined the powder in the packet. Song Joon was standing right outside of the door waiting when we exited the restroom, and we both quickly dabbed at our noses.

"That's $100," he said, irritated but confident that we had found it to be good quality powder.

Christy gave him the money, and we left the game room immediately, not knowing how to react to the contents. It would have looked really stupid if we had pretended to react to the stuff if it was actually bunk.

For Michael

I was mentally and emotionally exhausted, but it was getting a little easier to play the role. The only thing I was allowed to continue was my martial arts training twice a week, at a Shaolin style gung fu school. Although I had no rank, I had hung on to the training as a refuge and escape. It was the only thing left that had not been destroyed, and my gung fu brothers never pried into my personal life.

I was on my own this night, not on any assignment, and had found my favorite hideaway local bar on King Street to relax after a few hours of practice. There were no drugs or loud music at the cocktail lounge, just a jukebox of mostly solid-gold oldies. The early evening crowd consisted mostly of working people who stopped in for a few drinks before heading home.

Pauline the bartender was the mother of my high school classmate. She was in her fifties, slim, with natural blond hair and an Austrian accent. Pauline was gentle and polite and always served everyone with a warm smile. She reminded me of someone who would be working at a five-star hotel in Waikiki.

Janet had been a friend for years and managed the place in the evening, which was always filled with after-the-game sports enthusiast and small celebrations of one kind or another. I had looked forward to seeing her again, but unfortunately she was out sick this evening.

I hadn't seen Janet or Pauline for a long time and had looked forward to sitting with good friends. A karate tournament celebration had filled half of the room, and trophies, ribbons, and medals were on display at various tables. The celebrating customers were still in their karate uniforms boasting loudly about their martial arts expertise when three large men walked in and stood in the doorway scanning the room.

There had been a series of robberies occurring at the bars along King Street involving a group of drugged-out men who smashed and punched their way to the cash register and escaped with the money, always leaving their injured victims behind.

The men immediately gave Pauline a hard time, swearing and yelling about the overcrowded room, demanding a table, and obviously feeling good about their intimidation tactics.

They began to grab food from the tables even after Pauline had asked them to stop and offered to get them their own food. They didn't want to wait. The men were checking out each table, puffing up their postures as if looking for a challenge, and the once loud karate celebration became silent. Pauline asked them to leave, saying she didn't want any trouble, and began to walk back to the bar, when one of the men, large, unshaven, and dirty, grabbed and punched her.

A black-belted female karate student screamed and scrambled into the far corner of the room, in spite of the ribbons she wore around her neck. None of the men in the place or the karate group stepped up to help Pauline. Instead, they all sat there in shock and watched ... even the Karate Sensei.

I was outraged and got up from my table in the back of the room and started yanking and shoving the huge male away from Pauline. Pauline managed to get away to the phone and was trying to call the police.

The second guy punched my back as I was still trying to stop the first thug from trying to grab Pauline to stop her from calling the police. A mutual friend in the bar tried to pull the second guy away from me, but the third man in the group jumped up and interfered, blocking him and then pushing him all the way backward through the swinging doors that led into the kitchen.

The karate instructors all stood in the corner, as if protecting their students, who were screaming and huddled in the corner. Not even one had made an attempt to help Pauline. I felt my mind snap with rage as the emblems on the karate uniforms were burned into my memory. Their uniforms, medals, and trophies meant nothing without honor and courage. In my eyes they were all a disgrace to their school if they refused to help a helpless, innocent person from being assaulted in front of their eyes.

It was as if I was in a slow motion movie. Everything was surreal, and I was not myself. My mind snapped with anger and something had taken over, and I moved and fought with two of the men, who were twice my size, without thinking. Although I had no black belt or trophy, all I could think about was helping Pauline, but unlike a movie, I still felt the pain of the blows.

One of the men shattered a big glass platter of noodles across the left side of my head, and I felt my body start to crumple. The last thing I saw were the stars and bits of lights swirling around in front of my eyes and the other assailant ripping the phone off the wall

I focused back from the pain in my head and found myself pinned down on the ground. One of the assailants was kneeling next to me, pinning my shoulders down, as the other man stood up to go after Pauline again. I couldn't move against the weight of the oversized fat bully and could only bend my elbows. As the two men continued their assault, I instinctively reached up and grabbed the scrotum of the one still on his knees straddling me and trying to punch me. My fingers met, twisted, and yanked at the flesh I felt under the crotch of his jeans … just like Sifu, my gung fu instructor had instructed.

The huge bully dropped and moaned, and his friend left Pauline alone to help him.

The uniformed police officers had arrived just as the three men were trying to leave. One male, still screaming and yelling obscenities, had been placed into an ambulance. It was the male I had grabbed and twisted.

I found myself sitting on the curb outside, leaning against the wall and trying to wake up from a nightmare. I couldn't remember how I got outside. I finally began to focus first on the uniform standing in front of me, and then on the familiar face of the man who was wearing it. It was Michael Gartrell, a friend from high school.

This can't be real! I thought, still fighting to focus. Mike was a year older than me, and I suddenly remembered that he had joined the police force.

Mike recognized me immediately, too, but said nothing as we stared at each other, waiting for the other to say something first. Ice packs and questions. Mike watched me silently for a while as the drunken man with the smashed scrotum pointed at me. He yelled that he wanted to press charges after he and his friends assaulted Pauline and trashed the place.

Pauline and some of the other patrons were making statements as the karate club members left quietly, carrying their trophies, refusing to get involved and declining to make a statement to police.

"What's your name?" Mike finally asked looking at me intently and poised with his note pad and pen.

I gave him a fake name and address, and he wrote it down.

He looked at me and searched my eyes "Weren't you trying to get in?"

"I just haven't put on a uniform yet," I answered, and Mike nodded that he knew and understood.

"I'll call someone for you. Do you have a name and number?"

I gave Mike the only phone number I had, which was the telephone number of the Narcotics Office hotline. It was the only number I had for contact, and I prayed that someone would answer, which was not always the case. "Ask for Detective Stanley."

The paramedic came back with another ice pack for my left eye. "You're probably going to have a black eye," he explained, and there was a small gash on the side of my head just above my left ear.

"You better go to the hospital," Mike said after talking to the paramedics and looking at my injuries. "You look kind of beat up, and you might have a concussion," he said. "But what the hell did you do to him?" he asked, grinning as they watched the disorderly patient being stuffed into the back of the ambulance.

"I yanked his balls off!" I said quietly. ""He was punching out Jamie's mom and I had to jump in."

Mike knew Jamie from high school, too, but he didn't know that Pauline was her mom. He began to shake his head and laugh. "You're still the same!" he commented, and began to tell me that the three men had fit the description of the suspects of the robberies in the area.

Mike left me for a few minutes, and I watched him talking to the officer with the sergeant's stripes on his uniform.

"That's my sergeant," he explained after returning a few minutes later. "I'll take care of everything. Just go to the hospital, okay? Make sure you go to Queen's Hospital," he said with a reassuring smile. "We already called your office, and the paramedics said you should go in."

"Thanks, Mike," I said, but the words were inadequate for what I felt.

"You better go to the doctor!" he warned. "I know you, and you probably won't go! You look like shit! Promise me!" he demanded. "Or I'm going to drag you there myself or call another ambulance." Mike and I looked at each other for a moment, and we both broke into laughter.

I went to the hospital like I promised Mike but wasn't sure how to fill out the forms or if I had any medical insurance. After all, there was no record of me being a cop. I had just put the pen down when the detective walked into the emergency room.

"I'm sorry. I know you said not to talk to or trust any cops, but Mike is a good friend and I didn't know who to call. I thought I was going to get arrested."

"That's okay, girl," Stanley said, and then added, "Did you win?"

Moments later, the guy I had fought with was brought into the emergency room, screaming and swearing. He looked at me and yelled, "That's her! That's her. She's the one who ripped my balls!"

I walked out, and the detective followed. "I'm going home. I'm okay. I'll go to the doctor tomorrow if I have to," I said. I was more disgusted with the asshole than I was in pain.

I never saw my friend Officer Michael Gartrell again, and I never went to the doctor. I didn't know if I had any insurance or how to explain my injuries.

A few years later, Officer Michael Gartrell left Hawaii to join a mainland police department. He was killed in the line of duty.

No one knew what really happened that night or how his presence and his friendship had pulled me through a critical moment. News of his death had crushed me, and no one really knew why. I never got to say good-bye.

A few weeks after the incident, I went back to my gung fu training. It was my only escape, and I needed to heal my lingering physical wounds. Sifu Jose came up to me as soon as I entered.

"Do you know the two guys on the bar?" he asked, and motioned to the small lounge on the far side of the patio in the alumni club house.

"No I don't." I began to panic.

"Did you get into a fight at a bar a couple weeks ago?" Sifu Jose asked.

"Yes, I did. How did you know?" I asked apprehensively.

"They told me," Sifu answered, motioning to the two guys staring at us. "They were asking about you and have been waiting for you to show up for the last two weeks," Sifu Jose said calmly.

"Sorry, Sifu," I said. "I'll go see what they want."

"I don't want any trouble," Sifu said, but he walked up to the bar with me and waited a few steps away … just in case.

Clayton and Gary had somehow found out who I was and tracked me back to my gung fu club at this particular branch, out of all the numerous martial arts schools on the island. They were sitting on the bar at the lounge two weeks ago and had seen the whole fight. They had not come looking for trouble; they had wanted to join the same club I was learning from.

I explained the incident to Sifu Jose and showed him the bruises and cuts that had still not healed.

"Did you win?" he asked and smiled.

Clayton and Gary did join the club, but I began to stay away. It had been too easy to find me, and I was reluctant to admit that Detective Stanley was right. I had to cut all of my ties.

Chapter 5
North Shore Candy

The Haleiwa Candy Man

On April 25, 1980, Christy and I went to find the drug source at the West Side Bar and Grill. We sat in the lounge in the afternoon and cooled off from the bright North Shore heat. The ocean was turbulent with heaving swells of indigo blue, sending waves crashing against the large black rocks lining the shore. It was an awesome sight against the endless horizon of the ocean and sky. I thought of how nice it would be to jump into the ocean but knew I would probably drown.

Everyone seemed to know the man who walked into the lounge. He was Caucasian, very large, and five foot ten with a scarred face and curly brown hair. Several of his teeth were missing when he smiled.

Christy and I ordered a drink, and the man picked up the round. He raised his glass in our direction, and we gestured back in the same way to say thanks.

He sat a few tables away, joining the well-known politician we recognized immediately. They spoke seriously in hushed tones while still keeping an eye on us as we played the video game machines.

The man finally asked what we were doing in the place, and I answered lightly, "Just cruising." He invited us to join him at his table and introduced his friend, Augie, the politician.

"You want some soda?" he asked as soon as I sat down.

"What!" I looked at him in shock. "Are you joking?"

"No, no, no!" he exclaimed. "I'm the Haleiwa Candy Man!" he said proudly, and the councilman nodded in agreement.

The Haleiwa Candy Man passed me an amber vial and pointed to the restroom. Christy and I went, and Christy scooped about two-thirds of the little vial into the cellophane wrapper of my cigarette package. We returned to the table and pretended we had inhaled the precious white powder.

The Haleiwa Candy Man, who everyone called Freddy, continued to tell us that we should be good to him because he really was the Haleiwa Candy Man of the North Shore. He could get quality and quantity with no problem, he boasted.

Freddy told us stories about himself and explained how he had lost his finger. He had stuck it up between the legs of a Korean bar waitress and was cut by a razor blade that she had positioned to ward off unwanted intruders. Freddy bragged that his finger got infected and he eventually had to cut it off. He kept his severed digit like a trophy in a jar at home. He loved Asian girls, he explained, and I looked like someone he had been deeply in love with.

Freddy leaned over to me and whispered, "Come to my truck with me. It's right outside ... just you."

Christy and I looked at each other, and Freddy intercepted our doubt. "No worry!" he told Christy. "We not going no place!"

I followed Freddy outside to his truck, and the councilman walked out with us to leave for home. Freddy's truck was parked just outside the front door.

"Get into the passenger seat," he said as he moved around to the driver's side of the truck.

I opened the door and sat halfway into the seat, keeping both feet outside and on the ground.

"Close the door and open the glove compartment," Freddy instructed.

I did as instructed after he showed me that his car keys were on the dashboard, and not in the ignition. I glanced back at Christy, who was standing in the doorway of the lounge, watching me with a worried look on her face. My mind was already racing to plan a quick escape if I needed one, but I followed his directions calmly and opened the glove compartment. Freddy reached over and pulled out a bag of marijuana and a gram of cocaine. "That's for you," he said, and placed it into my hands.

"What's this?" I said in shock. "Are you for real?"

"Yup," Freddy said proudly. "I told you, I'm the Haleiwa Candy Man!"

I took the items and jumped out of the truck. Freddy looked surprised, almost as if he had expected a different reaction from me. I smiled and thanked him, and he followed me back into the bar. Christy and I finished our drinks and left. Freddy remained with a new crowd of his friends that had just arrived. Before we left him, Freddy and I exchanged phone numbers, and I promised to call him about the quarter ounce of cocaine we had talked about earlier.

On the way home, Christy and I laughed hysterically about the disgusting story Freddy had told us about his severed finger. It was laugh or throw up about the graphic details he had shared, and neither of us wanted to clean Christy's undercover car.

Indecent Intrusions

Freddy had told me to go to his friend's twenty-four-hour restaurant on the corner of Kapiolani Boulevard if I needed any ludes in the downtown area. The waitresses were all holding, he explained, and it was a heavy place to be. I found Yoshi's Restaurant and the little sports bar area inside that Freddy had described.

"Go check it out by yourself," Stanley said. "See if you can score."

Crystal was the waitress on duty and said she knew Freddy, but she had run out of her supply.

"Go down the street to the Lanai Restaurant," she suggested. "Go see my friend Billie, the bartender." The bartender was Crystal's source and was sure to be holding. I was familiar with the place and was comfortable sitting at the bar alone. It was the same restaurant where I had met Delia and Sarah. I ordered a drink from the female behind the bar and asked for Billie. The bartender brought me my drink, and I asked again, "Is Billie working today?"

"That's me," she said. ""Who are you?"

"Oh," I replied, caught off-guard, "I was expecting to meet a guy! Crystal from Yoshi's said I could come and see you."

Billie had a pretty face and a pleasant personality. She was a cosmopolitan blend with an Aloha type of smile that warmed up the place and could put anyone at ease. "How many?"

"Ten," I answered. "How much?"

"Sixty," Billie replied with a smile.

I nodded, and Billie disappeared behind the counter, returning a few moments later, placing a folded napkin on the counter. I placed $60on the counter and thanked her.

"Any time!" Billie said with a smile.

The deal was quick and easy, and as usual, I met the detective, told him my story, and gave him the pills.

I knew something was bothering the detective, but I didn't know what it was. I was not allowed near the police station and was never privileged to know anything about what was happening in the Narcotics office. My conversation with the detective was always nothing more than a debriefing and turning in the evidence. Stanley reminded me again, "I own you," but this time he added that *he* was in charge, not Christy, and that I was to take all my orders from him only. Christy was just a rookie footman, he explained harshly.

"When I'm with her, I follow what she tells me," I explained, "And then I follow what you tell me do to when I'm alone."

"Christy takes her orders from me!" Stanley retorted angrily.

"What's wrong?" I asked. "I don't know if she's telling me to do something without your approval. I thought you guys worked together."

"You don't understand, girl. I'm the one who's going to protect you. Not her. She's nothing. She's just a footman!" he yelled in a quiet voice.

"You're never around; she is!" I was offended at his slander of Christy, who was the only friend I had learned to trust.

Detective Stanley was startled at my reprisal and remained silent for a minute and then shook his head. Suddenly and out of nowhere, he asked me when I had my period.

"What?" I asked, highly offended and shocked at the intrusive question.

"What?" he asked, indignant at my reproach. "Beginning, middle, end of the month ... what?"

"Why do you need to know?" I demanded, feeling disgusted at his probing into my private life.

"Because I have to know when you're vulnerable," he explained.

"Oh come on, what are you talking about!" I began to feel totally outraged.

"Females get horny just around their time of the month and that's a fact! I gotta know so you don't get into any situations!" he demanded.

"That's bullshit!" I snapped. "Anyway, I'm not regular!" I was already uncomfortable around him and hated his mind games, but now he was just totally repulsive and going too far. I lied to get the interrogation over and get away from him.

Detective Stanley was obviously very angry and upset about something, and it had to do with Christy, but I didn't know why or what had happened. I was never told what happened behind the scenes and never allowed to talk to anyone else except him and Christy. Stanley was obviously trying to demean Christy, which was ridiculous because he was the one who had set us up to work together. But Christy was uncomfortable with him, too.

"He thinks he owns you!" she would often say after leaving the office to meet me.

When I told Christy that Stanley had asked about my menstrual period, Christy gasped and shivered. "He's getting weird!" she said, and I agreed.

Freddy's Surprise

April 27, 1980, Sunday. Christy and I went back to the West Side Bar, and Freddy said he was very glad to see me.

"How was the stuff?"

"Great!" I answered.

"I got something for you in my truck," he said, "but not now; wait for a while."

"What is it?"

"A surprise," he said and left it at that with a smile.

Christy shot me a look of caution and concern. "Be careful," she said. "He's in love with you!" she said half jokingly.

Freddy bought everyone in the bar rounds of drinks like a big spender. Everyone who came into the place seemed to know him. It was late afternoon, and the fishermen had come into the place to wash down the salt in their throats. I listened to fish stories and eventually even got to know the problems they were having with their girlfriends or their wives. It was a relaxing time, and the sun began to melt into the horizon.

It was in the early darkness of the new evening when Freddy finally asked me to go with him to his truck, alone. Christy looked really worried and said out loud that she would be waiting at the front door, watching. "Don't trip with him," she cautioned, and I nodded.

Freddy opened the passenger door of the truck and let me in. This time, he stood next to me on the passenger side and looked around first before he reached in to open the glove compartment in front of me. In my hand, he placed a letter-sized white envelope and said triumphantly, "That's the surprise!"

I held on to the envelope for a few seconds, afraid to know what was in it.

"Look inside!" he beamed happily.

The envelope contained a quarter ounce of cocaine, in half-gram heat-sealed packets, all ready and prepared for sale.

"What's this?" I asked in shock, and glanced over at Christy, who had seen my expression.

Christy was ready to jump over the drift wood railing to get to me.

I gave her a look that everything was okay, and she waited but still took a few steps toward me. By this time we had learned to communicate with our eyes and expressions. We didn't need words.

"Why?" I asked Freddy.

"I don't know," Freddy shrugged. "I usually don't front anybody, but I like you. I know I can trust you."

I knew in that moment by the quietness of his voice and the sincerity in his eyes that he was not only giving me his trust, but he was also trying to offer me his heart.

"I don't have the money!" I said quickly, trying to change the tone of the moment.

"Don't worry; you can pay me when you make your money back!" he said.

"But why? How do you know you can trust me?" I asked, wondering if I had somehow given him the wrong impression.

"I don't know," Freddy said quietly. "Guess I just like cute little oriental girls!" he paused, and when I didn't say anything, he lightened the conversation and added, "That's why I lost my finger!" he laughed.

"Thanks, Freddy! When do you want the money?"

"When you can. No problem. I told you ... I'm the Haleiwa Candy Man!"

Freddy reached over and gave me a hug, and I stared at him in alarm. He chuckled at my expression. "Don't worry. I'm not expecting any favors!"

I glanced over to Christy, who was almost beside herself with stress and ready to jump out of her skin to run over to the truck. I jumped out quickly to let her know that I was okay.

Christy and I left almost immediately when Freddy rejoined his friends in the bar. Christy almost fainted when I showed her the surprise, and she understood my feelings of guilt. We stopped to listen to the crashing waves of the ocean for a bit, and I breathed in the cleansing salt air.

"He's falling in love with you, girl." Christy had spoken the words that I didn't want to hear.

I soaked in a tub of very hot soapy water when I got home. I felt really badly when I should have been happy with the score.

"What's wrong with you?" my mother asked, but I couldn't even begin to explain, even if I wanted to. I knew that I was hurting my parents, too.

Kenji and Allen

April 29, 1980, 3:30 p.m. Christy and I headed out to McCully to look for Kenji at the parking lot. Allen was working the very busy parking booth, and Kenji was staggering around on the side, obviously totally wasted on some drugs. Kenji saw us and motioned us to a stall in the loading zones. He staggered over and hung onto the roof above the passenger door of Christy's undercover car to keep from falling.

"What? Ludes?" he slurred loudly, and I nodded.

"Allen got em in the booth," he giggled.

Christy and I walked up to the booth, and Allen glanced at us between attending to cars going in and out of the lot. "How many ... ten?" he asked, and I nodded.

Allen reached down into the booth and handed me a coin wrapper stamped with the name of a reputable bank containing ten white tablets.

I gave him $50, and he nodded good-bye without a word, getting back to the steady flow of vehicles.

"What about Kenji? He's totally wasted!" I asked.

"I got him," Allen said calmly and continued handing out change to a customer paying for parking.

My life has totally changed
The new identity is stronger ... I think I am, too
I still feel crazy at times, or dirty, or sick, or fearful
But I'm learning ... have to learn to handle this

Journal entry: April 27, 1980

✣

Chapter 6
Silent Tears

Nadine

April 30, 1980, 2:30 a.m., Wednesday. I went to the popular Waikiki discotheque called the Point After alone that evening, and headed for the bar.

"Go alone," Stanley had ordered, "but stay away from the back bar. There's another undercover officer in the place."

I felt conspicuous going to a disco alone but was getting very used to doing things I didn't feel comfortable doing. It was different from going to a local bar. It was standing room only when I entered the place, but a tall, handsome Chinese guy gave up his seat for me at the corner of the front bar. He was well dressed and well mannered. It would be nice to finally be in the company of a good guy, I thought.

Vic introduced himself and began to carry on an intelligent conversation about business and financial career opportunities. He was in sales and apparently very knowledgeable and successful in his field.

Still feeling uncomfortable about being alone and appearing that I was there to meet guys, I made an excuse that I was supposed to meet some friends, was in between jobs, and still figuring out what I wanted to do.

"You want to try something?" Vic asked, and without waiting for an answer, he slipped a rainbow-colored capsule into my hand.

My heart sank but I accepted the sample and said I would save it for later.

"Don't drink too much if you take that!" Vic cautioned, and then he asked me to dance.

Although I would have loved to dance, I was suddenly too disappointed and depressed, so I declined.

"Would you mind if I asked someone else?" he asked politely, and I was amused at his gentlemanly gesture to seek my approval.

"Go ahead. I'm just kicking back," I responded, and in a few seconds, Vic was on his way to find another dance partner.

Suddenly, everyone I met seemed to be doing drugs. Cocaine, Quaaludes, rainbow-colored Tuinals, and Black Beauty speed seemed to be everywhere. Vic had just slipped me a rainbow. Just once, I had wanted to be around people who were not into drugs. I had started to talk to Vic because I thought he looked like a clean-cut good guy who wouldn't be involved in drugs, but I was wrong.

I made my way to the women's restroom and found a Japanese girl sobbing and stumbling around inside with mascara and eyeliner running down her face. She was very badly bruised on her swollen face and had fading bruises on her arms. I helped her to the side as the other girls busied themselves with applying fresh makeup, totally ignoring her except when she bumped into them or tried to grab them to keep from falling.

Nadine was Japanese, about five inches taller than me, large-boned, but very skinny. Her boyfriend had beaten her again. He beat her all the time, she said, and she was trying to get it together in the bathroom but had taken too many ludes.

I helped her wipe the black streaks of makeup from her face, but even then, I could not tell what she really looked. Her eyes and face were badly swollen and colors of very fresh bruises were still darkening on her skin.

"Are you with friends? Can I get you some help?"

Nadine began to sob again and asked me if I wanted to buy any Quaaludes for $5.50 a piece because she was desperate and needed the money. "Please," she begged. "I need rent money!"

"Give me ten," I answered, unsure of what had really compelled me to buy the stuff, but it made the pitiful girl stop sobbing.

Nadine dug around at the bottom of her purse and started getting upset at herself again. The tablets had spilled out of their container, and she started to cry. But she stopped crying again when I gave her the money.

"I'll get you out of here and take you home," I offered, but Nadine refused. Her boyfriend was waiting for her outside and would probably beat her some more if she didn't leave with him.

I helped Nadine get it together in the bathroom for about half an hour and asked her why she got so wasted and why she was pushing dope.

"I don't know how to do anything else," she cried, and then explained that it was a way to make fast money.

"What if you get caught?"

Nadine didn't care about anything anymore. She wanted to get caught, to get arrested and put in jail. She wouldn't have to worry about anything anymore if she got busted, she explained: not rent, not food, not money.

"Call me," she slurred as she took forever to write her name and number on a paper towel. "You're a good friend and I need to sell my stuff," she added.

I promised to call her and then half carried her out of the restroom. She held on to my arm as she struggled to walk through the crowd to get outside of the place. We finally made it to where she said her boyfriend would be waiting for her, and she was delighted when she saw him standing in the corner of the outside lobby.

Nadine's boyfriend was raging and whacked her as soon as we rounded the corner.

I grabbed his arm when he tried to punch Nadine in the face, and everyone around us pretended they didn't see anything.

Nadine was against the wall, sliding down to the ground, sobbing and covering her face with her hands. Her already bruised cheek was starting to swell up again. Her small Filipino boyfriend tried to punch me, but he missed and I shoved him backward. He tripped over his own feet and landed on his ass. He was glaring at me with hate and rage as he tried to get up and started lunging at me, trying to hit me again. Nadine began to scream and yell.

The once crowded hallway was now empty as Nadine's wimp boyfriend threatened me.

"I going pound you!" he yelled but took a few steps backward when I stepped towards him. He was yelling and half crying himself.

Again he lunged at Nadine, trying to get around me, and managed to grab her by her long black hair. I shoved him backward again, and he started sobbing.

The bouncers arrived a few seconds later, shoved him face forward against the wall, and then dragged him out of sight. One of the bouncers helped me gather up Nadine from the floor to take her home. I noticed Vic standing in the doorway, watching as the bouncer and I practically carried Nadine to my car. He must have thought that Nadine was the friend I had planned to meet.

It took a few hours to get Nadine home since she kept passing out, crying, and giving me wrong directions. While driving in circles, Nadine told me that she was twenty-five years old, wasn't married, and had a son who was taken away from her. She refused to go to the hospital because the hospital would call the cops but promised to go to a doctor the next day. I wanted to tell her I was a cop, but it suddenly dawned on me that I didn't know what being a cop meant. No one would believe me, anyway, and I had no proof.

"Call me at home if you score," the detective had said, "No matter what time it is, you can't hold on to the evidence."

Stanley's wife answered the phone and was pissed off at me for calling.

"Who is this!" she demanded, and I tried to explain who I was and that I was following the detective's instructions.

"He was with you all night!" she accused me viciously. "I'm his wife! Can't I have him just for a little while?" she demanded.

"He wasn't with me. I was by myself!" I tried to explain. "I'm just trying to turn over evidence!" If I were with him, I wouldn't have had to call.

If he was spending his nights away from her, it wasn't with me. I couldn't stand him around me and hated his manipulating bullshit about how powerful and great he was. The detective's wife started yelling at me on the phone, saying that he had just come home drunk again, was sleeping, and she refused to wake him up. She slammed down the phone.

I had run the gamut of emotions that evening. Disappointment with Vic, pity for Nadine, disgust that no one would help Nadine, rage at Nadine's wimp boyfriend, and now, total anger and disgust for the detective and his jealous, accusing wife. I was angry with the detective for not answering the call after he had pounded it into my head that I had better call him no matter what time it was.

As usual, he had obviously gone out drinking while he had sent me out to score his dope. Maybe he was having an affair with someone and using me as an excuse. Whatever it was, he had not answered the call and left me to deal with his estranged and jealous wife.

My stomach was burning with the acid of anger and stress. I had no one to talk to and no way to diffuse, except through my journals, and I was now putting up with unnecessary drama and bullshit from the detective's wife.

I picked up my paychecks from the graveyards when he remembered or had the time. I made no overtime and spent my own money for drinks, video games, food, and gas while doing the deals. I found out later that the more than fifty blank expense vouchers he had made me sign were supposed to be money for me to use on the deals instead of my own money. Whatever money I was given in cash, I had kept separately to only use to buy the drugs.

"Get a private phone line in your room," the detective ordered. "Then you can give the crooks your phone number. We can reimburse you for the phone installation and the phone bill," he promised, but that was a lie, too. I also learned that he had turned in overtime cards when he sent me out alone at night with no backup. Stanley had kept me so isolated that I had no one to turn to when something was going wrong. I also had no way to verify that I was medically insured, since I did not exist in the City and County or the Honolulu Police Department's list of active employees. If I died, no one would know who I was.

"Don't trust your family. Don't trust your friends. Don't trust policemen. Don't trust Christy. She's just a footman and she doesn't know anything. Trust only me," he told me over and over again. The only thing I knew was that I couldn't trust him.

SPRING DAYS

Glimmer Glimmer
Drop and shimmer
Silent tears
No longer fall

Journal entry: April 28, 1980

Ernest

May 1, 1980, 10:50 a.m. Christy and I went to Ernest's apartment, and I knocked on the door. I could feel him peeping at me through the tiny spy hole in the door.

"It's me, Jo … Tricks' friend," I announced, and after a brief moment of silence, Ernest replied from the other side of the door, "Oh yeah," in recognition.

Ernest opened the door to let me in and abruptly shut the door behind me. I asked if Christy could come in, too, and he peeped at her through the door and agreed to let her in.

"I don't usually deal with kids," Ernest said, looking directly at me.

"I'm twenty-five years old!" I responded, and he stared at me in disbelief. I had no false identification, and all of my identification cards and my driver's license documented my real name and address. I hesitated but pulled out an old state ID, and Ernest glanced at the birth date.

"Damn, I thought you were in high school!" he exclaimed. "You want a half or a gram?" he asked.

"Half," I answered.

Ernest got up, went to his bedroom, and returned right away with a packet of powder and placed it on the table instead of my hand. I placed the $50 on the table, and he left it there as if he were afraid to pick it up.

"You want a lude?" he asked. Ernest then explained that he wasn't into Quaaludes but a friend had given him some and he had one left that he would give me for free.

Ernest went back into the bedroom and returned a few seconds later, placing the tablet on the table again as if he was afraid to place it directly into my hands. He always moved and talked the same way, which was a mellow low gear. We left in the next minute.

The drug deals were getting faster and easier, but the dissension in our so-called team began to grow. I was mentally and emotionally exhausted and looking forward to some down time.

There were only two people I was forced to depend on: Christy and Detective Stanley. But their differences and their discord were more apparent every day, and I felt I was stuck in the middle of their battle. It was Christy I trusted, and it was Christy who I was comfortable with. It was definitely not Stanley.

Detective Stanley sensed it, and it fueled the fire of his threatened ego. He called that night and sent me out again, alone, to score his precious dope as if trying to show me who was the boss and who controlled me.

The Blue Light

May 1, 1980, 7:00 p.m., Thursday. "Go pick up a quarter ounce from the King. Go alone."

I went alone to pick up the King. He was dressed in a white pullover shirt, white dress slacks, and a white Lauhala hat with a gold hatband that accented his gold earring. With a quick call, he directed me back to Marvin's apartment.

"It's $550," he said and again instructed me to wait in the car.

"Don't make me wait forever like the last time," I asked as I gave him the money.

"I'll be right out," he promised, and then to reassure me further, he explained Marvin's signals.

"If the blue light outside is turned on, that means the man is open for business. If it's turned off, he's not holding." The King pointed at an apartment with a blue light turned on outside the front door. This time, he came back in fifteen minutes and everything was cool. I dropped him off in Chinatown.

I thought it amusing that Marvin had chosen to use a blue colored light which was a recognized symbol of law enforcement.

May 2, 1980, 2:55 p.m., Friday. I was sent to score from Allen at the parking lot again. It was the first time I had ever seen him smiling and happy. He was back with his girlfriend, he announced when I asked why he seemed so happy.

"Ludes?" he asked.

"Ten" I replied, and I was on my way in a minute.

Liquor Store Ladies

May 3, 1980, Saturday. My private telephone rang early in the morning, and I knew it was either a crook or the detective. All I was sure of was that it was definitely not a friend calling. I shook myself awake and placed myself into character before I answered the phone. It wasn't difficult anymore. I had become totally engulfed in my new identity.

It was Detective Stanley calling with a new assignment. "Go to the liquor store on Liliha Street and ask for a Japanese guy named Jonathan. See if you can score some cocaine and Quaaludes."

As I prepared to go to seek out my new target, the fear of the unknown crept in and the anxiety churned in my stomach. Every day I faced unknown confrontations, meeting drug dealers, forcibly making friends for prosecution, and putting up with their questions and scrutiny. I had to constantly psych myself out to think, act, talk, dress, and become like someone else. I had to play the role well enough to be undetected.

Christy was worried. "It's not right! He's running you day and night!" she said. "He thinks he owns you!"

"Yup, he keeps telling me that over and over again," I answered. I learned that most of the other undercover officers bought dope once or twice a week at the most. I was being sent out day and night.

"That's wrong!" she would say, but we both knew that she was just the footman, and I was lower than that. I was just the undercover officer.

There was no one with me. No one knew where I was or what I was doing except the dictator detective. Even my family didn't know where I was, who I was with, or what I was doing. I was hurting them, and Stanley didn't care. My parents had stopped asking me questions. They knew I wouldn't answer. So many times I heard his words echoing in my head: "Don't trust anyone, not even your closest friend or your family. They'll hurt you and burn you!" Remembering the sound of the detective's voice made me cringe as I approached the liquor store. The real me would never choose to be associated with someone like Stanley.

I went into the liquor store and scanned the room, feeling totally alone and depressed. It took me a few minutes to approach the Japanese male behind the counter, but I finally erased my last personal thought and fully stepped back into my role.

"Are you Jonathan?"

"Nope, I'm Grant. Jonathan's not here," he said. "Jonathan comes in at night and closes up the store. He's the owner. I'll tell him you were looking for him when he comes in."

After all the preparation and anxiety, Jonathan wasn't even there! I left the store with an empty, light-headed feeling but didn't know why.

I called the Narcotics office and briefed the detective on what had happened, hoping that I was done dealing with him for the day.

"Go back in tonight at seven," he dictated.

I stayed in all day and mentally prepared myself for my role and thought of possible answers to the questions from Jonathan that I knew would be forthcoming. The day finally ended and evening came too quickly. I walked into the store again, still unsure about my preparation.

There was a different Asian male behind the counter with a Caucasian female. Grant was no longer around. A few customers picked out their purchases and paid for them on their way out. I waited until the store was empty and grabbed a can of soda as I watched Jonathan watching my every move. He even looked outside when I glanced out into the night as if he were trying to see what I was looking at.

I was alone and began to worry if he was going to check out my car parked outside and find out where I lived. For a brief moment, I was overwhelmed with concern about my family at home. Jonathan was staring at me so I hid my fears and doubts. I had learned very well how to cut myself off and put my thoughts away.

I paid for my soda. "Jonathan?"

He nodded his answer and asked if I wanted ladies.

"How did you know?" I asked curiously

"You look like the type," he smiled warmly.

"How much?"

"Five," he answered.

"Give me ten," I said.

Jonathan placed ten of the familiar white tablets into a small Ziploc bag. I paid for the ladies and turned to leave.

"How about some soda?" he asked and pointed to a small Ziploc bag filled with rice.

"What?" I asked, bewildered, and Jonathan placed the tiny bag of rice in my hand.

"Look between the rice," he coaxed and smiled.

I moved the rice around and saw a folded paper inside.

"Fifty for the half?" he asked.

I nodded and gave Jonathan another $50 for the cocaine.

Jonathan and I started talking, and he eventually invited me to a party that would be taking place later that evening. I declined with an excuse that I had to meet a very jealous boyfriend, and he shrugged his indifference but still told me where they were going to be, "just in case."

The deal had gone down too easily, and I felt uneasy about it. Jonathan wasn't at all what I had expected. He was about five foot eight, tanned with well-toned muscles, and a real clean-cut looking guy. He had smile lines tanned around his eyes and a carefree type of personality. He reminded me of a tennis player or a surfer.

I drove around for a while, watching for a tail, and then found a pay phone to call the hotline. "I'll meet you at the graveyard," the detective instructed after I told him I had scored both of the drugs.

The Nuuanu cemetery was deserted at ten thirty at night, but I had been there alone a few times before, to pick up my paycheck or turn in the drugs I had bought.

This particular graveyard was supposed to be haunted, and I began to remember all the ghost stories I had heard. I watched the shadows play with the moonbeams on the cement and marble stones until the detective finally drove up.

There had been many attempts to get to Jonathan, I was told, and I had been the first. "You did good, girl," he said, but I didn't feel good. In fact, I felt nothing at all, not even fear. But instead of letting me go home, Detective Stanley sent me out again to see if I could score at the Lanai.

Unexpected Empathy

May 4, 1980, 12:30 a.m. It was already Sunday morning. I left the graveyard and went back alone to the Lanai restaurant to look for Billie the bartender, but she wasn't working. Delia spotted me in the crowd and asked me to join them at a table, but I declined.

There was an incredible emptiness taking over my soul, and I didn't feel like joining a party. More than that, I didn't want to get too close to the girls. I knew it would be very easy to become friends and that eventually I would have to betray their trust. Delia was sympathetic and understood that I was feeling down just by looking into my eyes. She didn't push the invitation but I knew too that Stanley wouldn't let me go until I scored more drugs.

I asked if she was holding, and Delia told me to wait at the bar for a minute.

It was standing room only that evening, and once again, it seemed that I was the only one who had come alone. Delia was back in a minute, and I brought ten ludes.

"Too crowded," I said. I thanked Delia and left.

I found myself fighting the feelings of guilt that were beginning to tear at my conscience. My old identity felt that my deception was dishonorable, but my new identity fought back, saying that what I was doing was an honorable assignment: taking down the dealers. Or maybe it was the other way around. I didn't know which one was the real me anymore, so I erased them both and just did what I had to do.

There was a third persona emerging that had no thoughts, no conscience, and no emotions. It took over when my old and new identities were in conflict with each other. I didn't know where it came from, but it surfaced and stepped in when I needed help dealing with what I had to do.

After the debriefing with Stanley, I drove to Ala Moana Beach Park and sat alone in my car. The waves in the far distance were illuminated by the moonlight. Everything seemed so surreal except for the pounding headache, the incredible loneliness, and the hate I was beginning to feel for Stanley.

May 5, 1980, 1:35 p.m. Stanley sent me to see if I could score from Nadine again, but I drove to Nadine's apartment just to see if she was okay, not to score more drugs. I wondered if she would remember who I was.

Nadine was standing outside of her apartment and recognized me immediately. She had gone to the doctor, and the swelling and bruises were still visible but fading.

"How much?" she asked without hesitation.

"Ten," I said automatically, and Nadine entered her apartment, motioning for me to follow. Nadine was very sullen and pointed to the bed in the one-room studio. "Sit down and relax," she said.

Nadine walked to her chest of drawers and took out ten pills. She had all kinds of things stuffed in the drawer, including a picture of her son, which she pulled out to share with me.

"I got back with my boyfriend," she confessed, "I love him, and he loves me ... even if he's not my son's father."

I left Nadine and wished her the best. After turning in Stanley's precious dope, I went home and looked back into my old journals for an answer that I might have written for myself in the previous years.

All men are not created equal
Yet his Soul creates that equality
Is the purpose of man only to live, struggle, and die?
Are we only of human bondage?
What, then, is the meaning of existence?

FUTILITY?

Journal entry: 1975

Chapter 7
Nightmares

The Temple of Mirrors

May 7, 1980, 10:50 a.m. I bought a half-gram of cocaine from Ernest. It was more expensive this time because it wasn't cut as much, he explained. The drug purchases had become too easy, and I was troubled about it. *I should feel like I'm doing something evil*, I thought and then wondered about what I had become and what had happened to my real self. I was used to being alone on the deals most of the time and had even begun to go to dinner and to the movie theaters in Chinatown by myself in the evenings.

The only problem with working alone at nights was when I had to drop off the drugs to the detective. Every time I called, Stanley's wife would answer and send knives through the phone. I had done nothing to deserve her vicious verbal attacks and ridiculous accusations, which added unnecessary difficulty to the assignment.

Stanley was amused by the situation and said he would talk to her. If he did keep his promise, it didn't work. Perhaps Stanley was really having an affair, and I was a convenient excuse. The only thing I was certain of was that he wasn't with me. *I wonder if it would have made a difference if I was a guy*, I thought.

I had lost all contact with all of my friends and the gossip was getting back to my family that I was doing drugs and hanging around with drug dealer friends. I had nightmares, distorted ones of being discovered and trying to convince my family and friends that I was who I was not—dreams of running into a temple of glass and mirrors and having no reflection, of being shot and buried and no one knowing who or where I was.

Stanley said he would always protect me, and that made me laugh. He couldn't even protect me from his wife and had arranged for me to work with Christy, who he said I should not trust. I had no gun and no badge, and ran around alone with no surveillance except for when Christy was with me. *He* was never around.

All I had was a supply of coins and a phone number that unknown voices answered during the day, and a phone number that a vicious wife answered at night. But then again, that was only *if* I could find a pay phone and *if* the pay phone was working.

Glenn

May 8, 1980. My phone rang constantly at all hours of the day and night. It was wired internally for recording, and I had to sign a one-party consent for the monitoring. Freddy called, and negotiations began for one hundred Quaaludes. Glenn called today, too. I had seen him at the Point After disco in Waikiki, and he had approached me at the bar.

Glenn was Japanese, slim, and a very nice guy. He was an acquaintance from high school, and it was good to see someone I knew.

"I know what you're looking for," he had said, "but I don't have any."

I was surprised at what he said but relieved that he didn't have anything. I had never asked him for anything and had not seen him since high school, which was about seven years past.

We talked a bit and exchanged phone numbers, but I had already made up my mind to never call him.

Glenn surprised me again that morning. He called and invited me to drop by his house to talk about a business opportunity. He said he was ordering Lemmons in quantity, and he wanted to know if I wanted to order some, too, but I would have to front him the money before I could get the merchandise.

Glenn refused to accept the excuses I made that I was just an occasional user and didn't want to sell the stuff.

"Just come down," he persisted, and he gave me directions to his house.

I declined the invitation and explained I had no money.

Detective Stanley called as soon as I hung up the phone, and I informed him of the calls from Freddy and Glenn. I had never mentioned Glenn before and had never expected him to call. We had never talked or hung around together in high school, and our unexpected meeting at the Waikiki disco was a brief surprise. I got lectured on *loyalty*, withholding information, and fairness again after commenting that I felt guilty because Glenn was a classmate.

Stanley lashed out in anger. "He's not your friend! He's just making money off of you! He just wants to use you to sell his stuff. That's why he's asking you to front the money first."

Then the all-too-familiar interrogation began. "Did you ever go out with him? Was he ever your boyfriend? Was he a close friend? Did you hang around together?" The detective demanded personal information about my past.

I truthfully answered no to all the questions, and he snapped back with sarcasm.

"So what's the problem? Go pick up a sample. That's what you're here for, to get the drug dealers, and that's what he is! You're getting confused, girl!" he said with unsympathetic disgust. "You going to be fair or take care of the people you *think* are your friends?"

I prayed all the way to Glenn's house. "If this is what you want me to do, God, then so be it." I prayed on the way to every assignment. I had prayed that I would meet the people I was supposed to meet. I prayed for clarity, protection, and guidance, and then I said a prayer of thanks every night when I made it home safely. When I arrived, Glenn and John, another high school classmate, were finishing breakfast. Glenn led me to his bedroom to talk, and John followed.

"I thought you were trying to be a cop," Glenn asked.

"Yes," I answered, surprised that he knew so much about me. "I passed everything." John shot me a quick look.

"But I just had surgery in my left eye, so I have to wait. I'm just waiting to get into a uniform," I explained, trying to make Glenn think twice, but it didn't faze him that he was trying to set up a partnership to sell drugs with someone who was going to be a cop. I looked at John, and I was sure that he caught on to what I was saying, but he remained silent.

"I know what you were looking for at the Point After," Glenn continued and seemed to totally ignore what I said. "I can supply you with some bootleg for cheap, and you can make your money back in a flash. Sell them for $5, pay only $3.50 … maybe $3.75," he said.

"Nah!" I said. I was in shock at what I was hearing. Maybe Stanley was right.

"I was just cruising on my own. I don't want to push the stuff!" I explained, but Glenn was persistent.

He continued his sales pitch and showed me different types of Quaalude tablets in different sizes, explaining which ones were pharmaceuticals and which ones were bootlegs.

"Here, take this one." Glenn placed a free bootleg Quaalude in my hand as a sample. "Try it out later," he insisted. "It's not pharmaceutical; its bootleg so it's cheaper, but it's the same thing. Think about what I said," he urged. "You know so many people. You would do good!"

"I don't have the money, Glenn!" I protested.

"I can front you the stuff," he offered reluctantly after a moment of silence. "Just try the bootleg and call me back later if you like it."

Glenn explained that he got his stuff from a fireman named Roy and he could get cocaine from his brother if I wanted any. All I had to do was let him know.

I turned in the sample and told the detective that I didn't want to call Glenn back. Stanley was totally pissed off and shook his head.

"*You* don't have to call *him*," he finally said angrily, "but if *he* calls *you* and keeps pushing you, you better take him down. He's a dealer!"

I was supposed to call Glenn back that evening after I had tried the bootleg sample, but I never called him back. What was unsettling was how much Glenn knew about me even though we were never close friends, never talked in school, and had not seen each other for all these years.

Yakuza Fishing Boats

May 16, 1980, 6:10 p.m. Freddy, the west end Haleiwa Candy Man, was at Yoshi's Restaurant that afternoon and sitting with his friend Takeo. I had gone in to find Crystal to pick up some Quaaludes, and Freddy motioned me over to join him at his table.

Takeo was quiet and observant and looked like a middle-aged businessman from Japan. He was running Aku fishing boats at the North Shore docks. I listened as he and Freddy talked about killing informants, chopping them up, and throwing the body pieces into the ocean as shark bait. They were serious and spoke quietly. Takeo did not seem like the kind of person who would embellish a story or make one up to impress anyone, and I believed him.

"They can't prove anything without the body," Freddy said. When Takeo excused himself to use the restroom, Freddy took the opportunity to whisper that his friend Takeo was organized crime, too, just like Yoshi, the owner of the restaurant. They were both connected to the Yakuza.

Yoshi's wife stopped by briefly after Takeo returned to the table and greeted us with a polite slight bow. She was obviously from Japan.

Takeo gave me a gram of cocaine and a half bag of marijuana for free. I had never asked for anything. He just gave it to me without request or question.

When I briefed Stanley on what had happened and what was said about the Yakuza and killing informants, he responded that I was getting paranoid and shrugged it off like I was stupid.

Jonathan

May 16, 1980, 10:10 p.m. The call came in the early afternoon. "Call Jonathan and order some Quaaludes and cocaine for tonight," the detective instructed in an exceptionally loud voice. I could tell that he liked to bark out orders in front of the guys I could hear in the background.

I called Jonathan and asked if I could come by for the same thing, and he agreed without hesitation. I briefed the detective about the deal, and he informed me that *this time*, he would be watching me.

"This time?" I mused. Perhaps this time someone would know if I made it out of the store in one piece.

I went back to the store and nodded a greeting to Jonathan and Grant. I picked out an ice-cold soda again and drank some before I approached the counter. My throat was dry, and my hands were shaking. I had done this before, but I never had a surveillance unit. Instead of making me feel safer, it made me more nervous.

Jonathan waited for me at the counter, and I paid for my soda. He smiled pleasantly. "How you doing? Same thing?"

"Yup," I answered and watched him get the white tablets and small bag of rice from the cashier's counter. I checked between the rice, counted the tablets, and gave him $100.

Jonathan was in a nice mood, and we chatted for a while. The conversation put me at ease immediately. He seemed like a really nice guy; in fact, he even seemed to be honest. We joked around a bit before I left.

I started feeling a little light-headed again and sat in my car for a moment before driving off. Jonathan came out of the store, and I saw him looking at Stanley's car parked directly across the street. Jonathan hesitated, looked at me, and watched.

Stanley drove off, and I waited a while, pretending not to notice and to be organizing the interior of my car. The anxiety grew again, but when I drove off in the opposite direction from the Stanley, Jonathan smiled and waved good-bye. I circled around a bit and then went to the graveyard to wait.

It was 11:00 p.m., and a cool spring rain was falling. I could smell the freshly cut grass of the graveyard and was envious of the peaceful slumber of the buried. Shadows played across the gravestones, and the wet flowers left for departed loved ones glistened under the moonlight.

When Stanley arrived, I told him the story, turned over his precious drugs, and drove home in the rain. I had a funny feeling but didn't know what it was. I liked Jonathan and knew that under different circumstances, we could probably become friends. There was a silent loneliness creeping into my soul, so I cut myself off. I didn't exist.

Adonis

May 16, 1980, 12:30 a.m. The Sting was another popular discotheque in the heart of Waikiki. A long line of anxious patrons lined up on Kuhio Avenue, waiting to get in.

The man at the door was huge and solemn, looking like the perfect bouncer. He was wearing a tuxedo, and the look on his face said very clearly, "Don't mess with me." There was iron in his face and solid rock under his coat.

The cocaine dealer on the complaint was identified only as Adonis. There had been no description of the man or information about what he did, only that anyone could score the drug if they asked for him. Christy was with me tonight. When we finally reached the front of the line, we asked the bouncer if Adonis was in. The bouncer paused, looked at us intently, and asked why were looking for him.

"Just looking to pick up," I answered too quickly, and I expected him to kick us both back out, but he accepted my answer. The bouncer led us to the private VIP room on the second floor balcony and told us to wait, shutting the door behind him. Christy and I waited nervously for the man called Adonis to appear.

The room was luxurious with dark-colored walls and a thick dark blue carpet that sank when we walked on it. It was furnished with overstuffed blue velvet furniture and a low mirror-topped coffee table. A huge picture window overlooked the entire room just below us, but the blaring music seemed muffled and distant. We didn't know that we were talking to Adonis himself until he returned a few minutes later with a vial of powder, a gram, a small mirror, and a straw, and placed it on top of the table.

"Test it," he demanded. "In front of me!" His grim facial expression was a look of challenge and suspicion, and refusal was obviously not an option.

"How about dimming the lights?" I asked, looking into Christy's eyes. I knew her mind was racing as fast as mine, trying to think of our next move. It was the only thing I could think of to buy us some time.

Adonis looked at me curiously and explained that the huge window overlooking the crowd was a two-way mirror. He finally agreed when

I complained that I didn't trust two-way mirrors and was afraid that someone could still see what we were doing if the lights were too bright in the room. He chuckled at my paranoia and turned the lights in the room all the way down.

Christy took the test vial and the straw and began preparing a small line of powder on the mirror Adonis had provided. She turned her back to him when he glanced at her, as if huddling in embarrassment.

I distracted Adonis by talking to him about the two-way mirror, trying to draw attention away from Christy until I heard her inhale deeply and quickly.

Adonis turned abruptly to look at Christy, who was dabbling at her nose, and he was satisfied. The deal for a gram of cocaine was concluded quickly and with a smile. He took our drink orders and left, saying he would send a waitress.

As soon as he left the room, Christy raised the lights in the room, looking around nervously. There was white powder all over the blue velvet furniture, and we frantically tried to dust it off the thick fabric until it blended and dissolved.

Adonis opened the door a few seconds later and flashed us a winning smile. We had dusted most of the powder off but it was still visible, so we both quickly plopped down on the sofa to hide the discoloration. I suddenly gasped at the thought that there might be a hidden surveillance camera in the room.

Thankfully, he had just popped his head into the room to announce that the first round was on him. We both managed a smile in spite of our fearful hysteria.

My first drink went down quickly, and I felt the adrenalin begin to ebb.

The place was packed, and I suddenly felt like the world and everyone in it was closing in on me. I drove home in the first light of early morning with the wind and the rain in my hair, blowing through my opened car window.

꧁꧂

Chapter 8
Truth

Just the Facts ... Not Truth

May 17, 1980. I received all of my reports back from Stanley and was told I had to do them all over again. I had never written a police report and was learning the hard way: accuracy, brevity, and clarity. I had written an essay instead of an investigative report, which was unacceptable.

"Take out all the fluffy stuff. Keep it short, accurate, and to the point! Don't use ten words that mean nothing."

I was frustrated. I had written the truth about what each suspect had told me, including what was going on in their lives, such as divorces, problems with boyfriends, and selling dope to make ends meet, but that was going too far. Police reports only dealt with the facts that document the criminal conduct, and each fact had to be supported by evidence.

"Go back and pick up from Jonathan," Stanley ordered after handing me a package of yellow canary-colored papers to type my reports all over again.

I went to see Jonathan that afternoon and bought ladies and soda again. Jonathan noticed that I was agitated and asked if I wanted to go to a party in Kaimuki. I graciously declined and excused myself with the description of a jealous boyfriend.

"He follows me around sometimes," I explained. "He monitors everything I do and say. He thinks he owns me, but he's married. He even gets mad if I get too close to my girlfriends!" I realized I was describing Detective Stanley and felt sick about it.

May 19, 1980. I bought a hundred ladies from Jonathan as instructed.

It was only $4 a tablet because of the quantity. "The more you buy, the cheaper it gets!" Jonathan smiled.

Jonathan talked about his pending divorce. He seemed like he needed to talk to someone, but I didn't want to stay to listen. I thanked him, made an excuse, and left quickly. It was difficult getting to know the dealers on a personal level. I was beginning to find out that they were not that different from anyone else. They had the same problems, the same hang-ups, and some had very easygoing personalities. The only difference was that they had made different choices for themselves.

I used to think that drug dealers were mean, nasty, and heartless. Almost everything I believed in was crumbling, but I was beginning to learn, too. But I didn't know exactly what it was that I was learning or what the final lesson would be.

I knew I had changed. I had always thought it would be really easy to take down drug dealers and put them in jail. I hadn't counted on identifying with them, understanding them, or even liking some of them as friends. I was getting to know their ups and downs, their problems, their laughter, and their fears. I could no longer hang on to the concept that they were evil and that I was different from them and doing a good deed. The line I had always drawn that separated good guys from the bad guys had begun to dissolve. Nice guys sometimes did bad things, and bad guys sometimes did nice things.

"Don't get too close!" Stanley had warned, but he forced me to see them every day and every night. He forced me to become like, identify with and befriend my targets and no one else. I had been forced to realize and confront my own prejudices and judgments and had then watched them slowly dissolve.

Stanley was always bragging about his knowledge and expertise and how he intimidated everyone in the office with his ability and his power. He demanded my loyalty and always spoke about who was loyal to him. "With drug dealers, it's all about the money and nothing else," he said in an all-knowing tone.

But I knew he was wrong. If money were all that mattered to the drug dealers, then he wouldn't need me. *He* could go out and buy the dope himself. All he would have to do was flash around some beaucoup bucks! In the streets, like anywhere else, it was about being accepted, gaining trust, and establishing friendships and loyalty … and it was that ultimate betrayal of loyalty that he would probably never be really capable of understanding.

There was no vast separation between good and evil anymore, and I realized that I could have so easily fallen into this lifestyle simply by making a choice. The nightmares increased along with my drinking as I watched everything that I used to be and all my beliefs destroyed.

My new undercover identity was now stronger and more dominant. I had to perfect my undercover personality in order to be successful and survive, yet it was destroying who I used to be and what I believed in. I had to hold on to the fact that I was a police officer, but the real truth was that I never even knew what that meant in the first place. I learned too that facts don't always portray the truth. Hot showers didn't wash off the day, but drinking helped to numb the pain, stop me from thinking, and make the escape of sleep come quickly.

LOYALTY

A driving force able to move nation against nation
Able to justify prejudice, killing, destruction
A powerful commitment of devotion that can instill
Eternal friendship without question, Support against the odds

It can be demanded
A concept threatened from the ranks of insecurity
It can be commanded
A concept earned from the ranks of respect
Wrongly used, the power grows through blind faith, oblivious to truth
Rightfully gained, each man is still true to himself
Loyalty … a dark force … a white light

Journal entry: April 15, 1987

May 20, 1980. It was 4:00 a.m., and the Point After disco was closing. I met Bill this morning. He was of Spanish ancestry, forty-five years old, and one of the managers of the disco. He was a gentleman and very professional. For the last several hours, he had moved back and forth through the crowd, but always returned to sit with me at the back bar. He wasn't feeling well tonight, he said, and had asked me if I had anything that would make him feel better.

I offered him the aspirin that I always carried in my purse for my incessant headaches. I had also used the aspirin as a prop to pretend to drop Quaaludes, whenever I had to convince someone that I was trustworthy.

Drinking was my excuse for not smoking grass, and dropping an aspirin and pretending it was a Quaalude was my excuse for not doing cocaine. "I don't want to mix the highs," I would explain, and saving it for later was always an accepted excuse. I was learning the art of the deception too well, and I was uncomfortable with that.

Stanley had told me many times to "out-scam the scammer and always be one step ahead," but he never told me how. I had to figure out how to accomplish my assignments as well as keep my identity a secret—on my own. There were no rules of this game, no how-to books on the art of deception in the streets, and Stanley had sent me out on my own to learn from the streets. He constantly talked about loyalty and demanded mine. But I had already learned before I met him that true loyalty had to be earned … it could never be demanded. Loyalty worked both ways, and I knew he never understood that.

Bill had refused the aspirin I offered and explained that he was looking for some cocaine. Feeling really stupid, I said I didn't have any but was looking for some, too. He had disappeared into the busy demands of the disco after our conversation and didn't reappear until I was leaving.

From behind me, Bill called out and ran up to me just as I was about to exit the front doors. He was slightly out of breath and led me to a dark corner near the pay phone just outside the doors of the discothèque.

"Give me fifty bucks. I got the stuff!" he said anxiously.

"From who?" I asked, totally surprised.

"The man doesn't want to meet anyone. Just wait right here."

Bill ran back into the nightclub, and the doors closed behind him. A few minutes later, he was back with a folded paper and a small spoon he had removed from the breast pocket of his long-sleeved dress shirt. He was nervous, out of breath, and anxious as he took two spoonfuls of the powder and inhaled its white powdery contents with quick, deep breaths.

"Whoa, is that my stuff?" I asked, as he was about to take another spoonful.

Bill sighed and folded up the small paper and placed it into my hands. He held on to my hands for a moment with a look of deep gratitude.

"Thanks. I feel better. I really needed that, and I knew you wouldn't mind. You're a loyal friend." Bill looked deeply into my eyes and smiled, ran back to the front doors, and disappeared inside. I was stunned for a moment and just stood there, bewildered at what had just happened and sad at the desperation I had seen in this man.

Stanley's wife answered again, yelling at me and hanging up the phone. This time I called back, and this time I wanted to talk to her. I was tired of the bullshit and knew that Stanley had not taken care of his problem with her like he said he would.

Stanley's wife answered the phone again. I explained that I had no intentions on her husband and, in fact, I didn't even like him, but I needed to drop off the dope and if she had a problem, I would meet her in person or she could tell her husband to make other arrangements for me.

I was outraged and told her that I had been out around the clock because of her husband's assignments and hadn't slept all day. I had always been alone and was never hanging around or drinking with him. If he had been with me and providing some kind of back up, I wouldn't have had to call to drop off the dope. Furthermore, I said, "I don't like him, and he doesn't turn me on!"

The detective's wife had listened reluctantly but finally apologized, saying that he had just gotten home drunk again and he was passed out.

Stanley finally got on the phone and told me to meet him at 5:30 a.m. to drop off the cocaine. I was tired but had to wait for an hour and a half and hang around in Waikiki alone. "You wait for me, but don't ever make me wait for you!" I remembered his command.

The Waikiki beach was across the street from the disco, so I walked along the beach side of Kalakaua Avenue, trying to stay awake, dissolve my anger, and kill some time.

At 5:30 a.m., the sun had already risen. "I'll talk to her," he said, when he finally arrived, but I found no credibility in his words.

I didn't remember driving home or finally falling asleep. It didn't matter that I was running around alone on the streets with drug dealers. It didn't matter how I was getting hurt. All that mattered was that I was buying his precious dope and making him look good though my efforts.

"You don't realize how much I care about you," he said ... and that made feel worse.

May 20, 1980. The skies were a clear cornflower blue, and bright. It was one of those beautiful days in late spring, and I remembered wistfully how I used to go to the beach on days like this. Stanley sent me to pick up a hundred ladies from Jonathan. I had already called him to order the quantity.

"No problem!" This time the price would be $4 a tablet instead of $5.

It was nice of Jonathan, I thought, to give me a discount. I went into the store and picked out an ice-cold soda from the refrigerator. I was thirsty again, or maybe it was just a habit that mentally prepared me for the encounter. I paid for my can of soda, and Jonathan removed a waxed paper sandwich bag from behind the counter filled with white tablets. I checked out the tablets and paid Jonathan the $400.

"Come back tomorrow," he said, explaining that he had run out of the cocaine today but his supply would be coming in.

Again I went to tell my story and turn in the tablets, but I was not myself. I was the undercover person and stuck in character. It was getting harder to separate my identities. I had realized that when I felt sick, dizzy, or nauseated, it was because my real identity was reacting to what I was doing. Today I felt different. When I left Jonathan, I didn't get sick. I didn't know why.

Chilled winds
Blow ice
Through my broken spirit

Journal entry: 1980

Pushing

May 20, 1980, 5:50 p.m. Glenn called me as soon as I got home from the deal I had just done with Jonathan. He was extremely upset that I had never called him back. He had tried to reach me numerous times, he said, but I was never at home.

I apologized and made an excuse that I had no money so I didn't want to order and that I had been out looking for a job and was going to start working pretty soon.

Glenn had taken the liberty of ordering Quaaludes for me and was holding ten Lemmons for me for quite a while. His source had fronted him the Quaalude tablets and now he had to pay him back.

"Meet me someplace," Glenn almost demanded. "I got ten for you. I gotta sell my stuff and pay the guy back! Meet me at the game room on Kalakaua Avenue."

I met Christy and explained what had happened and told her that Stanley was very upset at my reluctance to have anything to do with Glenn and had lectured me on my obligations, withholding information from him, and loyalty.

"He thinks he owns you! That's why everybody calls him the ayatollah. You should hear him bragging about you in the office. Some of the guys think he has a crush on you!" Christy blurted out.

She understood the reluctance and anger I felt toward Glenn, and didn't get on my case the way Stanley did. I It had become very obvious that Glenn was pushing me into this and wouldn't take no for an answer, and that had disgusted me. Of all the people I met so far, he was the one who pushed me the most. But he also sounded desperate to pay his source. We decided to meet with Glenn and pay him for the ten he was holding so he could pay his source. He must have been eating his profits if he was so desperate for payment of ten tablets.

There were only two other patrons in the small game room on Kalakaua Avenue when Christy and I arrived. Glenn was not there yet, so we played a few games. Christy had become an ace at the video games since we started hanging around together.

Glenn finally arrived and stood by a machine at the entrance for a moment, looking hesitantly at Christy, but I didn't go up to meet him. I was hoping that he would just leave, but he didn't.

He finally motioned me over to him, and I explained that Christy was a friend.

Christy put him at ease immediately with her playful personality.

Glenn placed the tablets on the video table, and I lost my last starship in the video game. I paid him what I owed for the pharmaceuticals just as Christy was excitedly placing her name on the machine next to me as the high scorer of the day.

"You can do this, too! Would be easy for you. You can make fast money!" Glenn urged me again.

I was getting disgusted at his pushing and explained that I had just gotten a job at Yoshi's Restaurant and didn't want to get into selling drugs. Glenn shook his head in disappointment.

"Call me," he said, but I never did.

"Cute Japanese boy!" Christy responded. "He's really pushing you to sell his stuff!"

"Yup, and I'm trying to shine him off. I feel sick, He just won't take no for an answer.

I felt very uncomfortable about what Christy had said, and I was totally disappointed and sick about Glenn's pushing.

Each day I wake
And try to destroy
The great turmoil
The incredible loneliness.
I think I'm very sad
And sometimes enraged
But I'm not sure
Of anything anymore

Journal entry: 1980

The Man in the Trench Coat

May 22, 1980, 7:10 p.m. It was a humid, muggy day—not sunny, not raining, but in between—and the air was heavy and thick.

"Call Jonathan; see if you can pick up a quarter ounce of cocaine," Stanley said officiously.

"Come to the store at four with $600. Make sure you come alone!" Jonathan said, and I promised I would.

"Take Christy into the store with you," the detective commanded, totally disregarding the arrangements I had made with Jonathan.

It didn't matter what I felt. It didn't matter what I had to say, even if I was the one who would be up front and would have to answer to Jonathan for the subversion.

Jonathan stared angrily at me and was totally upset that I was not alone. He shook his head and folded his arms across his chest as he watched Christy with intense suspicion. It seemed that he was about to kick me out of the store, but he relaxed a bit when I introduced her as my party buddy.

I made up a quick excuse and explained that I had borrowed some money from Christy and that Christy wanted to make sure it wasn't a rip.

"What are you talking about? You should know me by now! This is my store. I cannot run away!" Jonathan was very offended and highly agitated at me.

Jonathan went outside and looked up the street for a few minutes and then closed and locked the front doors of his store when he came back inside.

"The guy lives right up the street," he said, "but he didn't deliver yet."

Jonathan went behind the counter and nervously used the phone. A few minutes later, he came up and whispered to me, "That's him over there," nodding towards a car pulling up to the curb outside.

"Be cool!" he said nervously and then went to unlock the door for the man.

The man was large and wore a long trench coat in spite of the humidity of the day. He wore a T-shirt, shorts, and rubber slippers underneath it, and a baseball cap covered his long hair. He never took off his dark glasses or his trench coat the entire time he was there, and he and Jonathan disappeared into a back room.

Christy ran out to get the man's license plates and got back into the store just as he and Jonathan exited the back room.

Jonathan seemed to humble himself in the man's presence. He began silently stacking a few cases of beer on the counter and held the door open for him when he walked out. The man paused a minute to stare at me through his dark glasses without saying or word or paying for the beer.

When the man had driven off, Jonathan relaxed and told me to follow him into the back office. He told Christy harshly to wait outside, and she looked at me with a worried stare. I swallowed my fear and followed him into the back room. Jonathan shut the door behind us and then turned to me with a playful smile. "You're not afraid to be alone with me in this room?" he asked curiously.

"No. Why?" I lied.

Jonathan looked at me for a moment and then chuckled and said, "Nah. Here." Jonathan gave me a white envelope with a large packet of white powder in it.

"Thanks, Jonathan!" I said and opened the door just as he was starting a conversation.

Things hadn't been going too well for Jonathan, and I was already beginning to feel sympathy and compassion for him, so I left him standing alone, in the threshold of the front door of his store.

He was going through a divorce, and his wife was trying to take his business away. He was dealing heavier now to get some money put together for his lawyer, and also just in case she took everything from him. If he ever got busted, he would have to answer to the man, who was a real bad ass and heartless. I trusted and believed Jonathan without a doubt.

Once again, I had to tell the detective just the facts and turn in the very expensive powder.

Jonathan was actually a very nice guy. Feelings of guilt and regret began to creep into my soul, so I drowned them out by blasting my car radio on the way home.

I didn't want to think, I didn't want to feel, and I was getting pretty good at erasing myself and becoming empty and void. It was easier that way. It was obvious, too, that Stanley made a decision that put me in jeopardy and could have gotten me hurt or screwed up the deal. But he didn't care as long as I scored his precious merchandise.

I was beginning to hate Stanley for his mind games, manipulation, and selfishness. It seemed as if the dealers I met were more up front and cared more about my safety than he did. One thing for sure was that Jonathan seemed to care more about my safety than the detective.

Clarity of Emotions
To respond, not to react

To be without fear, anguish, and anxiety, and to control
To be of Truth, and only Truth
I long to be Free
My life!

Journal entry: May 25, 1980

The Pimp

May 30, 1980. I went back to Yoshi's Restaurant. Freddy said he had fixed me up with a job through his Yakuza friend, Yoshi, who owned the place. Yoshi was a close friend of Freddy's, "Since we were kids," he said.

"He's a real heavy, so be careful!" Freddy warned and then explained further that they were looking for a mule to transport some stuff to Japan. "Go down to Yoshi's and ask for my friend Sharon. She can help you apply for the job."

"Take the job!" Stanley insisted. "If you're working somewhere, nobody's going to think you're working for the police department. You can secure your cover," he explained. "But you just have to sign your pay checks and give it to me," he added.

I was already trying to identify with three different personalities: my real self, my undercover drug identity, and being a police officer. Now Stanley wanted me to add another identity to this game, hold an additional job, and turn over my earnings. *He's just like a pimp!* I thought angrily.

Christy was shocked when I told her that Stanley wanted me to take the job at Yoshi's. "Are you making any overtime?" she asked again. "He's running you ragged!"

"What's overtime?" I shrugged. "I even have to sign and give my paychecks from Yoshi's to him!"

Freddy's friend Sharon was working as a bartender in the restaurants' small bar that afternoon when I reluctantly went to apply for the job. She was in her early twenties, five foot four, and a very attractive cosmopolitan blend of ancestries with a feisty personality.

She provided me with an application for a job and sold me a gram of cocaine, too. Freddy had told her I was coming in, and Sharon was confident that I was trustworthy because of his referral.

During the job interview with the owner, Yoshi, Freddy arrived unexpectedly. After a quick interview, I reluctantly accepted the job. Freddy and I had a few drinks in the bar while Yoshi took care of some of the paperwork.

"She can run some stuff to Japan for you!" Freddy said to Yoshi when he joined us in the bar.

Freddy and Yoshi talked about how easy it would be for me to be a mule.

"Come look for me anytime on the Ewa side," Freddy said, just before he left the restaurant with Yoshi.

Christy had come to the restaurant to check on me. She challenged me to a Space Invaders game to lighten my spirits as we watched the steady flow of customers buying more than drinks from the bar. Sharon, we learned, was the undefeated champion in the ongoing video game tournament.

⚛

Chapter 9
Integrity

Turtles

Christy and I went shopping for turtles that afternoon. I was getting very lonely and was beginning to get depressed. It was a different kind of loneliness I had never felt before. It wasn't about having a personal relationship. I had lost myself in the numerous roles I played and didn't know who I was or where I belonged anymore.

I knew that taking the job at the restaurant would push me over to the other side and that I would lose myself to my undercover identity, especially if I started transporting stuff to Japan for the Yakuza. I was suddenly afraid that I wouldn't be able to get back to normal.

Stanley was either totally ignorant of what he was doing to me or he was too full of his own agenda to care that he was hurting or destroying anyone else in the process of attaining his own success.

I had continued with my journals to document my changes so that I could follow them backward and hopefully undo the changes in my identity. I had no one to talk to so my journal became my most trusted friend. It was my only safeguard against crossing the line, and I thought it would later be my way back home.

Christy had become my only friend and ally against the dictatorship of Detective Stanley, but Christy had her own life, too. She had two sons who she always talked about, and it was clear she loved them very much. She was married to a policeman, and she already had a few years of experience in the police force. Christy had often talked about the other detectives and officers in the Narcotics Vice Division and how they shared jokes, laughter, and friendship at the office. But Stanley had made it all too clear that I was to have no contact with any friends or cops, not even the officers in Narcotics. He even tried to convince me to distrust Christy!

"Get a pet!" Christy suggested, happy that she had found a temporary solution.

Turtles! They were silent but always appeared to be listening when you talked, and were easy to maintain. Thus, we began the day in search of turtles instead of drugs.

After failing to find a new friend at several pet shops, I was finally informed that no one was allowed to sell the little water turtles anymore because they carried a disease. Christy looked heartbroken when she saw my disappointment, so we went to the beach to talk for a bit instead of doing the daily assignment from the Stanley.

"You should only run when you have backup," she said. Christy had argued with Stanley about running me around the clock with no backup and had always lost.

His expected response had been, "I'm the detective. I'm in charge. You're just the footman!"

She felt badly for not being with me at nights because of her family.

"It's okay," I assured her. "I'd rather work alone than have Stanley watching me. I can't stand him anymore!" I confided. "But the only problem with working alone is that every time I try to turn in the dope, his wife answers and gives me a whole lot of shit."

Before we parted company for the day, Christy gave me a priority assignment to think of another pet. I laughed in spite of wanting to cry.

June 2, 1980. I called Yoshi's to see if anyone was holding, and Crystal answered the phone.

Crystal was twenty-one years old, a blend of Portuguese and Hawaiian, five foot two, tanned and slim. She always wore a sweet smile and kept her long brown hair pulled back neatly. She was getting a supply of Quaaludes that evening, she said, so I could come by anytime. At 11:30 p.m., she was just getting off her shift as a waitress on the restaurant side of the business.

"Thought you weren't going to make it down," she said sweetly. She was getting off early because business was slow.

"Only four tonight," I said as we sat at a table in the dimly lit lounge. "I don't have that much money."

Crystal smiled in understanding, sold me the four tablets, and went back to her duties in the bright lights of the restaurant. She was a really nice person, and I would have never guessed that she was selling, too.

Outside, the rain was falling in a midnight mist as I stood beneath the partial cover of a white-blossomed Plumeria tree. I watched a uniformed female cop walk into the restaurant and smiled at her when she walked past, but she responded with a grim-faced stare and looked at me like I was stupid. I watched her curiously, trying to identify with her as a police officer as she sat in a booth. I had never seen a female cop in uniform before.

The female was tall and stocky, with short hair and light eyes. I turned away when the officer glared at me through the window with a look that seemed to say "What the fuck are you looking at?" I immediately thought of Christy and knew she wouldn't have reacted to a smile that way, dressed in uniform or not, and then I realized that I was supposed to be a cop, too.

The Conflict Begins

Christy and Stanley's verbal attacks against each other's credibility had escalated to hostility, especially when they each had informed me about the numerous arguments between them at the office. Each described the other as incompetent, ignorant of how to do the job right, and trying to be macho. Both told had told me that the other was just using me to make them selves look good. Both told me not to listen to the other person who had no clue what was happening and would get me hurt.

It was the only team I had contact with and the only two persons I had to rely on for guidance and direction. I was still not allowed to go near the police station or have contact with any other person or police officer. Christy thought that it was Stanley's way of keeping me all to himself and really had nothing to do with my safety.

I ran around with Christy during the day and was alone at night. The detective was usually out drinking until I called him on the hotline, or he was at home, sleeping it off, when I had scored some drugs.

"Christy's trying to be macho," Stanley said. "She's just a footman. She doesn't know what she's doing, and I'm the one who's running this operation!" Again, the lectures on loyalty, and again, "You don't know how much you mean to me, girl. I'm the one who's going to protect you, not her!"

Besides the detective giving Christy a hard time at work, she was having problems at home, too. She was trying to hold her life together after she had just discovered that her cop husband was having an affair with another female cop who was her trusted friend. For several days I watched Christy catapult between outrage and devastation. There was nothing that I could do except watch Christy's broken heart bleed from the wounds of betrayal and hurt, and it crushed me to see her pain.

One day out of the blue, Stanley demanded to know to whom I was more loyal and with whom I was more comfortable. He was speechless with anger when I answered honestly that it was Christy.

"You're *my* UC!" he snapped angrily, turning away. "You belong to me, not her. She's nothing. Nobody wants to work with her! She's dangerous!"

Detective Stanley always made me feel extremely uncomfortable with his all too frequent statement, "You mean more to me than you know."

There were no rules or procedures to follow and I had no one to talk to outside of the team, which had become extremely dysfunctional.

Russell

June 2, 1980, 6:45 p.m. An anonymous complaint came in about all kinds of drugs being sold at Slim's Lounge and Poolroom in Kailua. The complaint had said that everybody was dealing, including kids. The call was from someone who was always at the lounge, possibly someone working in the lounge who was afraid to be identified.

Today's assignment was to go to Kailua and look for a biker named Weasel. It didn't matter if I felt it was too close to home and that I would probably run into people I knew who might confront me openly about what I was doing.

I sat on the bar, tended by a heavy-set middle-aged female, in a room of men in their forties and fifties. The lounge was one big room with stained cement floors and a limited capacity. It was furnished with a few scarred and battered pool tables and a few video game machines.

A voice called out my name from behind me, and I turned apprehensively to see who had recognized me. It was Russell, who had gone to the same high school and was a few years younger.

"What's happening?" he said as he sat next to me on the bar and introduced me to his friend Ken, a large Caucasian man in his fifties.

"Since when did you change into a bad girl?" Russell teased. "Student government, all kinds of awards!" he continued as everyone in the lounge looked at me suspiciously.

I tried to change the subject, but Russell continued with how he thought I would be a social worker or a lawyer one day instead of hanging out in a place like this. Ken look at me curiously, swallowed his beer, and went outside to check the parking lot. I knew that he was looking for undercover surveillance units. Russell was in a happy mood, ordered a beer, and passed me a half tab.

"Test it out!"

He was selling Quaaludes he explained, and if I liked it, I could order more.

I looked at him in shock, and he smiled back.

"Why?" I asked.

"Money," he answered dryly.

I finished my drink quickly and left with the half tab.

This island is too small, I thought. I kept bumping into people I had known and who I had believed to be good people who would never be involved in drugs. Russell was always a little on the wild side, but it was still hard to accept him this way.

Weasel

June 5, 1980. Christy and I went back to Slim's Lounge to look for the man called Weasel.

Weasel was a Portuguese guy who looked like he was in his forties but I couldn't really tell. He openly discussed being an ex- heroin hype and showed me his hypodermic needle track marks up and down both arms. He was tattooed, skeletal, and he walked with a limp. His rotting teeth were noticeable, and his stringy, long hair was graying with ragged ends stopping just below his shoulders. He spoke of riding in different Harley clubs and claimed that he was an awesome biker who once rode with the Sons of Hawaii.

I had known some of the members of the Sons of Hawaii, and none of them looked like Weasel. The bikers I knew were all good guys who had a deep concept of loyalty. If you had earned the respect and honor of the members within the club, then you had earned their loyalty, too.

The loyalty within the their club, was not like the "loyalty" that Detective Stanley had constantly demanded from me through his control and attempted intimidation. The bikers I knew were well-built, good-looking guys, with lots of charisma. For them, Loyalty worked both ways.

Weasel and I started talking about riding Harleys, and Christy slipped into the conversation with ease. He talked about bikes, burglaries, and the jail time he had spent at the Halawa Correctional Facility. He bragged about his assault and robbery rap and being an expert at pool. The stories he told didn't make me feel like he was an awesome type of guy like he tried to portray himself to be. Instead, his lifeless eyes had no depth behind them, even when he told his fantastic stories. I found myself feeling sorry for him. It seemed as if he had lost his soul, had no life except in the past, and was a hard-luck type of guy.

Christy thought I was too sensitive, and I knew she was right. Christy bought secobarbital black beauties from him, and we left.

I am working at the restaurant under a false name
I am learning things that I would never have experienced in my lifetime
I am a cop, but I am not
I am a drug dealer, but I am not
I am me, but I am not
But what will tomorrow be? I don't know … I have lost expectations.
I have erased all familial ties and the false
Illusions of the separation of Good and Evil
There is only the understanding of Truth and Honor left to find

Journal entry: June 8, 1980

Feds or Friends

June 12, 1980. This time, the assignment came from the FBI, and the target was a man named Damien.

Detective Stanley and the federal agents had already prearranged a meeting for me to meet up with this big cocaine source in Kaneohe. I had not been included in any of the arrangements, but at least Christy would be allowed to accompany me on this deal.

Damien came into the restaurant and met me for the first time. I had no backup story or knowledge of how the arrangements for the meeting had been made. It was the most uncomfortable assignment I had ever done. I didn't know what he was told or by whom. Stanley kept all that to himself and felt that the information I asked for was on a need-to-know basis. I had no clue about how I was going to answer any of Damien's questions.

Let him do what he expects me to do, I thought bitterly, but then again, I knew that Stanley was too arrogant and abrasive to be able to score drugs from anyone. It was all too obvious that he had a very high opinion of himself, and he often bragged about his intimidation, supremacy, and reputation as the most feared and respected detective in Narcotics. He would probably never gain a rapport with anyone on the streets.

I put my mutinous thoughts away when Damien came in and joined us at our table. He was tall, slim, and blond with blue eyes. He looked like he had a lot of money, and his mannerisms were very polite.

Damien apologized to me that he didn't bring any stash with him because he didn't know who I was. All he was told was to look for a small Japanese female, but just by looking at me, he knew that I could never be a cop and he was comfortable. He spoke freely about a yacht and moving drugs between the islands. I was supposed to gain his trust and attempt an inter-island run on his yacht. Damien didn't stay long and said he would call me later to sell me some good quality cocaine.

Later that evening, Christy and I met with the federal agents and were surprised to find, that they had been there in the room the entire time. You would never know to look at them, that they were the feds.

Damien called me a few days later and said he had been trying to call me all day. He told me that a good friend of mine named Kevin was holding a gram of cocaine for me to taste and had volunteered to bring me the powder.

Kevin was the boyfriend of Christine, who was one of the girls in my high school social club. I had often listened to Kevin's problems in high school and thought of him as a younger brother. When I begged to be removed from the investigation, the FBI agents looked at me with disdain. They had heard too many stories about Honolulu cops taking care of their friends.

Detective Stanley got on my case again about loyalty, and my request to be removed from the deal was of course denied. It was a joint investigation with the feds, and there was no way I would be allowed to ruin the case because I previously knew the dealer. I would dishonor the Vice Division, as well as embarrass the Honolulu Police Department, if I didn't do this deal.

"You're being monitored, too!" Stanley threatened.

Christy went with me to meet Kevin and tried to help me convince him to let me deal straight through Damien. But Kevin was insistent on being a player. He even offered to get me better quality merchandise for a better price than Damien's and then tried to push me to become involved in a pyramid scheme. Kevin began to name all of the people I knew who were participants in what was already being publicized as an illegal investment scam.

"You know a lot of people. You could make us a lot of money. The more people you bring in, the more money we make!" he pressed.

After the first deal, Kevin began to call me constantly to get me to invest in the financial pyramid. He was disgusted and angry that I had refused to join the group who met at Christine's house.

"Kevin is just a little rat!" Stanley raged. "Take him out! Go join his pyramid scheme!" Detective Stanley was upset with me, too. He had tried to force me into bringing all of the narcs into the pyramid and then planned to raid Christine's house and arrest everyone for criminal charges. That would have meant that Christine and her parents would have been arrested, too. Stanley even wanted to do a media event to publicize the raid and the arrests.

Kevin and Stanley continued to pester me about joining the pyramid scheme as news of victims who suffered substantial financial losses continued to hit the newspapers. I was totally sick and disgusted with both of them.

The more I tried to walk the line of impartiality, the lonelier it became. I had always hated favoritism and prejudice of any kind. I hated knowing that money or connections had allowed some people to get away with all kinds of crimes, and now my beliefs and ideals were being put to the test. The only thing I was sure of was that I would have to live for the rest of my life with the results of every decision I made, and they too would someday have to answer for the decisions that they had made. I realized too that no one would understand my commitment and sacrifice for what I believed to be the ideals of justice and the true meaning of truth and honor.

❦

Chapter 10
Judge Me Not

Thomas

June 12, 1980, 11:00 a.m. The popular fish market in Kaimuki displayed rows of fresh fish prepared in different Poke-style flavors and trays of sliced sashimi. "Pick up some Quaaludes from a Japanese guy named Thomas," was the assignment for the day.

Thomas was Japanese, in his twenties, and husky, with thick, short black hair and a clean-shaven face. He prepared fish for a living, slicing and mixing different ingredients and flavors with the fresh delicacies from the sea. He wore a white apron stained with the blood from the catch of the day, and was skilled with the big sharp knife that he wore on his waist like a saber. Thomas was serving customers behind the busy refrigerated counter, and it was finally my turn to order.

I ordered the shoyu flavored Poke fish I had just watched him prepare, warm musubi rice balls wrapped in paper-thin dried seaweed, and Lemmons. Thomas reached for the fresh lemons on the counter, and I stopped him, saying softly, "No, not that kind."

Thomas paused a moment and then smiled. "Follow me."

Thomas led me to a storage room in the back and sold me five Quaaludes. The usual questions were asked, and I supplied him with the answers that had worked so many times before. By the time we left the storage room, Christy had already started eating the fresh fish but was careful not to devour my portion. It was the best Poke we had ever tasted. The market was very busy and the fresh fish and the boiled peanuts they were famous for had disappeared quickly.

It was one of those clear beautiful summer days, and Christy and I feasted in the sunshine at a park nearby.

June 13, 1980, 1:15 p.m. "Go hang out with Freddy. See if he can get you Quaaludes. Go down by yourself."

I made arrangements over the phone for a fast pickup of Quaaludes from Freddy. I didn't want to spend any more time with him than necessary, because I didn't want to give him the chance to be misled about my intentions.

The Ocean View Inn was built on the Haleiwa seashore. Sea foam had left its patterns on dry land after splashing high into the air against the large rocks at high tide. The salt air was healing, and the waves of the ocean heaved powerfully in ageless depths of indigo blues.

The deal went quickly, and I declined the offer of a drink. I could tell by his reaction that Freddy had realized and already accepted that we were only business associates.

The Tourists

June 13, 1980, 10:15 p.m. Stanley sent me out alone to the discotheque to see Adonis. I found him at the back bar with three girls hanging on to his arm and rubbing him everywhere on his body. The bleached blonde girls were groping his crotch and trying really hard to turn him on. I could tell the girls were tourists by their sun-burnt skin, Waikiki-styled aloha-print dresses, and uninhibited conduct. They were working really hard to impress this massively built local Hawaiian boy.

Adonis smiled at me with a Cheshire cat's grin, knowing that I knew what his score for the evening was going to be. He shrugged off the girls for a moment to talk to me privately.

The girls were very angry that I had taken their trophy away from them. When I couldn't help laughing at their visible disappointment, they pouted and sulked. They were totally wasted on something more than alcohol.

Adonis loved it. He had scored a Haole tourist every night, he bragged, but he had never had three at the same time!

"Half?" I asked, and the sale of cocaine went quickly. Adonis smiled and returned to his waiting entourage of thrill-seeking females.

I stood in the corner alone, nursing my drink as the song from Santa Esmeralda, "Don't Let Me Be Misunderstood," vibrated in the room and echoed in my head. Adonis came by and silently slipped a black beauty in my hand without saying a word. We got along like longtime friends, and it made me sad. If circumstances were different, I knew we could have become good friends. One of the females in his fan club glared at me, jealous of the unsolicited attention I had received from Adonis, and yelled, "Damned fuckin' Jap!"

For a moment, I wanted to slap her, but instead I just shook my head and laughed as Adonis got on her case for the racial insult. She sulked in the corner for a minute and then snuggled up to him and stroked his chest explaining in a babylike whimper, that she was angry and jealous because he had paid too much attention to me. Adonis looked at me and winked, and I nodded that I knew he was watching my back.

Adonis was a Hawaiian in ancestry and carried himself like a warrior.

June 14, 1980. Crystal came up to the front desk at Yoshi's Restaurant just as I was taking a reservation for dinner over the phone. I was working the night shift as a reservationist and hostess. She shyly slipped me a handwritten note on a napkin saying that she had black beauties for sale.

"How much?" I asked when I hung up the phone.

"Four a piece," Crystal answered.

I bought one to test and promised to buy quantity if I liked it, and that seemed to make her happy.

Crystal was selling drugs on the side to make ends meet. She seemed like an innocent young girl with a very sweet heart, and I had never seen her stoned, wasted, or high.

I hated my job at Yoshi's, and I felt I was getting too close to my suspects. Detective Stanley didn't care. He would hurt anyone to succeed, even his own subordinates.

June 16, 1980. I went to the fish market to see Thomas and ordered a half-pound of shoyu Ahi Poke and ten Quaaludes. Thomas had weighed out about a pound of the carefully prepared fresh fish but only charged me for half a pound.

"Nah! That's okay," I said. "Don't get in trouble!"

"No problem," Thomas answered lightly. "I own part of this business."

Thomas was mild-mannered but handled his long knife like a skilled assassin. He told me to wait outside by my car for the Quaalude tablets, and I complied.

I ate and finished my gourmet meal as I sat alone in my car waiting for about thirty minutes. Thomas finally appeared in the front door of the market, and I waved him over. He glanced around the parking lot and then jumped into the passenger seat of my car, looking around nervously at the interior of my car. Thomas appeared to be satisfied that everything was okay and gave me a package containing the ten white Lemmon 714 tablets. He relaxed a bit, smoking a cigarette, and talked about the rising costs of fish.

"If you own the place, why don't you just package it and slip it over the counter?" I asked. "Then you wouldn't have to be so obvious and leave the counter.

Thomas explained that his parents would be totally pissed off if he carried on his side business so openly, and I nodded in understanding. A large van drove up, and Thomas jumped out of my car. He had to accept the delivery of fresh fish, and the delivery guys hated to wait. I watched as he greeted the large driver, who had already unloaded the containers of freshly caught fish, lined up in neat rows on beds of ice.

He worked hard at his job and obviously respected his parents, but it also seemed that they knew what he was doing. I couldn't understand why he was selling drugs, but then again, I couldn't understand much of anything anymore.

Team Support

June 19, 1980. Weasel woke me up at 9:00 a.m. He hadn't seen me for a while and asked where I had been. He had scored some cocaine and would be at Slim's Lounge all day if I wanted any. I told Weasel that I might drop by to see him later in the day.

I couldn't find Christy, but I found Detective Stanley in the office and briefed him on Weasel's offer.

"Go pick it up, girl," he instructed, and he promised he would tell Christy where I was. I met Weasel about an hour later. The lounge was empty, and he was shooting pool alone on one of the battered tables. His face was bruised and swollen with fresh cuts and lacerations.

"What happened to you?" I asked, realizing that he was pretty badly hurt.

Weasel walked gingerly to the bar and sat down carefully, nursing his ribs as if they were broken.

"You all right?" I asked, and he nodded his answer, smiling. He had gotten into a fight last night and was beginning to feel the pain today.

"You got time for a drink? Weasel asked.

I paid for his drink and listened to his story. After finishing his story and two drinks, Weasel handed me two matchbooks for $50 each. Each matchbook concealed a half-gram packet of cocaine, and I bought both. Weasel was very pleased, and I knew he needed the money. When I got home, I found a handwritten note from Christy attached to my gate.

"If you finally decide to do some work today, call me at the office ... half of the day is already shot!" she wrote sarcastically. Christy had apparently waited for me, for half an hour and she was really pissed off.

I was tired and upset and called Stanley to tell him I had scored a gram from Weasel. I also told him about the note I had from Christy and asked why he hadn't told her where I was. Stanley explained that, like me, he hadn't been able to find her either, and she had not checked into the office like she was supposed to.

"Forget about it," he laughed with delight at our misunderstanding. He then told me that Christy couldn't score by herself and had never done this type of work before, no matter how hard she tried to impress everyone. She was only brought into the unit because they needed a female as a cover unit for me, but now Christy was trying to run the show and she couldn't because she had no clue about what she was doing. "It's her own fault!" he declared in a final comment. "She knows she's supposed to check in with me first!"

Christy had finally gone to the office and learned that I had gone out to do a drug deal on my own. She never brought up the incident or the note, and never apologized for the accusations.

It was intermediate school all over again, and it appeared that the supervisor was fanning the controversy between the members of his own team.

The Burglary Boys

June 20, 1980, 7:30 p.m. Danny, a.k.a. the Burg Boy of Kailua, was sixteen years old, heavyset, and known as one of the main sources of Quaaludes in the area. He had been in and out of the Koolau Boy's Home and had a rap sheet that was twice his age.

Danny hung around at the Kailua game room and acted as a bouncer for the place. He said nothing when he heard us asking if anyone was holding any Quaaludes, but followed us out to the parking lot when Christy and I were leaving.

Danny called me over to his new red Mustang in the parking lot and showed me a glove compartment full of the tablets. I bought five, and he and his juvenile friend, Guy, showed me jewelry and cameras they had just stolen from a house. The boys bragged about their organized crime affiliations and said that all cops were shit.

We had no money to purchase the stolen items and missed the opportunity to snag a burglary ring.

The two young boys were way beyond the turning point and there was no way back for them. They looked forward to a successful career as criminals. They had gotten off easy with the juvenile system, which they already knew inside and out. The profits and rewards of their criminal endeavors had brought them everything they wanted, like the Candy Apple red Mustang. There would only be a small price to pay if they ever got caught. Judgments against juveniles were always lenient.

Connections

June 20, 1980, 7:50 p.m. Kevin called to let me know that he was getting his cocaine from a different source and not from Damien. He then added that he and Damien had gotten into a heated argument about who was going to supply me with the merchandise.

Damien was the manager of an auto dealership in Kaneohe, and Kevin was a salesman. The argument had taken place on the sales floor right in front of a few customers and finally ended when Kevin told Damien that I was his friend and that he had known me longer.

He was holding a quarter ounce of cocaine that I had never ordered from him for $600, and I could have a sample if I wanted.

"I'd rather have Damien's stuff," I complained, explaining that I had already tested it and liked it.

Kevin was stubborn and wouldn't listen. He had basically intercepted and taken Damien's line. I finally told him that I would have to check with Christy because it was her money, too, and Kevin accepted the stall for time. I couldn't believe how self-centered he had become, just like Glenn.

The FBI agents were shocked and very upset that Kevin had interfered with their federal investigation. "He's a greedy little rat!" the agents said, seething with anger. "He stole Damien's line!"

"If he wants to play, take him out. Go get the sample! You got a problem with that?" Stanley challenged, glaring at me.

I went to meet Kevin, and it cost me $100 for the sample. I was disgusted at how greedy and pushy he had become and couldn't stand to be around him. He was not the same Kevin I knew as a friend. The other sources I was dealing with had always given out samples for free. Even Glenn had at least done that.

Kevin commented on the stress and fatigue he saw on my face and showed me six white tablets of speed—pharmaceuticals, he said. "They're great." He didn't realize that he was the immediate source of my stress and that it was also the disgust and anger I felt for him that was showing on my face.

Kevin pushed and insisted that I take the tablets, and this time gave me the speed for free, for helping him out on his deals.

He began to push me again about joining his pyramid group, explaining that I had a lot of friends and connections and could bring them in to help push him to the top. I was irritated at listening to his money-making sales pitches.

"Nah," I declined. "I hear about all the guys losing money. It's all over the newspapers."

"Don't worry about it," he said. "With all of your friends and connections, we would be on top real quick, and we wouldn't be the ones out of money." Kevin continued his pitch, saying that he wasn't worried about the undercover busts because all of his investors were friends and family.

Kevin's greed was showing, and it was obvious that he wanted to use my connections to make himself some fast money. Again, he insisted that I come to the meetings at his Christine's house. "Bring Christy, too!" The sound of his voice was beginning to make me sick. My stomach was turning, and I felt like I was actually going to heave.

"Take the speed! It's going to make you feel better," he coaxed.

I went straight back to the feds, and this time I noticed them on my tail. Christy was waiting at the debriefing and looked at me with concern. She knew I was sick and totally stressed out without me saying a single word. "You all right?" she asked, but I didn't answer.

The agents and the detective shrugged with indifference. "He's a greedy little rat using you to make his money!" they said coldly, and I knew they were right. All Kevin had talked about was fast money schemes and using me for my friends and connections to make it happen.

A couple hours later, Christy and I drove back to complete the quarter-ounce deal for $600. It was making me sick to look at Kevin and listen to his non-stop talking as he tried to convince Christy to join the pyramid scheme, too.

I had never seen this side of Kevin before, and I hated what he had become. Perhaps he had always been this way and I had just never seen him for what he really was. It seemed like he would step on or use anyone to make his money. He had even cut Damien out.

Kevin had said what Glenn had said: "You know a lot of people. You have a lot of friends and connections. If you jump in, we can make fast money!"

Everyone, including Detective Stanley, was using me because I knew a lot of people and because I could make the connections. I suddenly felt like I was the sacrificial pawn for everyone to use for their own selfish agendas.

I wondered if anyone would ever know the truth of what took place behind the scenes, and then I remembered: "Just the facts!"

Clarity of vision and clarity of emotions. I needed to see the truth—not what I remembered Kevin and Glenn to be like or what I thought they were like in their hearts and souls. I had to see the truth of who and what they were today, and it was very hard to deal with the truth I had found.

Christy and I returned to the debriefing site to turn in the evidence from Kevin. I watched Stanley acting macho in front of the FBI agents, and it was making me sick to watch and listen to him, too.

Stanley ordered us back out again to score at Slim's Lounge, even though he knew that I was sick, tired, and exhausted.

One of the agents looked at me sympathetically and smirked at the detective's obvious attempt at being impressive.

"He's just using you," Detective Stanley said about Kevin.

And so are you! I thought spitefully.

I was on shut-down mode as we waited for Weasel at Slim's Lounge. I was filled with pity for him when he came in limping. I couldn't bring myself out of my depression to do another deal, especially with Weasel, who looked so beat up and pathetic and was still healing from his wounds.

Christy did the cocaine deal instead, while I sat at the bar trying to drink away my thoughts and emotions.

This time, the scotch didn't work and the numbness never came. This time, I couldn't step into my UC identity. Instead, even to my surprise, I watched my real self burst into tears and couldn't stop sobbing. I desperately wanted to tell everyone the truth of who I was and what I was doing.

Christy told everyone that I was stoned and dragged me out to the car. The large older female bartender glared at me and started berating me in front of the other customers at the bar.

The bartender never took the time to find out why I was hurting. It was way easier to judge and kick people around when they were down. Instead, she volunteered to be a character witness for Weasel during his trials. I was later told that she was probably the anonymous caller who had turned him in and was trying to avoid discovery by testifying on his behalf. I would never know.

Barry

June 22, 1980, 10:30 p.m. It was a quiet Sunday evening, and I was on duty at Yoshi's' restaurant at the front desk and surprised when Barry, the night manager, slipped me a matchbook with a gram of cocaine carefully concealed inside. He seemed like a very straightforward, clean-cut Japanese guy, and I had been discreet with my purchases from the waitresses out of respect for him as my supervisor at Yoshi's. My judgment of his character had been totally wrong.

It was $120 for the gram, he said, but I didn't have the money. Barry said it was okay with him to be paid later since I had never ordered the merchandise in the first place.

I placed a quick call to the Narcotics office, praying that someone would answer.

"Go out into the parking lot in a half hour," Stanley instructed. "Someone's going to be dropping off the money. Give him the matchbook."

Time moved like molasses, and the tension built as I imagined everything that could possibly go wrong. I didn't know who to expect or what he looked like and began to panic at the thought of someone seeing me give the dope to a narc. The time finally came, and I left the front desk and the cash register unattended to sneak out into the parking lot.

I was playing three different roles now. I was a cop but I was not, I was a dope dealer yet I was not, and now I was holding a legitimate job at a restaurant, which was just another front. I missed the simplicity of things. I missed knowing exactly who I was, and I missed the comfort of ignorance. Even working a legitimate job at Yoshi's was still in an undercover capacity.

I had been given the social security number of an unidentified person who had already died and had provided a fake last name on my job application, as instructed. Every day I wondered if and when I would be confronted about that, too.

Stanley was always monitoring me and forcing me to stay in my role. He had successfully brainwashed me to listen and obey without question, and then left me to figure out for myself the rules of engagement when dealing with the confrontations from the dealers I met.

It was raining outside, and I stood in the darkness, feeling the cold of every raindrop. A man drove into the parking lot, and I prayed that he would leave quickly before I did the exchange. But he parked his car and didn't get out.

I watched him watching me as I stood in the darkness and the rain. I was relieved when he finally started his car, but began to panic again when he drove up in front of me and stopped. He had long, wavy hair and a mustache and was wearing dark glasses at night.

"You got something for me?" he asked.

"Like what?" I asked stupidly.

"Stanley sent me," he answered, but I still couldn't believe this guy was a cop.

"Who's Stanley?" I asked, trying to sound brave.

The narc showed me his badge and the exchange went quickly. He was a detective, but I would have sworn he was a hit man. I hurried back to my workstation just as Barry rounded the corner.

"How did you get the money?" he asked in surprise when I paid him for the cocaine.

"Borrowed it from a friend," I explained and busied myself with unimportant paper work to escape any further questions. I felt my face flushing with fever and turned away.

After dragging through the dinner shift, Barry stopped by again to pick up the profits of the evening, "Coke, Speed or Quaaludes" he smiled, "anytime."

❧

Chapter 11
Ethics

The Glass Bird Cage

I was exhausted, mentally, physically, and spiritually, when I went to Waikiki alone that evening. I had a sudden impulse to run—anywhere—just run and run and run, as fast and as far as I could go. But there was nowhere to go. The Chivas went down smoothly, and the much needed escape it brought came quickly.

There was no black and white anymore, no good vs. evil. I had crossed over the threshold separating the two, and it had disappeared behind me. I felt I was spending too much time with my suspects, but the detective didn't see it that way. I knew he could never understand what he had never experienced himself.

The job at Yoshi's forced me to get closer to the targets, and now I had grown to know too much about them, their families, and their ups and downs. It was destroying me, but Stanley didn't care. He was stuck in his macho role and greed for success at my expense and efforts.

I had learned from Christy that although he told me that I couldn't let anyone know who I was, especially cops, he was telling everyone about me, and they had been driving into the parking lot to see what I looked like through the large glass picture windows of the restaurant.

I had become a bird in a glass cage and wanted desperately to fly free. The only escape I had left was to continue to write in my private journal and the scotch.

I could feel myself changing too fast and hoped it was a way to go back to who I was when this was over. My journal and my constant prayers were the only things left in my life that hadn't been destroyed, and I clung to both as my only source of redemption. If I could document the transition, maybe I could undo what I had become.

Some of my suspects had talked to me about going to church. They did their Sunday rituals of memorized praying and singing and then forgot about truth, honor and the Ten Commandments for the rest of the week. For me, it was a way of life, and I took God with me every day to wherever I was sent. The universal father had become my only source of guidance and protection in this selfish "use and abuse" world.

I had begun to see the arrogance and prejudiced judgments of those who preached and lectured but were blind to truth. I wondered too if anyone would recognize God or even feel his presence if they saw him sitting on a stone wall on Hotel Street in the middle of Chinatown at night; or would they scorn him and think he was wasted on drugs if they saw him crying for the world he saw? Who would see the heart of a man instead of the façades?

Glenn's Gift

June 22, 1980, Glenn called me at Yoshi's during my evening work shift.

"I have a surprise for you. When do you get off?" he asked happily.

My shift ended at midnight, and Glenn said he would be there to meet me after work. He arrived alone just before midnight, wearing a great big smile.

"What's the reason?" I asked, dying to know why he was so happy and what the surprise was.

He sat in a booth next to my cashier's station and just smiled. "Wait till you get off. It's in my car."

I began closing out my cashier's drawer while we talked, sharing bits of information about the high school classmates we had lost contact with through the years.

Glenn was dressed up and looked handsome that evening. He led me to his car when I finished my shift and opened the passenger door for me to get in. He got into the driver's seat with a triumphant grin. I looked around in the car for the surprise but couldn't see anything unusual.

"Open the glove compartment!" he said, still beaming with excitement.

I reached into the glove box hesitantly, expecting something to spring out at me. Glenn seemed in such a cheerful and playful mood, I was expecting a practical joke.

"This is a joke right?" I asked when nothing popped out.

Glenn reached over, pulled a small brown paper bag out of the glove compartment, and placed it into my hands.

"That's for you!" he said.

I hesitated at first and then opened it slowly, afraid of what was inside.

"I didn't order! This is not mine! I don't have the money!" I blurted the words out in protest. There were a hundred white tablets in the package, and I stared at him in disbelief.

"Just give me what you got on you right now and you can pay me the rest later," he said, genuinely pleased with his surprise gift.

"Just give me ten," I suggested, but he wouldn't accept the return of his gift.

"You're going to make your money fast and then just pay me later. Sell 'em for $5 and just pay me $375," he said happily.

I fought my conflicting feelings of friendship and of doing my job fairly regardless of connections and ties. I wanted so desperately to yell and scream at him, and my mind raced back to all of the other people I was dealing with.

Some of them were very nice, some were married, and some had families. I thought of how unfair it would be if I selectively busted only the people I didn't know before I took the undercover assignment—those who had sold me smaller quantities than Glenn and had not pushed me to buy after I had declined.

He's just like Kevin, I realized sadly. I had already turned him down, never called him, and never ordered the large quantity, but he kept on pursuing me to sell his drugs. Swallowing my heart and erasing my feelings, I accepted the gift he refused to take back, giving him all the money I had on me.

"Want to trip to Waikiki?" he invited.

Five minutes ago, I would have been happy to join him. Although I had hardly known him in school, I had gotten to know him in the last few months and was beginning to feel comfortable with him. Now, everything had changed. Glenn looked at me curiously when I could not disguise the abrupt change in my mood. I could see the confusion on his face and the questions in his eyes at my sudden depression and silence. He wasn't smiling anymore. I made a whole bunch of excuses and declined his invitation.

He must have seen the overwhelming sadness I couldn't hide as he watched me walk away. I knew how much I would end up hurting him, and my heart broke. But I wondered if he would ever know how much he had hurt me, too.

"He doesn't give a shit about you. He just wants to make some money!" Detective Stanley snarled. "Did you read the newspaper today?"

The twenty-year mandatory jail term for all Class A felonies became effective at eight o'clock that morning. "Glenn's case will be the first to be tried under that statute," Stanley said with a smirk of delight.

Everything I believed in was being put to a test, and I had to confront myself for the answers. I was dying inside. The person I had been, the one who laughed and had feelings, could not exist anymore in order to survive and continue.

I never went anywhere except to do my assignments. I was afraid to bump into the wrong people, afraid to see anyone I knew, and afraid to be seen with my old friends and my family by the wrong people. I was being monitored twenty-four hours a day because Detective Stanley needed to know exactly where I was and what I was doing in case anything came up. I had no gun, no badge, no training.

No one knows who I am or what I'm doing, not even me.

The Stuffed Tomato

"Go to the Stuffed Tomato nightclub," Stanley laughed, "Just pretend that you're gay."

The few gay friends I had could spot frauds and fakes before I ever knew that someone was putting on an act. I knew there was no way I could do a gay act without being discovered, but I followed his orders.

The dark gray walls of the patio-styled bar were dimly lit, with a revolving silver ball hanging in the center of the room over a bare concrete floor. Colorful Christmas lights strung up along the perimeter of the ceiling appeared to be used as additional permanent lighting and decorations. It was a full house but not overcrowded that night.

I stood at the open door, which was gated by a thick rope, waiting to be allowed entrance, and watched the activity inside. I could see that there were no Asian females in the place. I wondered if I should turn around and leave when a few of the patrons looked at me standing in the doorway as if I was at the wrong place by mistake.

"I'm looking for my friend Jerry. He hangs out here," I said, trying to explain my questionable presence to the bouncer, who looked at me doubtfully. It was the first name that popped into my head.

The bouncer relaxed. "Lots of Jerrys. Go take a look," he said, and dropped the thick rope to let me in. I had passed the bouncer's scrutiny, and it seemed to put everyone at ease.

Too many people had tried to get in only to harass the gay patrons.

My gay male friends were artistic, sensitive, and compassionate, and more honest and sincere in their hearts than the macho egotistical guys who were everywhere.

"Go see if you can score from some queers," Stanley said when he gave me my new assignment. He had also referred to them as half-a-dicks. The words he used had infuriated me, and he saw my response.

"What?" he asked sarcastically. "They always have ludes. They take that so that they can fuck each other in the ass. It loosens up the muscles in their ass!"

The detective would never come close to being "good people" like my gay friends, Billy, Jerry, and Frank.

Several patrons approached me as I sipped my drink at the bar, so I put my thoughts away.

"Straight?" they asked

"Yes," I answered. "Just looking for some friends who might be here," I explained, and the bunch of local girls at the bar listened to my response and accepted my answer.

"Who you looking for?" they asked.

"Jerry," I replied, staying with the name I had given the bouncer.

The name Jerry ended up being a good random choice. It could have been the name of a male or female, whichever I needed it to be. A few minutes, later a totally wasted straight guy stumbled up to me at the bar to ask me to dance, and I politely declined.

He was skinny, tattooed, in his twenties, and could hardly stand up.

"What!" he slurred, indignant at my rejection. "What's your fuckin' problem?" he demanded.

"Just waiting for my friend and looking for some ludes," I said, knowing that he had probably dropped a bunch of the tablets. I would score the drugs and leave quickly, and this time I had no qualms about taking down this obnoxious guy.

"I'll be back!" he said and stumbled back through the crowd on the dance floor, intentionally bumping into people as he pushed his way through to the other side of the room.

"Watch out for him," the girls at the bar warned. "He can get some, but don't front him the money. He rips, too!"

But the warning came too late. He was already stumbling back towards me, aggressively pushing people on the dance floor out of his way. He was pissing people off as they stepped out of his way.

"Give me the money!" he demanded "Then I'll go get it."

"Nah, that's okay. I'll pay you when I get it."

"That's right, sister!" the females at the bar voiced their approval. "Don't front him the money. See the stuff first!" they warned.

"Shut up, you fuckin' dykes!" he yelled, and a war of slurs and insults erupted between him and the girls.

The creep suddenly grabbed my wrist and started pulling me off my bar stool towards him. In a flash, one of the girls smashed a beer bottle across the side of his head. Glass was flying, and bar stools were falling. I was yanked backwards by the waistband of my jeans. One of the big girls had pulled me out from the middle of the brawl and smiled at me.

"No worries, tita!" she smiled. "Get out of here before the cops come. I've been waiting for the chance to break his face for days!" She grinned, pushing me out of harm's way onto the slippery dance floor.

The entire place had erupted into an all-out no-holds-barred war between the straight wasted dope dealer and his friends, and the gay patrons.

I kept slipping on the baby powder that had been sprinkled on the dance floor, making it harder to make my way through the mad rush of patrons trying to escape in a hurry. The bouncer was the only one pushing his way through the crowd in the opposite direction, toward the chaos. He grabbed my arm and pushed me out through the only door.

"Get out of here," he smiled calmly. "The guy had it coming. They push their dope in here and always cause trouble, too!"

The gentle giant disappeared into the commotion of breaking glass and screams. I glanced back into the room for a moment before I was pushed out into the streets and caught a glimpse of the dope dealers and the creep getting their asses kicked. The patrons who remained to watch the barroom brawl began to cheer.

Everyone was running away from the place as the sound of police sirens neared. One of the females at the bar had gotten out too, and she abruptly pulled me into a dark corner just as the uniformed police officers arrived on their Cushman vehicles.

"Wait a little while," she said as we stopped to catch our breath. "Then just be cool and walk away. Don't run in front of them! The cops always raid this place, and they grab everybody—especially if you run!"

"What happened?" the detective asked at the debriefing. "They got the whole sector at the place."

"Pandemonium," I answered without explaining further.

"You involved?" he asked.

"Not really. Just sort of."

"You got a bunch of glass in your hair," he said blankly, and then he started to laugh.

"Wasn't my fault!"

"Go home," he said, finally releasing me for the night.

I was very glad that he didn't send me out again. This time, I laughed on the way home.

Burnt by Cops

June 27, 1980, 10:10 p.m. Adonis looked at me and then behind me, scanning the people in the area with a grim expression. His demeanor was abrupt and nervous instead of his usual calm and cool manner as he led me inside to the bar.

"What's up?" I prodded.

Adonis explained that he had heard some rumors about Charlie's Angels on the street, working in the discos in Waikiki and buying drugs. He paused and looked intently into my eyes.

"One Haole and one Japanese. How's your friend Christy?" he finally asked. "How long have you known her? Where's she from?"

I answered Adonis's flurry of questions, explaining that I had met Christy at a disco and that we had been tripping around together for several months.

"Watch out for her!" he warned and slipped me a half-gram of cocaine. "I'm trying to dump my stash fast. I heard they were in here already and the narcs are planning to raid the place!"

I looked around nervously, too, and then left right away, and this time, I wasn't just pretending to be upset and worried. Adonis was trying to watch out for me, and as I walked back to my car alone, the feeling of a deep empty void swallowed my heart.

Detective Stanley was upset at the debriefing when I told him about the Charlie's Angels rumors.

"Somebody's chirping!" he said. "And I know exactly who it is!"

"Wasn't me!" I said defensively. "I don't talk to anyone!"

Detective Stanley said Christy had been bragging to everyone that I was her UC and then giving out details about what I was doing, who my suspects were, and where I was working. Stanley sped off in a quiet sizzling rage

July 8, 1980, 10:30 a.m. Stanley sent me out alone to see if Ernest had heard the rumors, too. The half-gram deal went quickly and smoothly without question.

Ernest didn't get out much, and he didn't care much for Waikiki. He was down to earth and mellow and didn't like the hustle he saw at the discos. He stayed away from Waikiki, he explained. If he wanted a little action, he just tripped to town but mostly kept to himself. He liked it that way.

Protection in the Streets

July 13, 1980, 11:44 a.m. Delia called me early that Sunday morning. It was kind of unusual since she usually stayed out late on Saturday nights, partying. She had never called me before.

Delia invited me to her apartment explaining that she was trying to sell her stash of Quaaludes and asked if I wanted any. "Just come down," she invited and gave me directions to her apartment.

"Go get it," Stanley ordered, ignoring my apprehensive feelings. "Go alone."

I went to Delia's place to pick up the ludes. Her apartment was full of beautiful clothes overflowing from her closets. Delia told me that she had heard the Charlie's Angel's rumors on the street and she wanted me to know that she wasn't worried. She talked openly about working with the cops as an informant for a murder case. It was a quick and easy deal, and I repeated the story for the detective during the debriefing.

Stanley never told me if Delia really was an informant. Instead, he reminded me that Delia was gay and that Sarah was her lover. I didn't want to hear whatever more he had to say about their relationship and told him that I didn't want to know any more about my suspects than I had to.

"The cops owe me," Delia had said, looking at me intently, and she wasn't afraid of getting caught. She just wanted me to know that.

July 14, 1980, 2:35 p.m. Delia called again and said she had just picked up a new batch. "Just come by to my apartment," she invited.

"Go get it. Go by yourself." Stanley refused to stop the investigation and thought nothing of sending me out alone, even knowing that we had already been identified.

I went to pick up the Quaaludes and Delia looked at me sympathetically.

"Look," she said, "if you ever need protection, just let me know. I can call my boys. They're not afraid of anything. They already killed somebody, and they're not afraid to kill cops, too."

"Thanks. I'm okay!" I replied and left.

How ironic! My suspects were offering me protection and friendship, and Stanley didn't seem to give a damn. He had to know that he was sending me into a critical situation alone, but he didn't care. He just wanted to continue his operation at my expense. I wanted to see *him* do what he sent me out to do.

July 16, 1980, 2:15 p.m. Christy went with me to the fish market that afternoon. Stanley was throwing his weight around and had her chained to the office, typing up her cases, she said. We hadn't seen each other for quite a while because he was trying to keep us separated "*to save his operation.*" He also wanted us to know that *he* was the boss.

We picked up the Quaaludes from Thomas and then feasted on the fresh fish and warm steamed rice while I filled her in on what I was doing. It was very clear that Christy and Stanley didn't like each other. It had become a competition between them, and I felt like I was stuck in the middle.

The team that had never been a real team was gone.

Women's Intuition

July 17, 1980, 3:15 p.m. Barry called me at home and asked me to meet him at his house that afternoon. He was holding some Lemmons and needed to make some fast cash.

"Go get it, girl!" Stanley said, and I drove alone to his house on Nuuanu Avenue.

Barry introduced me to his wife and newborn baby. His wife was Caucasian with shoulder-length light brown hair, and she still carried a little bit of weight around her waist from her recent pregnancy. I wasn't sure why she told me that she was a few years older than Barry, but I saw the puffy circles under her eyes from either sleepless nights or crying. She was still dressed in her long terry cloth bathrobe and sat next to me on the sofa, whispering that she needed to talk to me. She began a casual conversation and waited until Barry left the room to confide in me quietly.

Amanda told me that she wanted Barry to stop dealing. She had a funny feeling that he was going to get caught, and she couldn't shake the fear and worry about his drug activities. He wouldn't listen to her, she said sadly. He had been doing it for so long that he was getting very lax about it. She smoked a little grass now and then, but Barry was getting carried away and sometimes came home totally ripped and violent. They needed the money, she admitted, but now he was bringing people to the house.

"Can you talk to him? At least tell him not to bring anyone to the house," she pleaded with desperation in her eyes.

"You're right. He's probably going to get busted," I said. I told her that I understood her concern and that she was right to worry.

Barry apologized about his wife when he saw me at work a few days later. She had confessed that she had told me about her fears and had asked me to talk to him. They had gotten into a huge fight about it.

"She's right, Barry," I said, and the conversation ended.

⌘

Chapter 12
Honor

The Yakuza Offer

July 18, 1980. It was 1:30 p.m. in the hot summer afternoon and, as ordered, I went to see Thomas and picked up ten more Quaaludes. I didn't order any fresh Poke this time, but Thomas slid me a container of the gourmet delicacy he had just created.

Freddy had called earlier and told me that he would be meeting some really heavy people at Yoshi's Restaurant, and that they had already been checking me out. The heavies, he said, wanted me to pack and move some drugs inter-island and maybe to Japan. If I accepted the job, I would get some really big bucks for being the Yakuza mule.

I hated the hostess/cashier job at Yoshi's. I never saw my earnings and never knew what Stanley did with the money after he cashed my checks. I was working around the clock and never got compensated for it. I wasn't even allowed to get away from him on weekends like a normal job would have allowed. I no longer existed.

The Yakuza job offer sounded good to me, and I thought for a moment about how great it would be to walk away from Stanley and all the bullshit and work for them on my own. But I forced myself to shrug it off and reminded myself that I was supposed to be working for the police department and actually an undercover cop.

July 20, 1980. "Go score some coke from Tricks tonight," Stanley had instructed. "Go alone."

I was uneasy about going to see Tricks alone at night, especially after what had happened the last time. I remembered Tricks' anger when I refused his invitation to share some whiff with him in his apartment, but Stanley didn't care.

I had periodically checked Tricks' apartment all evening, and he finally returned home at 3:30 am. Tricks smiled happily when he saw me and said he needed to pick some up, too.

Tricks and I went to Ernest's apartment, and he disappeared inside while I waited in the car. When Tricks didn't come back out for a long time, I knocked on Ernest's door to see what was going on.

"That was your stuff?" Ernest asked apologetically. "He's gone. He just ripped you off."

Ernest commented that he had wondered why Tricks had left through the back door, but sometimes Tricks was flaky. "I'll go talk to him about this when I see him," Ernest said helpfully. "We'll see if we can get your money back."

I had never been ripped off before, and Stanley was upset, but there was nothing he could do about it. There had been no one with me and no surveillance during the deal.

"It's not your fault!" Christy said. "He should never have sent you out by yourself. This wouldn't have happened if you had backup!"

July 22, 1980, 11:30 p.m. Crystal and I finished our shift at Yoshi's and went to the Lanai Restaurant to see her friend Billie. We had a couple drinks, and I picked up more Quaaludes.

There was a large Samoan man sitting at the bar in a leather coat, watching me the whole time. When Crystal left for home, he came up to me and whispered quietly.

"I know who you are. I used to work in vice. So what are you going to do if I don't let you out of here?" he asked and moved his body in a position to block my exit.

He had been sitting at the far end of the bar but moved to a barstool two seats away from me, which placed him directly between me and the exit. Every time I moved in my seat, he moved as if he was going to follow me and block me from leaving.

I used the pay phone near the ladies' restroom and called the hotline, praying that someone would answer, but no one did. The former vice cop had gotten off his seat when I went to use the phone, but sat back down when he realized that I wasn't leaving. He turned his seat around to face my direction, making it obvious that he was watching me. I hated calling the detective at his house, but I didn't know what else to do, and sure enough, his wife answered. She finally gave him the phone after interrogating me again about why I was calling.

If the Stanley was fooling around on his wife, it surely wasn't with me. I was stranded and couldn't get out of the place and was sure that the ex vice cop wanted a confrontation or would tail me.

Stanley was drunk again, and I knew I was on my own as usual. "Just get his license plates!" he slurred.

I finally walked out with a bunch of girls and hid in the dark corner of the parking lot. I watched the ex cop leave the lounge a few seconds after us and walk to a black Cadillac parked in the middle of the crowded parking lot. He scanned the area before he finally drove away, but I never got to see the license plates from where I was hiding.

Stanley knew exactly who I was talking about by the description I had given him of the man and his black Cadillac.

"He was trying to scare you. He was probably just playing around with you."

"So how did he know who I was?" I asked, but there was no answer.

Blind Dates

July 24, 1980, 10:50 a.m. Barry sold me ten Quaaludes at work and then tried to fix me up on a date with his friend, who had seen me several times at the restaurant. I convinced Barry that I was seeing a very jealous guy who had a mean temper. Barry asked why he had never met him, and I made up an excuse that he was married and only saw him when I could. Barry shrugged and accepted my excuse, and we left it at that.

July 25, 1980, Friday. Freddy set me up to meet with the Yakuza heavies he had told me about.

"They want to meet you!" he explained, and he had arranged an introduction for that afternoon at Yoshi's.

Yoshi was sitting with them at the table when I arrived. Masa seemed like he was a very respectable Japanese businessman. He was quiet, reserved, and didn't really talk that much. It was agreed that I would be a mule for them and they would let me know when.

Stanley finally confirmed that the names I gave him were connected to the organized crime group from Japan. He said nothing about calling me paranoid when I had first told him about them. He kept the rest of the information about them to himself because, after all, he was the detective, I was just the UC, and it was on a need-to-know basis.

The Jealous Tyrant

July 26, 1980. Christy had a whole bunch of personal errands to do that morning. She drove us to the Kaimuki branch of her bank and introduced me to a friend she had bumped into in the parking lot.

I said hello to the young man Christy introduced me to, and they walked off together, talking.

If Stanley didn't call me by a certain time every day, I was ordered to call the hotline everyday to check in for my assignments. Sometimes there were different voices on the other end of the line, but I had never met them. A few days later, the male voice answering the phone asked if I remembered him. I had never met any of the Narcotics officers and was sure I didn't know him.

"I met you yesterday with Christy," the voice explained, and he reminded me of the uneventful meeting in the parking lot of the bank in Kaimuki.

I had only said hello, and didn't remember if Christy had ever told her who he was or his name. I couldn't remember his name or what he looked like, so Harvey introduced himself to me again.

Christy had told Harvey how difficult things were getting and how isolated and depressed I had become. Harvey started calling me just to talk, and I was grateful for the conversation. He was the only person I could talk to who wasn't a target or involved in the investigation. We talked as friends, and always only on the phone and never in person. I thought I had finally found a friend.

Harvey asked me to meet him for a cup of coffee once, but I declined his invitation, knowing Stanley would be enraged. We talked about martial arts mostly, and things that did not concern or involve what I was doing. I was thankful for the moments of escape from my reality.

About a week later, I got a call from Stanley, who was raging with anger. "Meet me at the zoo right now!" he yelled and slammed down the phone. Stanley was obviously upset about something but wouldn't tell me what it was about on the phone.

I met him in the parking lot of the Honolulu Zoo and found him sitting in his car, flushed red with anger.

"You want to tell me something?" he said with reproach, looking straight ahead instead of looking at me.

"Tell you what?" I asked, baffled at his question.

"Okay, if you're going to do this, that's it!" he threatened. "I can't work like this! I can't trust you! Where's your loyalty!"

"What the hell are you talking about?" I demanded, bewildered at his verbal assault. I was frustrated, disgusted, and angry at all the mind games he played.

"You know what I'm talking about!" he yelled.

"You know what? I can't take this shit. I quit. Let's end this!" I snapped. "I can't take it anymore!"

As I started to leave, Detective Stanley stopped his attempt to coerce an unknown confession from me.

"So how long you been having an affair with Harvey?" he asked sarcastically. "You going to tell me about it or just keep sneaking around behind my back?"

"What the hell are you talking about?" I tried desperately not to yell. I was shocked at his accusations about my new and only friend, and outraged at his attempt to dirty our innocent relationship. I was already fed up at the accusations of his wife, and now he was accusing me of disloyalty and having an affair with Harvey. No one asked for or wanted to hear the truth. It was easier to jump to conclusions and to yell accusations.

"I quit! I hate what I'm doing, and I hate all your stupid mind games!" I blurted out in anger. "You know what? Believe what you want. I quit. Just tell me what I have to do to get out of this!"

Stanley said the whole office was talking about the affair and the special secret relationship I was having with Harvey. He had just heard about it this morning.

"So how long has this been going on?" he demanded again.

"You know what?" I said trying to contain my anger. "Christy introduced me to him once for a few seconds, and I don't even remember what he looks like! We talk on the phone, that's it! He's a friend! Call Christy and Harvey right now and ask them!" I demanded.

"I just wanted to hear it from you," he said, failing at his attempt at a soothing tone. "I was the last to know!"

"That's bullshit. There's nothing to know. I'm the last to know. I quit! I don't need these stupid mind games everybody's playing. I've had it!" I hissed with my contempt for him and drove away.

I drove to the nearest pay phone to call Christy and Harvey at the office. I was outraged and asked why I was being accused of having an affair with Harvey. I wanted to know who was starting the rumors, and I informed Christy and Harvey that I wanted quit immediately.

"He has a crush on you!" Christy gasped. "He thinks he owns you and he's jealous. There's nothing wrong with you having a friend to talk to!"

It had been incredibly difficult to do what I was doing, and now I had to put up with mind games, rumors, and false accusations. The hot humid weather caused visible heat waves to rise from the asphalt on the paved roads, and the stench of the zoo animal feces in the steaming heat added to the ugliness of the day.

Stanley called a few days later and apologized. "You don't understand how much you mean to me, girl." He was drunk again, and added in a soft, slurred voice, "You don't realize how much I care about you and how hurt I was."

The sound of his voice and the words he spoke made me feel sick, but I had no one to talk to about it. I was banned from any contact with Harvey and Christy, who Stanley felt had conspired against him behind his back.

"They're going to hurt you!" he said. "Don't trust them! You keep this up with Harvey and he's going to get kicked out of vice!" he threatened.

Christy had already informed me that there had been a huge blow up in the Narcotics office about the nonexistent affair. Harvey and Stanley were actually going to throw some blows before they were stopped. Christy had taken a couple days off. The growing animosity and controversy between the Stanley and Christy, about who knew better about what was best for me, and who had control over me, had grown out of control. The team that I had to rely on was not only totally dysfunctional, it had become extremely hostile.

Stanley had demanded that I cut all contact with Harvey and Christy, especially if I didn't want to get Harvey into trouble.

At the onset of the investigation, I had failed to ask how I could quit if I wanted to get out. *How can I quit if there are no records in the personnel department of me being a police officer? I even get paid from a slush fund account instead of the city and county and never entered the academy. If I got killed, they could deny my existence easily. Even I can't even prove who I am!* I thought to myself miserably.

I had been working with Christy during the days, when Christy was available and wasn't in court. I worked nights at Yoshi's, when I wasn't buying dope all over the island. Every moment of every day had been filled with turmoil and anxiety, and my head spun with the multiple identities I played. I couldn't remember how things used to be or who I was anymore. Scotch, prayer, and my journals kept me going, as well as the belief that I was doing what was right by taking down the drug dealers.

All I had was a detective I hated, and a footman that the detective said was dangerous and incompetent. I had told Stanley that I wanted to end this, but he didn't want to listen.

"I'm the detective. You're just the UC. You can't just quit until I tell you to stop." Christy and Harvey knew I wanted to get out, but he had blocked me from them, too.

The power is not found in gender
Nor in the loyalties
But rather in the thought
Or desire or belief of a dream
It is not the dream that is important, ultimately
But more so the desire of that dream
And the pursuit of the desire
And the sincerity of that pursuit
That when it is ended
We can be fulfilled
Not in only in the attainment of the dream
But in the sincerity
With which it is was pursued
And if all dreams and desires
Identify what we have not yet attained
Then true fulfillment
Is the acceptance of what we already have
It is the expansion of the self
Not the separation
It is the encompassing of all things in the universe

Journal entry: August 1980

Outrageous Betrayal

The small Japanese bar on King Street was crowded that evening. I was finally given the undercover car to use since Christy was on vacation, and I drove it to the debriefing. I had been to the bar to drop off the evidence once before, when Detective Stanley was with his friends and girlfriends. He had introduced me to everyone as his UC.

It had been wrong for me to talk to my close friends, and it was wrong for Christy to introduce me to Harvey, but it was all right for Stanley to introduce me to his friends in a bar

The table he sat at was cluttered with empty bottles of beer, and he had stripped and peeled the labels off of each bottle. He was by himself this time, and he was very drunk.

Stanley stared at me from across the table as I placed the dope I had bought in front of him.

"Talk to me, girl," was his opening statement to me every time we debriefed, and I began to tell him about the deal.

Stanley scraped the label off another bottle of beer he had gulped down. I could see that his thoughts were far away, and I knew he wasn't really listening to what I had just told him. He was pounding the beers nonstop, and instead of new instructions, he began to defame Christy again.

My time with Stanley and Christy had been spent in part listening to each of them demean the other. I had slowly become a pawn in this game as they each tried to convince me about who was better at the job.

I was always comfortable with Christy and trusted her as I would trust a friend, but I had grown to despise Stanley and had never learned to trust him. He started talking about loyalty again, and lately, he was always asking to whom I had given my loyalty.

This time I answered that I was loyal to the ideals of justice, and my answer made him snap. I had never told him that I was loyal to him, and that was the answer that I knew that he was waiting to hear from me all these months.

"Are you loyal to Christy?" he demanded, raising his voice.

I answered that I felt close to Christy, and he cut me off from finishing my answer.

"Why?" he yelled, oblivious to the heads that were beginning to turn towards us.

The older Japanese female manager, who everyone in the bar referred to as Mama, looked at me with concern. From behind him, she silently mouthed the words of warning, "He's drunk," and shook her head.

Stanley yelled at her for another beer, and Mama reluctantly brought him another, telling him he was drinking too much and too fast. Stanley became belligerent and wiped the numerous empty beer bottles from the table on to the floor, demanding that she clean up the table and mind her own business.

"Policemen think they can do anything they want to!" she said with a scowl. Mama walked away in a huff and glanced back at me for a moment with a worried expression.

Stanley glared at me when I stood up and told him I was leaving. His conduct was outrageous, and I was embarrassed and repulsed to be sitting at the table with him.

"Sit down!" he said, raising his voice. "You'll leave when I say you can!"

One of the customers sitting at a few tables away had been listening to the detective yelling at me and saw me trying to get up to leave.

The young man was in my line of sight and sitting at the table directly behind the detective. He had begun to stand up to help me just as Mama was coming down the aisle past his table. She blocked him in and told him, "Don't get involved. He's a policeman!"

Stanley was staring at his emptied beer bottle, scraping off another label with his thumbnail, oblivious to what was happening behind him as I stood up to leave.

I glared at him when he stood up and began to reach across the table, either to slap me or yank me back into the seat.

The guy behind him stood up again to help me and started arguing with Mama, who was still blocking his way. I sat back down, asking the Stanley to stop making a scene.

Stanley stood up, puffed out his chest, looked the place over, and started yelling at everyone in the place to mind their own business, calling out anyone who had a problem with him.

Mama pushed the young guy back into his seat as he was preparing to answer the challenge. I knew if I tried to leave at that moment, there would be a fight, and Mama motioned for me to wait a little while.

I knew that Mama was worried about what was going to happen if I tried to leave. Even if the young guy kicked Stanley's ass, the cops would come and probably help the detective. The young guy, who was trying to help me, would probably get hurt.

Stanley finally sat down, but only after I did, and for a few silent moments, we glared at each other across the table. He must have seen the burning hate and anger I had in my eyes, and his rage suddenly turned to sadness.

It was apparent that everyone in the place knew that he was a cop and that no one was going to do anything to help me. The one guy who tried was still upset and said in a loud voice, "I don't give a shit if he's a cop!"

Mama sat next to him, blocking him into the bench seats, trying to calm him down. Stanley was again oblivious and just sat staring at me with glassy, bloodshot eyes.

The whole place had become silent as the tension in the air began to thicken.

Mama rushed over to offer me a drink, and sat across from me, next to Stanley. With a nod of my head, I silently thanked her for staying at our table for a moment. She responded with a slight bow of her head and sympathetic eyes.

After sitting a minute longer, she hurried away quietly to bring me a drink on the house.

I gulped the scotch down when Mama returned, and began to wipe the mess of spilled beer from the table. She left and rushed back with another shot of scotch.

A short, skinny, elderly Japanese man approached our table with bento boxes of prepared Japanese food and placed them on the table in front of the detective. He sat next to Stanley, across from me, and began talking in a hushed voice about TVs and other items he had in his possession. It gave me a few moments of reprieve to think about how I was going to leave and get away from the disgusting tyrant.

A few groups of patrons began to leave. The young Asian guy who had tried to help me asked if I was all right as his two friends pushed him backward toward the door. I nodded. The detective was still listening to the Japanese man, who appeared to be offering him more than food.

Detective Stanley was a big man who liked to intimidate and manipulate people. He often bragged about the control he had over others and had often asked if I was afraid of him like everyone else was. My answer was always no, and he knew it was a part of the control over me that he had not yet achieved. He would justify his inquiry by telling me that I needed to realize that only he would protect me.

The small Japanese man had left, and Mama kept bringing full glasses of scotch as if to keep me there to pacify the detective's belligerent drunken behavior. I gulped each one down, trying to erase my thoughts and numb my feelings. It was a methodology I had used to prepare for drug deals with a suspect I was uncomfortable with. None of my suspects had made me feel as uncomfortable and disgusted as Stanley did.

Part of me was screaming silently for help, but I knew that no one could help me.

I drowned out the sound of my own screams and forced myself back into my UC identity to deal with the moment at hand. I often had to pretend to be comfortable and have a good time with people I didn't like, and that UC identity had always kept me safe.

This time, it was the detective who was the bad guy I didn't want to be with.

I would play the good little UC role to survive this scene and then would casually walk out in a few minutes and escape. I had never seen him this drunk or belligerent before, but then again, I had never actually really spent time with him. He never went with me on deals like Christy. Tonight, he was bouncing between rage and depression. He was supposed to be my guidance, support, and protection?

Stanley stared at his bottle for a moment, scraping off another label with his thumbnail. When he finally spoke, it was in a sad and pathetic tone.

"You don't know how much I care for you. Talk to me, girl."

"About what?" I didn't know what to say or what was going on with him.

"You're cold!" he said sullenly and stared at me, scraping at a label.

He suddenly stopped scraping the bottle and looked at me as if he had come to a realization "You're not afraid of anything, are you? Not even me! But I know what would get to you!" he said triumphantly. "I would kill your family. I would kill your mother and your brother," he said in an even tone. All he would have to do, he said, was to call his brother in prison, who would do it for him without question.

He had won the mind game and had pushed me into a flash of rage, and I couldn't hold on to my composure.

"What do you want from me!" I demanded.

"Calm down, girl!" he smiled at triggering a reaction.

He went on to explain that he wanted to be close to me like Christy was. He wanted me to confide in him, trust him, and be loyal to him. He wanted to know what I talked about with Christy and not him, so I told him.

"Sometimes I feel guilty. I feel like I've changed. I don't laugh, I don't cry, and I feel an incredible loneliness that I never felt before." I answered honestly, but it was a mistake, and my answer threw him suddenly into a rage again.

"What are you trying to do to me?" he yelled and pushed himself backward from the table, glaring at me.

"What the hell are you talking about now?" I snapped back. "I'm not trying to do anything to you. You asked what we talked about and I told you, and this is why I don't ever talk to you about my feelings!" I stood up to leave.

"Wait, wait, wait," he pleaded. "Just sit down!"

"I can't take this anymore. You always play these mind games, and I'm stuck in the middle of you and Christy. I quit! Get me out!" My head was spinning, and the scotch did not help me to control my emotions.

"You want to quit?" he snapped back with a sassy tone. The patrons in the bar glanced apprehensively in our direction and then turned away, pretending not to hear.

He was in a rage again and wiped the bottles and dishes off the table with one swipe of his arm. "Stay!" he yelled at me as I stood up to leave.

"Give me the keys to the UC car," he yelled when I wouldn't listen to his commands to sit back down.

I dumped the keys on the table in front of him.

"Give me the buy money!" I dumped all the money I had, including my own, on the table between us.

Detective Stanley pulled out his revolver and slammed it on the table, yelling, "Shoot me if you hate me that much!"

A waitress screamed and ran into the kitchen as the customers sitting in the nearby booths scrambled to leave.

Humiliation and rage filled every pore of my body as I glared at him in disbelief. My reproach and indignation instead of fear seemed to pull him back to awareness.

"Please!" he begged in a drunken slur, "just sit down. You don't know what you're doing to me. This has never happened to me before. I'm afraid of you, girl!" he slurred. "I don't know what to do!"

"I don't know what you're talking about. I'm not doing anything to you!" I retorted.

"You're cold!" he said again. "I'm trying to tell you, but I can't reach you!"

I didn't know what was happening but began to panic with a desperate need to get out. Even if it meant he would shoot me in the back, I knew I had to get away from him.

"Sit down," he pleaded and almost seemed sober. "How are you going to get home?" He offered me the car keys.

"I'll find a way," I said and refused to accept the keys from him, knowing that it would give him the feeling of my dependency on him. Instead, I walked out, leaving him saying, "I'm sorry … I'm sorry."

There was a slight drizzle when I stepped out of the doorway into the street. It felt like I was stepping out of a horror movie. I didn't know where to go, but I kept on walking. The anger and humiliation I had just gone through replayed like a broken record in my mind. The disgust and hate I felt for him escalated with each step I took, growing more intense with the quickening sounds of my footsteps on the pavement. I began to run to escape the filth I felt from the months of working with him, but I couldn't shake it off and I didn't know where to go. I suddenly realized that I had dumped every last coin I had, including my own money, onto the table at the bar. I didn't even have money for a pay phone. I ran to the nearest intersection on King Street at McCully Street, afraid that he was following me.

Just when I thought I had escaped him, he came up behind me, blasting the horn in his car and yelling for me to get in. I ignored him and ran to the opposite side of the street, but he continued to follow me. I kept walking down the street, trying to look for an open business with a phone I could use. He followed me, yelling his apologies and demands for me to get into his car.

"Leave me alone! I quit!" I kept yelling back. "Stay away from me!"

Cars were slowing down to stare and watch, but he continued to follow me, blocking traffic in one lane. He didn't care. He was a policeman and could do anything he wanted. I wanted to run and hide.

The UC identity in me said to follow directions. The other half said to run and hide. I realized that Stanley had become the biggest obstacle I had to overcome in the entire investigation.

Cars were beginning to pull over to watch what was happening. My mind was spinning with panic. I didn't know where I was and I had nowhere to run. I didn't know what to do, and I felt my mind snap and go blank. I couldn't think.

Stanley refused to leave me alone, and my refusal to get into his car was causing a scene. I was totally stranded.

"If I get into your car, just take me back to the UC car," I bargained.

"I promise!" he said. "Just get into the car!"

"Please!" I begged, not totally trusting him. "Just take me back to my car!"

"I promise," he said again. "Trust me!"

When I finally got into his car, my mind went blank at the relief that I was going back to the UC car and getting away from him.

Time seemed to be passing in rifts as I watched the streetlights flying past outside of the passenger window.

"Let's talk," I finally heard him say and realized I was still with him.

I focused on where I was and was furious when I realized that he had not taken me back to the car as he had promised. We were at Waikiki Beach. I was wrong to have believed and trusted him. He had lied to me and broken his promise to let me go and leave me alone. Instead, he had gained his control over me again.

The streets were deserted and dark, and I got out of his car but still didn't know which way to go. I tried to shake myself back to reality and looked around, not knowing how much time had passed. I wasn't dreaming, but I couldn't escape the nightmare that was still continuing.

I found myself sitting under a coconut tree at Queens' Beach, and I couldn't figure out how I got there. I think I was sobbing and Stanley was telling me how he had fallen in love with me and how this had never happened to him before.

I couldn't remember how long he had been talking. My mind had blanked out and I couldn't figure out if I was stuck in a nightmare or a tragic reality. He was accusing me of making him go crazy and screwing up his life and he didn't know what to do.

I was getting sick and began to feel how I had never felt before: desperate.

I was unable to focus and kept trying to disappear to make the nightmare stop, refusing to accept what I was hearing and what was happening. From out of the darkness, the silhouette of a thin man with layers of clothes and matted long hair walked up and asked for a smoke.

"Watch this," the detective bragged and pulled out his gun, pointing it at the man. "Beat it!" he said, and the black silhouette of the man raised his hands up in submission.

"It's cool, man. It's cool!" he said as he walked backwards a few steps and then disappeared back into the darkness.

"We should go somewhere else," the detective said.

"I want to go home. Just take me back to my car!" I pleaded.

In a moment of clarity, I realized that I was in his car, and it seemed as if I had experienced another rift in time. It was as if I was outside of my body and was watching myself crying. I was separated from myself. I was empty and void, and nothing seemed real.

There was a battle between two identities fighting in my mind, and I had stepped back to watch, trying to grasp what was happening. This time, it wasn't Christy and the detective fighting with each other to get control of me. It was a battle between my two identities, switching back and forth, trying to tell me what to do. I stood back helplessly and watched the battle from some place afar.

The detective was talking, but I couldn't hear him. Instead, I watched the two identities fighting over how to react, what to say, what to do. The UC identity began to listen to his instruction when he told me to take off my clothes. The other identity was screaming. I stopped.

"This is wrong. I can't do this. Just take me back to my car!" I pleaded, but he wouldn't listen. I remembered that I was nothing. He owned me. He was the detective, and I was just the UC.

"Don't be ashamed of your body," he instructed. "I'm not going to hurt you. I would never hurt you. I'm the one who's going to protect you and no one else."

The UC identity was saying over and over, "Follow directions. You are not you. You belong to him. This is not real." The other one was screaming hysterically at me. I was a puppet, unable to make my own decisions.

He had named his penis Big Henry, he had bragged when he hurriedly pulled down his pants.

He pulled down my pants, moving me around like I was a lifeless rag doll, and I didn't fight. "Come on top of me," he ordered as he lifted me on top of him and pulled me down onto him.

A voice screamed in my head, and another said, "Follow directions. He owns you. He's the detective." But my voice was silent. I couldn't speak. The pain I felt brought me a moment of clarity, and I pulled myself away from him. I wasn't turned on, and it had hurt when he tried to force himself into me.

"I can't do this. This is wrong. Just take me home!" I pleaded, but he wasn't listening. He was almost frantic.

He got into the back seat and lifted me easily into the back and began to push himself inside of me again. Time was passing in rifts again, and I didn't know how long it was before I watched myself begin to sob and he finally stopped.

"I don't want to hurt you, girl! You're just not used to big guys like me." He had repositioned himself in the back seat and was pulling my head down towards his crotch, still frantic for his release. "Just suck on me," he instructed.

"I can't do this!" I said again, trying to gain back control of what was happening. Suddenly, there were flashing blue lights and high-beamed headlights blinding me.

"It's the beat man!" he said and jumped out of the car, zipping up his pants hurriedly.

I still had my blouse on, and frantically found my pants and panties and yanked them back on.

I didn't remember getting home. The last thing I remembered was watching him talk to the beat officer in the parking lot of what I recognized a year later to be Fort Ruger.

Christy came back to work and finally parked the car to ask me what had happened. I didn't even realize I was with Christy. I didn't know how long she had been gone or how many days had passed since the incident.

"What's wrong with you? What happened when I was gone?" she asked, and I began to sob hysterically. I suddenly realized that I had lost time. I had lost conscious awareness.

"I gotta quit. I hate him!" I said.

Christy peered searchingly into my eyes. "Did he hurt you?" she demanded.

I began to tell Christy of my hurt, shame, and anger.

Christy flew into a rage. "I knew it," she said. "I knew he was in love with you. That's why he's so jealous!"

"Get me out Christy, Please just get me out." I begged.

"He fuckin' raped you is what he did!" Christy was screaming and began crying in fury. "He brainwashed you, got you drunk, and used you! I can tell what happened just by looking at you!"

"I didn't fight him off, Christy," I said in shame. "I couldn't figure out what was going on and if it was really happening."

Christy took me home and said she would help me quit. "He can't get away with this!" she said. "And he had the nerve to accuse me and Harvey of getting you hurt!!"

"I don't know what to do. I don't even know how to quit," I said.

Christy said she would take care of it and would go to the lieutenant. She called me later that night and told me she had gotten into a heated argument with the detective after finding out he was going around telling everyone how much I was in love with him.

Christy knew that I hated him and couldn't stand his macho intimidation and how uncomfortable I was every time I was around him.

"She's not in love with him. She hates him!" she tried to tell the guys in the office.

Christy knew the detective was covering his tracks with lies, but no one believed her, she said. "If they saw you they would know he hurt you!" she said, and Christy started to cry.

"He's covering his tracks! He's turning this whole thing around before anybody finds out what happened!"

Christy said she would talk to Lieutenant Okimoto and tell him to call me.

When he failed to call a couple days later, Christy gave me his phone number. It was obvious that the lieutenant was reluctant to talk to me or to hear what I had to say.

Even the Narcotics Vice Division's secretary had confronted me on the phone asking me what I was trying to do to Detective Stanley, who was her very good friend.

I had seen what the detective was really like behind his macho manipulating façade. I knew too that there were others who knew the truth about what had happened and the truth about what kind of person he really was. He was out of control, and I had been victimized for it, even though I had done nothing to him.

Stanley knew too, what he had done to me, and how his conduct as a supervisor had been totally outrageous.

The Man Pact

I finally met with Lieutenant Okimoto. I told him I wanted to quit and wanted to know how to get out of the UC assignment.

He was aloof and said up front that if I didn't want to press rape charges then I should just stop talking about it.

I was outraged at his response. I wanted to know how to quit and I hadn't talked to anyone else about what had happened, but he was blaming me for the story going around all over the office. He looked at me with reproach.

"Maybe it was the beat man or all the people in the lounge or on the street when he was following me with his car," I said angrily. "I didn't talk to anyone except Christy, and she's just trying to help me quit! I'm not trying to make a complaint," I repeated. "I'm trying to quit!"

Lieutenant Okimoto didn't seem to care what I had to say. He also said he was meeting me on his own time and wasn't happy about it. I knew I would have no help and no understanding or support.

"You know what, I'm really sorry but I don't know who else to talk to," I finally said as he continued to chew his food, not even looking at me. I told the lieutenant again that I wasn't seeing him to make a complaint but I didn't want to be anywhere near Stanley and wanted to quit, but he wasn't listening to what I was saying.

Okimoto continued, in his dull voice, to advise me that if I made a complaint, it would never fly because the detective was very well liked and respected. No one would believe me, and if I was in love with him, this is not the way to get back at him. He was a good detective and a family man.

I was outraged and knew that the detective had gotten to everyone and spread his lies.

"I can't stand him!" I said. "I don't like fake macho guys like him; I never did!"

For a moment, Lieutenant Okimoto stopped chewing and looked at me like I was a pain in his ass and lying.

"If you quit, you will ruin it for all the females coming in. The department will never allow females in Narcotics again, especially if you make a complaint. You're going to ruin him, his family, and the chances for the other females," he said in a harsh, patronizing tone, and then he added, "Did you go to the hospital? Do you have proof?"

"What?" I asked in shock.

"Did you go to the rape center?" he repeated his question coldly.

"Listen to me! Can't you hear what I'm saying? I just want to quit. I don't want to be near him or have anything to do with him anymore! I hate him! I'm not trying to make a rape case; I know I'll lose. But I got hurt and it seems nobody wants to hear the truth or help me!" I was almost hysterical with disbelief at what was happening and half crying with rage.

"You guys are all siding with him! Christy and Harvey know the truth," I said, seething with rage and disgust at the man who was supposed to be a police officer and Stanley's supervisor.

I knew that I would be blamed, that no one would help me, and that no one wanted to listen or hear the truth, not even the lieutenant.

"Look" he said, "I don't want to get involved in this if I don't have to. I don't want to talk to you if you're not going to press charges. I shouldn't even be talking to you now and meeting with you like this," he said.

I was shocked at his cowardly and feeble response. I was his officer, but he was definitely unable to handle the responsibility of being my supervisor.

"So you're telling me that if I don't press charges, I have to continue to work with him and you won't do anything to help me?" I asked incredulously.

Lieutenant Okimoto continued to chew his food and thought about it for a minute.

"We'll just shut down the operation then. Can you handle until that?" he asked coldly.

"As long as you keep him away from me!"

The lieutenant finished his food, dropped some money on the table, and walked out. It was obvious that he didn't want to get involved or know the truth. His only concern seemed to be protecting the detective's reputation and completing the investigation. I got word the next day that I would be working with Christy and she would be my direct supervisor and no one else. Christy would relay all instructions and I would never be alone with the detective again.

Christy told me that she was getting harassed from the guys at the Narcotics Office.

I told her how evasive, insensitive, and reluctant the lieutenant had been during our meeting.

Stanley had manipulated everyone at the office with his lies and had even gotten to the lieutenant. He had already created a story making me look bad, to cover up what he had done to me, even though I had never made any complaint.

I had heard about the "brotherhood in blue" always covering each other's ass. I had always thought it was only a rumor, and that there was still honor and integrity in the police department, especially in the higher supervisory ranks. What I had learned from Detective Stanley and Lieutenant Okimoto's conduct made me believe that maybe the rumors were true.

Perhaps they all expected and wanted me to give up, quit, and disappear. My hate for Stanley and disgust for Okimoto made me vow to never quit and to somehow never let this happen to any other female UC again, but I didn't know how to put this behind me and continue. I couldn't understand how it had come to this point after what I had already sacrificed and lost for the success of the investigation. I couldn't understand why Stanley had done this to me.

Every day and every night, I psyched myself up to erase what had happened. I couldn't deal with the feelings of outrageous betrayal. I wondered how many other females in law enforcement or male-dominated fields had faced this nightmare and had been left to face the ordeal alone.

Let Truth be my sword
For my sword of vengeance no longer exists
Let my staff be my wisdom
For that is true strength

And true art be a reflection of heaven
There is no separation of heaven and earth
There is no threshold to cross
Except through the door of the soul

Journal entry: 1980

Tainted Badges

July 29, 1980, Christy and I went to Yoshi's. It was my day off at the restaurant. It was a cool summer night, and the drizzling rain outside quenched the thirsty shrubbery outside. We went into the lounge and sat at a small table in the center of the room.

James, the bus boy, just out of high school, challenged Christy to a video game.

Sharon joined the game during breaks from serving the few customers in the bar.

I ordered some Lemmons from Sharon and asked what else she was holding. She was out of cocaine, she answered, but would be getting some speed in later that evening.

Barry stopped by at our table to tell me that he was expecting a shipment of cocaine and told me to give him a call later. I nodded, and he went back to work as the night manager.

The small lounge area was getting crowded. Several males entered the bar and sat together at a big table. They were Sharon's friends.

"They look like cops!" I said.

Sharon laughed. "No worry. They're my friends!"

One of the males brought a phone to our table and plugged it into a phone jack under the table, near our feet. I never knew that there were phone jacks under the tables even though I worked there.

Sharon explained that the phone lines were illegal and were used to place gambling bets, but no one was supposed to know about it.

The male using the phone called the police station. Christy and I listened as he identified himself to a sergeant and asked for comp time off because he was sick.

Doug smiled when he hung up the phone. "You girls want to join me for a smoke later?" he invited

Christy looked at him doubtfully. "What do you do?" she asked suspiciously.

"I'm a cop," he answered proudly and without hesitation.

My mind was racing. "What's going on?" I whispered to Christy when Doug left the table.

Sharon came over with cocktails, and I asked her if all the guys at the table were cops.

"Yeah," she laughed, explaining that they were all cool. They protected her from getting busted because they all did dope, too.

Doug came back to the table to call the police station again.

"I got CT or what, sarge?" he asked the person on the other end of the phone.

"But I'm sick!" he complained and motioned for us to be quiet. When he was assured that he had been awarded time off, he hung up the phone and plopped himself down in a seat at our table.

"So do you want to go out now for a smoke?" he smiled. "I got some choice stuff in the car."

"You're a cop! Are you joking?" I asked, truly shocked at his invitation, and Doug assured us that he wasn't joking.

"I keep my stash in my car parked at the police station!" he laughed confidently, and then added, "Nobody would suspect that!"

Doug went back to his table, where a gray-haired older man was staring at Christy.

We both looked away when the gray-haired man passed our table several times to look at us. He sat at a table with a heavyset Caucasian female who had been sitting alone on a table in the back of the lounge, but he continued to stare at us. Christy suddenly turned pale, and the blood seemed to drain from her face.

"We're burnt!" she whispered nervously. "He's a detective. His name is Harrison, and he knows me!"

I looked at Christy in alarm. She had her back to the detective, and I began to describe exactly what he was doing with the female who was with him. The female was wearing thick black-framed prescription glasses and had passed Detective Harrison a large envelope. I watched him counting the very large bundle of currency it had contained. Then he put the envelope into his shirt pocket.

"Maybe he's doing undercover stuff, too?" I offered hopefully.

"Nope, he doesn't do that type of work," Christy said grimly.

The female had long hair with dark brown roots growing out. She too began to stare at us.

Christy went to the restroom to use the pay phone on the wall to call the hotline just as Yakuza Masa came in unexpectedly with a few friends. They waved me over to their table, but I motioned for them to wait.

Sharon had just walked back to our table, and Harrison the detective yelled at her to go over to his table.

"Wait!" she exclaimed in a huff, but he called back to her urgently, "Come here, now!"

The heavyset female also started to call to Sharon, "Get over here right now!"

"What! You cannot wait?" Sharon answered back half jokingly. She had noticed the alarm in their voices and demeanor and looked puzzled.

"I'll be back," she told me and went to Detective Harrison's table.

Christy had returned to tell me that the hotline was busy and she couldn't get through, just as Sharon started yelling, "Narcs?"

"He's burning us!" I told Christy. "Leave now!"

Christy left the bar to try the hotline again, and I waited to see what was going on.

If we both left, I knew it would be an admission. I had to pretend that I didn't know what was going on and could hear Sharon trying to back me up.

"Nah, not Jo. She works here. I know her!" she argued.

Harrison continued whispering, and the heavyset female, who Sharon later told me was his girlfriend, stared at me and smirked.

Sharon was swearing when she left the back table and went straight back to the bar instead of returning to my table. I waited to give Christy time to make a phone call and get out of the place and then went to the bar to get another drink.

"What's up?" I asked Sharon, who was a slamming a glass down on the bar.

Sharon started asking me how long I had known Christy and if I had ever actually seen her do any drugs.

"I've known her kind of long. We just trip around sometimes. Why?" I asked, trying to play dumb.

"More than a year?" Sharon asked.

"No." I paused "Less than that. We just trip around sometimes," I explained. "Why! What's going on?" I asked again.

"My friend Harrison is a detective," Sharon said, "and he said he knows that Christy is a narc, and you're probably one, too!"

Sharon was half yelling, and the sudden silence in the lounge was deafening. Everyone was looking at me and listening to every word Sharon was saying ... including the Yakuza guys who were going to arrange for me to transport the dope. I chose my next words carefully, and the nervous confusion I had was real.

"What you talking about?" I asked, pretending to be in shock and offended. "I know her. Your friends are the cops, not mine!"

Doug and Steve, the other two cops who had arrived with Detective Harrison, called Sharon to the opposite end of the bar and started talking to her softly, and she listened intently.

Sharon came back and pleaded. "Please, Jo, tell me the truth. Is Christy a narc?"

I wanted so badly to tell Sharon the truth, but Christy might get hurt, too.

"Nah, no way!" I said instead. "We've been tripping together and partying! I don't trust cops!" I scrambled for the words. "They're the cops!" I said, pointing to her friends, and added what I had too often heard in the streets, "All cops are dirty!" But this time I believed the words I was saying, outraged at what was happening with the cops in the room and remembering my hate and disgust for Detective Stanley and Lieutenant Okimoto.

"Listen, Jo," Sharon said, "my friends told me that if I sold you so much, it would be a Class B felony, but if I sold more than that, it would become a Class A felony. They should know because they're cops and they're trying to help me out and tell me what charges I'm going to face if I sold drugs to *you!*"

The walls seemed spin and the ground felt like it was about to give way under my feet. I suddenly felt sick and didn't try to hide it. My mind went blank again, and there was nothing I could think of to do except to walk out.

"I don't know if they're your friends, Sharon, but I don't trust cops," I said, meaning every word, and stood up from the bar, trying to figure out what to do next. Hopefully, Christy had gotten out and got through to the Narcotics office.

I walked past the Yakuza table and paused a moment. I knew they had heard the entire confrontation, and they looked at me in silence.

"I'm out of here," I said angrily. "Too many cops in here!"

Shawn was sitting at the first table near the entrance of the bar and stuck his foot out to block my exit. He placed his handbag on the table and traced the outline of the gun he had in his bag while he watched my expression.

For a brief moment, I glared at him, daring him to shoot me. He was Sharon's boyfriend, and I had met him once before.

"What's going on?" he asked me with sarcasm in his voice.

"I don't know!" I snapped back and stared into his eyes. I looked at the cops in the room and couldn't hide my true feelings of contempt and disgust.

The room roared in silence as everyone watched me intently.

Shawn eased up and shrugged "Watch out!" he said, smiling and moving his foot out of the way just as Sharon yelled at him to let me go.

I never knew if his warning was on my behalf or a threat against me. All I could think of was tainted badges.

In the months that had passed, I had continued to do my job no matter how difficult it had been, because I believed that I was doing the right thing and that I was a cop. But in that moment, nothing made sense anymore and I found myself hating all cops.

I checked for Christy and was relieved to learn that she had made it out of the restaurant. I couldn't find her in the parking lot and the UC car was gone, too, so I just started to walk. It was like a dream again.

This only happens in the movies! This is not real. It can't be! I had heard of dirty cops, of pay-offs, and favors, but had refused believe it was true. Maybe it was just that I had never wanted it to be true.

Christy found me on a street corner a few blocks away. She had finally gotten through to the hotline and had been driving around in circles for a while to check for a tail.

There were several detectives at the debriefing this time, and seeing Stanley filled me with hate and I couldn't talk.

Christy began to explain what had happened up to the time she had left me in the lounge. I filled in the rest of the story, with the confrontation with Sharon and Shawn, and explained how I had walked away from the Yakuza guys.

All the detectives knew immediately who Shawn was. He was the brother of one of the Narcotics detectives who was with us at the briefing.

I was suddenly sick and dizzy and tried not to heave when I looked at Stanley, who had pounded it into my head that he would protect me. Bullshit! Everything he said had been a lie.

There was no one else except Sharon backing me up in the bar and trying to tell the real cops that she trusted that I was not an undercover cop. It was she who had given me the chance to get out by vouching for me.

I realized that if anything had happened to me, no one would ever know that I was an undercover cop. I didn't exist. The police department could merely deny knowledge of my existence and it would be readily accepted. I had nothing that could prove that I was working for the police department. Like Lieutenant Okimoto had said, "Do you have any proof?"

The only person who was there to help me was Sharon, and she would get arrested in the end. I suddenly trusted my suspects more than I trusted the detective or any other cop.

The few days that followed were blank pages in my memory. I had died that night. There was nothing left. I felt betrayed by the police department and couldn't identify with anyone or anything anymore, except my suspects. And in the end, I would betray their loyalty and friendship.

During the next few weeks, Stanley sent me out everywhere by myself, "to salvage the investigation." He refused to stop, in spite of everything that happened. Okimoto had lied; Stanley was still controlling me.

I had heard my suspects talking before, that the best way to escape a drug rap is to take out the witness. I was the witness and was probably already identified, but Stanley didn't care. He just wanted to continue at any cost, as long as it was me taking the risks and the fall and not him. Stanley never had to pay the dues levied in the streets. I would be the one to pay the price.

Word had spread fast on the streets that Charlie's Angels were running around in Waikiki and town, a Haole lady and a small Jap. I hated the reference to the glorified Hollywood production.

"You fit the description of the Jap, and Christy fits the description of the Haole." I could not deal anywhere on the island. No one would talk to me. But Stanley still did not want to terminate the investigation.

Christy had told me a few days later that all the police officers in the bar had been identified. She was worried about her children's safety, as well as the safety of my family.

"If the cops are against us, then we're totally alone!" she said, and we both knew that we could never count on Detective Stanley or Lieutenant Okimoto.

Detective Harrison, unlike Detective Stanley, had admitted what he had done and was suspended for one day. Harrison never lied or trumped up a fake story to make anyone else look bad or take the blame. Even if he had compromised my undercover identity and put me in jeopardy, he had acted more honorably than Stanley and Okimoto and had accepted responsibility for what he had done.

Stanley had demanded that I bring my friends and suspects to justice and force them to answer for their conduct, yet he could not do the same and hid cowering behind his lies.

Instead of despising Harrison, I ended up respecting him and believed him to be an honorable man, in spite of what had happened.

❧

Chapter 13
Reality

Police Brutality

Detective Stanley sent Christy and I back to Kailua to see if we were burnt ther,e too. Instead of shutting down the investigation and setting me free, he still wanted to continue.

Christy negotiated a deal with one of the young guys hanging around at Slim's place, and he tried to run off with the money. We chased the suspects with the help of an off-duty police officer who had recognized Christy and jumped in to help.

Stanley told Christy to arrest me in front of the game room to try to keep my undercover identity, and Weasel came out and stared.

The burg boys, Danny and Guy, had also been watching and sped off in their red Mustang, not in fear but to spread the news of what was happening.

Christy called the Narcotics Vice Office from the Kailua police station and left me handcuffed in the back room.

"Don't answer any questions," she instructed, and I sat in the room silently in handcuffs.

About an hour later, Christy came back into the room with Stanley and told me to give her a hard time and to refuse to answer questions during the interrogation she would be conducting.

While Christy asked me questions for the booking sheets, numerous uniformed officers came in and out, including a patrol sergeant who kept staring at me and saying he recognized me from somewhere.

Christy began to treat me harshly, and I played the defiant game, refusing to answer her questions. After booking me for narcotics charges, Stanley escorted me out, still handcuffed behind my back, to his car. He had told everyone at the station that he would be transporting me to the main police station.

The sergeant talking to Stanley continued to stare at me the entire time that Christy interrogated me. Stanley was doing most of the talking, and he was mostly listening and nodding. He suddenly began yelling at me as I walked out of the door into the parking lot of the Kailua police substation.

"Hey! Hey, you!" he yelled, and Stanley told me to ignore him. I could hear the sergeant's footsteps quicken as he approached me from behind. I ignored him as instructed and continued to walk to the police car with Stanley holding my handcuffed arm. I hated being near him, and Christy looked at me with empathy.

She was just about to get into the driver's seat of the UC car. She was standing frozen in anticipation, watching me with a look of fear on her face.

"Eh, you! Turn around!" the sergeant yelled angrily when he had finally caught up and was standing behind me. But I refused, waiting for Stanley to unlock the car.

Stanley had taken his time opening the door and had watched the agitated patrol sergeant continuing his approach but did nothing.

The sergeant, who obviously lifted weights, grabbed my hair and yanked me backward. He pulled my head back until he had forced me to turn around and face him. Stanley again did nothing and just stood watching. I glanced at Christy who was biting her lip with tears in her eyes, helpless as the detectives allowed the scene to continue.

"I know who you are!" he yelled at me angrily. "You're the one! You're the one who got arrested last week and punched the hole in the door at Kaneohe Station!" he accused.

"Wasn't me!" I said angrily at his misidentification, outraged at Stanley, who seemed to be enjoying the abuse I was taking.

The sergeant moved forward to hit me, and Stanley still did nothing.

It was Detective James who finally stepped in and stopped the belligerent patrol sergeant from giving me a backhand. I recognized Detective James immediately. He was the detective who had dropped off the money at Yoshi's Restaurant.

I glanced at Christy, who was watching with a horrified look in her eyes. I knew that there was nothing she could do or say. After all, she was just the rookie footman.

Christy could read me like a book without me saying a word. She saw the rage in my eyes at the sergeant for yanking me around, and saw the escalating hate and revulsion I had for Stanley for doing nothing.

Detective James and Christy left in the UC car, and I had to ride, still handcuffed, in Stanley's car. I could see the fear and alarm she had for me as she watched me getting into the car alone with Stanley. "Follow me!" I mouthed, and she nodded.

I burning with hate and rage until Stanley finally broke the silence and asked in a sarcastic tone, "How are you feeling?" His tone made me wonder if he had staged the whole incident.

I didn't answer. I couldn't stand hearing his voice, looking at him, or being near him, and he knew it. Instead of answering his question, I asked for the name of the sergeant, who Stanley had only identified as "his very good friend."

As soon as we got to the debriefing, I jumped into Christy's car and refused to talk to anyone. After Christy talked to the detectives for a few minutes, we drove home in silence. It was Christy who told me Sergeant Melvin's name. It would prove to be a name, face and incident I would never forget.

My mom looked at me anxiously when I walked into the house. I hadn't seen her for days. I was gone almost around the clock, seven days a week. When I came home, I usually went straight to my room and slept.

My mom sensed that something was wrong and turned away when she saw my face. "I was worried," she said quietly.

"Whatever you're doing, I hope you're all right," she said without looking at me. She couldn't stand to see the hurt and stress that I couldn't hide from her anymore.

My parents had just been told that I was working undercover and that Christy was my partner. It was decided that because the situation had become critical and that I might have been identified, I would finally be allowed to tell my parents the truth in case the suspects followed me home for a confrontation. I watched their disbelief and confusion turn to concern and fear. Their disappointment in me was easier to handle than seeing the helpless fear in their eyes. Stanley instructed them to call the hotline in case something happened and hopefully someone would answer.

"How's your friend Christy?" she asked

"Fine," I lied. "We had fun today."

"That's good," she said, not believing my answer. "Eat something and get some sleep. You look terrible."

"Thanks, Mom," I said as I watched her busy herself preparing a meal for me. I wanted to tell her I loved her. I wanted to apologize but couldn't. I would have burst into tears, so I went to the bathroom instead.

It looked like I had been in a fight, and I tried to wash off the signs of the confrontational day. The long, hot shower I took did not wash off the dirt and filth I felt from being near Stanley or the aches and pains in my neck and body from his "very good friend" Sergeant Melvin.

I began to sob hysterically in the shower, and I didn't know if it was from hate, anger, futility, or hurt. When I finally came out of the shower, my mom looked at me and asked if I was crying.

"Nope," I lied again. "Just got some soap in my eyes." My mom looked away, choking down the tears I could see welling up in her eyes.

"Your food is ready," she said with her voice slightly cracking. "Eat it while it's still hot."

I looked at the carefully prepared plate of hot food and realized immediately that my mom was trying to tell me how much she loved me. When she had found out that I was an undercover cop, she didn't complain, no matter how much it worried her, no matter how much anxiety she was going through. She and my dad had held their fears and doubts in silence.

My dad came into the house and looked at me. "How you doing?" he asked, trying to mask his concern and worry. I knew I still looked like I had gotten into a fight and knew he could tell that I had been crying.

"Fine," I lied to him, too. "Just tired." My voice cracked.

I hurried into my room and lay down for a while to erase myself and control my need to cry before I faced them again. I fell asleep. I woke the next day at noon and found my plate of food carefully wrapped in the refrigerator. I wanted to cry again, but this time the tears did not fall.

I had never expected or foreseen how much my decision to take the undercover assignment would hurt my parents.

Stanley had told me over and over again not to trust them because they would be the ones to blow my cover. He had lied. He had told me he would be the one to protect me. He had lied. I had learned the hard way that it was wrong to trust him and how dishonorable he really was.

My parents were suffering now because of what I had chosen to do. No one had ever told me that my family would be deeply hurt and affected, too. I had been too trusting in the honor and integrity of the detective to foresee the devastation, betrayal, and abandonment. It was too late now. I had learned the truth, and in my mission to do something good, I had been forever destroyed. I was learning how to cry without tears.

I have a friend who has never complained
Of difficulties seen or lost, forgotten dreams
I have a friend who's been with me through the years
When others in my lifetime have slowly disappeared

She dared to speak the Truth because she cared for me
And when I failed and stumbled, she cried silently
She tried to teach me Honor and tried to make me see
That life was what we made it and it's what we chose it to be

I would like to say I'm sorry for the things I could not see
For taking her for granted and the life she gave to me
For the times I made her angry and the times I made her cry
For the times I made her worry because I wouldn't try

I would like to say thank you, though inadequate it would be
For all the love she gave me and the things she's done for me
For all the times she struggled and denied who she could be
To give me all she could to make a better life for me

What did she want to be when she was growing up?
Is there a treasured dream that she might feel she's lost?
I would give my friend the world and grant her every wish
And to wipe out every tear, I would do my best

The love in her heart is as endless as the sky
The beauty of this lady will surely never die

I love you, Mom
Thank you for being ... My Friend

Journal entry: 2004

Terry

I learned a few days later from Christy that on the very same afternoon I was arrested, and almost at exactly the same time, another undercover officer working in the Chinatown area on the other side of the island had also been arrested and severely beaten by cops. He was in the cellblock for hours before the Narcotics detectives realized he was missing. Like me, he had usually run without backup.

Terry Bledsoe had his jaw wired shut, and Stanley asked me to meet with him because he had stopped talking with everyone.

"I don't blame him," I smirked. "Why the hell are you calling me?"

Stanley clarified that it wasn't him asking for the help, it was the detective of the other officer. He also wanted to use my parents' house for a meeting.

"Why here?" I snapped, incensed that he was using my parents now, too. "Why don't you use your own house or go somewhere else?"

"My apartment is too small. Your house is the only safe place for the meeting. It's for the UC," he coaxed.

The sound of his voice was sickening, and I only agreed because I wanted to meet someone like me.

Stanley wanted me to talk to Officer Terry Bledsoe to bring him back out of his silence, and I thought it was ironically outrageous. After all, he was the awesome macho detective supervisor, and we were just the UCs.

"Why would I do that?" I had asked sarcastically.

"I'm not asking for me. I'm asking you to help the other UC."

A few days later, for the first time, I finally met another undercover officer.

Terry had arrived with the detectives, and without saying a word, he had walked straight into the patio and sat facing away from everyone in a hunched over posture. Just by looking at him, I knew that it was more than his jaw that had been shattered.

Terry did not move from the corner and had refused the invitation to eat the steamed fish and that his detective had brought. He was making it clear that he wanted to be left alone.

"Go talk to him," Stanley pushed. "See if you can bring him out of his shell and get him to talk."

I cautiously approached the officer I had been waiting to meet. Terry turned around to look at me when I introduced myself, and I finally saw the face beneath his short afro hairstyle. I was surprised to see a flash of outrage and defiance in his eyes instead of hurt and depression. Terry informed me in an abrupt tone that he had nothing to say to the detectives and could not stand being near them or looking at his detective. I immediately understood what Terry was feeling. Instead of trying to coax him to join the detectives, I stayed in the corner of the patio with him and we began to talk.

During our conversation, I learned that Terry had already completed the Police Training Academy, and that we shared the same feelings of animosity towards our detectives, who were supposed to be our backup and protection. I knew too, that he felt the same outrage and betrayal at having been hurt by other cops. The pain of his injury was nothing compared to the pain of his broken spirit. I knew we were sharing something that the detectives would probably never understand or experience.

"They want me to tell you not to quit and not to give up," I smirked, and Terry snickered.

Stanley finally asked me if I had convinced him not to give up.

"That's up to him," I said, and walked away feeling dirty and violated again.

I didn't see Terry Bledsoe again until a few years later. But I knew that evening that we would meet again someday and would become lifelong friends. The wounds of betrayal would leave deep scars in both of our lives.

Up From Under

August 1980. The operation was officially terminated, and I was overwhelmingly relieved and thankful. Preparation for the arrests, secret grand jury indictments, and signing arrests warrants had begun. Stanley made it a point to tell me how hard he was working on the paper work. I was finally allowed in the station and met the people behind the voices on the Narcotics hotline.

I was surprised to find that they were not overbearing, manipulative, and dishonorable tyrants like Stanley. I knew that the other detectives would never have hurt me.

Howard was a Narcotics officer. He was like a Japanese samurai, and he looked like one, too. He was strong and outspoken but had the sincerity and honesty to back his words. I never heard him brag about how good he was or how many people were afraid of him, even though I could tell that he could kill someone in a flash if he had to.

He acted like a grouch sometimes but always had a twinkle in his eye when he was yelling and screaming about one thing or the other. He was like a mischievous child.

Max was Hawaiian, level-headed, and sensitive. You could tell he had a big heart and a clean spirit. He too never bragged about how great he was or how many people feared him. He was quite a gentleman. Max was more solid than a brick wall, and he could not only cook but he could sing, too. Max never bragged. He didn't have to.

Elroy was Portuguese, very quiet, almost shy, but you could still see the goodness inside his heart. He didn't waste his time on mind games and chirping.

Detective James was Portuguese and kept to himself. He looked and acted like someone who would be on *Miami Vice*. I knew I would never forget how he helped me.

Gary, Shawn's brother, was Caucasian/Korean. I rarely saw him, and when I did, I just kept a comfortable distance even though he was really nice guy.

Steven was Japanese and was the most like Stanley in character. He carried an air of arrogance and you could tell by what he said that he thought very highly of himself. He too liked to play mind games and reminded everyone that he had a college degree. He had asked me to come over to his house one night to discuss possibility of working under his supervision. I had honestly thought it was because I was going to be temporarily assigned to him, but when I arrived, he was alone, and he had prepared some drinks. I left when I realized that I wasn't there to discuss an assignment. He just wanted to spend some time alone to get to know me, he explained, when I said I was uncomfortable and stood up to leave. I had learned my lesson too late with Stanley, but I wasn't going to make the same mistake again.

"I'm just testing you," he said, "And now I want to see if you're going to tell anyone about this." I wondered again if Stanley had staged the whole thing.

Now I fully understood why everyone in the office had called Stanley the ayatollah. He had none of the qualities of a leader but he truly believed that everyone worshipped him. I knew without a doubt that if I had been assigned to someone else, the investigation would have been twice as successful and I wouldn't have been hurt and destroyed.

The one thing almost everyone had in common was that they had all described the lieutenant as a weak supervisor.

A good supervisor, I realized, was someone who was not only willing but also able to do what they expected their subordinates to do. And they definitely should never cover up the dishonorable conduct of their subordinates. Honor above loyalty.

Green Harvest

The entire Narcotics Division rode around the island in unmarked vans as the helicopters flew above like dragonflies.

Thousands of marijuana plants and trees were pulled and yanked mercilessly from their prepared beds of fertile soil as their growers bit their lips in speechless anger.

The precious weed was found in hot houses, fields, pigpens, and dog kennels. At one location, numerous two-foot-tall budding plants were growing in ten-gallon black rubber planters, hanging in the thick branches of the mango trees like ornaments on a Christmas tree. The green leaves of the branches had created a protective canopy, keeping them from being spotted by any choppers flying by, and units on foot were searching the grounds looking down instead of up towards the sky.

Farrell was a clown. They let him drive the van every day, even if he kept banging into trees, mailboxes, and fences. He was artistically gifted with charcoal drawings and paintings, but not with driving skills.

Some of us were poisoned by unknown chemicals that the growers had vindictively sprayed on the plants after hearing that the harvest was headed their way. Our skin burned like fire when we grabbed the stalks of the plants and brushed up against the leaves.

A large pit bull urinated on an officer's head when he walked through an underground tunnel beneath the kennel of the dog guarding the area. The tunnel led to an old bomb shelter filled with beautiful budding marijuana plants.

Bribes of every sort were being offered, and Internal Affairs spotters were everywhere to make sure that none of the offers were accepted. The Vice guys were scrutinized from dawn to dusk until every plant and seedling had been systematically logged, photographed, tested, and then destroyed.

I met the men in the Gambling Detail for the first time during the weeks of Green Harvest. They were so different from the Narcotics team. Most of the members of this Gambling team would remain my close friends till the end of my career.

The Gambling guys were all buff-bodied and had to be to carry the illegal gambling machines and to bust down reinforced doors on raids. Kevin was sensitive and kind, and went out of his way to try to make me feel comfortable by trying to include me in their conversations. Ben was his best friend. They lifted weights and clowned around like brothers.

Kevin was Caucasian and blonde with fair skin, and Ben was Filipino, had wavy black hair, and was darkly tanned. They reminded me of twin titans, day and night. Ben loved to laugh and play around, and Kevin was shy in contrast.

Maurice was the handsome Hawaiian rebel, Donald was spiritual and sensitive, and Derrick was the one with the caring heart who would later become part of the Critical Incident Unit, created to help officers.

The Roundup

The arrests of all of my suspects went well, and the news media expressed their curiosity about the secret identity of the unidentified undercover officer. The newscasters on the evening news reported that they had estimated that there had been close to one hundred felony indictments, and arrests were being made all over the island. Before the day was done, about forty-five suspects had been arrested, and the cellblock was overflowing.

I had driven all over the island that day, pointing out and identifying the suspects in pool halls, game rooms, and bars, and then went home alone. I was banned from the police station again, which was ridiculous since all of the suspects now knew positively that I was the undercover narcotics officer. It wrenched my heart to watch some of my suspects get arrested. The media cameras hung out at the cellblock, filming all the suspects arriving and then being released on bail pending further investigation.

I received nonstop warnings and threats on my phone in the weeks that followed, but Stanley didn't care. He had targeted them but had sent me out to do the dirty work, and now I had to answer and stand alone against the wave of their hate, with no gun and no badge. He didn't care that all the suspects had my phone number and could easily find out where I lived. He was too busy taking bows.

No one from the police department called to say thank you or even checked to see if I was okay. Everyone protected the anonymous complainants and informants, but no one called to see if me or my family were all right.

Stanley received numerous commendations for one of the most successful undercover operations ever. He had called me to brag about his recognition, but he never said thank you for my sacrifices or for not making a formal complaint against him. He was getting promoted soon, he boasted, and added that I better get ready to testify in court and prepare for the Police Training Academy.

I told him about the threats and suspect showing up at my home, and his callous response was, "You're just getting paranoid. Nobody hits a cop!"

He and Christy weren't getting any calls. No one knew their phone numbers. Christy always had a UC car, and Stanley never made a drug buy.

It would be true justice, I thought, if one day he would come to know the fear of being identified and hurting his family because of what he did and who he chose to be.

Kevin showed up at my house to scream at me like a kid pulling a tantrum and accused me of setting him up. He was demanding an apology, and I refused.

"For what?" I demanded. "You pushed your way into a federal investigation no matter how many times I tried to turn you away. Grow up! Think about it. You called me. I never called you! You got pissed off that I wouldn't jump into pyramid scheme with your family and friends. Your whole family would have been busted, too!"

He was silent for a while and stomped away. "Fuck you!" he said. I never saw him again.

Some of my suspects at Slim's Bar called to invite me to party. "No hard feelings," they chuckled. "Just come down." They would never realize that it had been their own friends who had turned them in on complaints.

Rumors began to circulate among my high school classmates about how I had set up Glen and Kevin and "forced" them to sell me dope. My family had heard the rumors, too, as well as the warnings that I would be killed before I ever had a chance to testify.

Laurie always did my mother's hair in the salon. She kept talking about all the rumors she had heard about what I had done and asked if my mom was worried that I was going to get killed. My mother came home and burst into tears and never went back to get her hair done by Laurie again. I would never forget Laurie's outspoken insensitivity.

I was held back from starting the academy to bust prospective police recruits who were selling dope. One candidate was still selling pounds of marijuana in Haleiwa one week before he was scheduled to start the Police Academy.

No one in the department cared about what me or my family were going through.

No one cared that I was following orders from Detective Stanley. He was left blameless, as were the people who had turned in anonymous complaints about their friends pushing dope.

It was ironic, but I heard it was not uncommon that some of the anonymous tipsters would later show up in court in support of their suspect friends, to hide their involvement.

Today is September 15, 1980
It marks the beginning of the transitions I had waited for, endured, experienced, sacrificed,
suffered, and disciplined myself for. This moment and its learning and revelation . . .
And this revelation does not separate me from anything but has instead infuses my being with
everything else. I identify with nothing. My identities have merged into a oneness. There are no
more thresholds or barriers to cross. They do not exist. Therefore, I do not belong in one place or
another. I follow my own destiny.

Journal entry: September 15, 1980

Chapter 14
The Dark Side of the Badge

Internal Affairs

I've finished my undercover assignment.
I've learned unbelievable lessons of life.
It seems that all the tests, opposition, limitations I needed to face were confronted at this time.
I'm preparing for court now, and my reflections of myself are so totally new ... different.
I have no real identity ... no home. I am empty. Perhaps it is life that I have finally come to balance ... not separate.
We are one with the universe and not separate.
I am getting back into my writings and my art.
I balance with my past. My memories will balance with time. How amusing to see how things come to be. I work with different angles. It's called no angles.
I remember my past life, but I need more stability and strength.

Journal entry: September 18, 1980

November 3, 1980. I heard from Stanley, and again it was to ask me for help. This time, he wasn't bragging about how many bows he had taken or how many people he had impressed. He was asking me to do another assignment in spite of the fact that he knew I hated him and had no loyalty or respect for him.

"Why?" I asked, unable to hide the disgust in me voice. "Who's asking?"

"This is coming straight from the chief!" he said excitedly. The chief had asked him to do the assignment, he gloated, seeming very pleased with himself. "Yes or no? I can't tell you about it until you say yes and help out the chief. It's not for me. I can't tell you anything. It's on a need-to-know basis."

The sound of his voice was disgusting, and he knew very well that if it were him asking me for help, I would refuse.

"This will be the most dangerous assignment you'll ever work. Another UC already turned it down, but it's the chief asking. You don't ever say no to the chief!" he pressured.

"Why you?" I asked, and he was silent for a moment at my reproachful challenge.

"Because they know I'm the only one who can do the job!" he gloated.

"So why are you calling me?"

"I have to know right now!" he said, changing the subject. "I can't tell you anything about it until you agree to do the assignment. You'll be working with Internal Affairs, not me."

"If it's for chief and I'll be working with Internal Affairs and not you, then I'll do it," I said.

That afternoon, I met with the lieutenant and detectives of Internal Affairs in the quiet dining room area of a popular family restaurant.

"Is this the girl?" one of the three men seated at the table asked, and Stanley nodded.

Lieutenant Richard Fujita was Japanese-Portuguese-Hawaiian-English. Detective Wallace Akeo was Hawaiian-Caucasian, and Detective Clarence DeCaires Jr. was Portuguese-Hawaiian. The members of the Internal Affairs unit were well-groomed, well-dressed, and solemn.

"What's Internal Affairs?" I asked and then felt really stupid for asking, especially when Stanley glared at me for speaking and the IA team all turned to look at him in shock.

Detective DeCaires looked at me with surprised concern and then asked Stanley if he had told me what the investigation involved.

Lieutenant Fujita stared intently at Stanley, who wasn't answering the question.

"You didn't tell her!" he said, looking at him with reproach.

Stanley put his hands up in the air and shrugged but still did not answer.

"I don't know anything,'" I announced. "I had to say yes first, and I still don't know what this is about except that the chief was asking for this investigation."

I had finally met policemen who seemed to be straightforward and honest in their conduct instead of playing manipulating mind games. Stanley's "I'm the man" game had just been exposed. It was obvious that the Internal Affairs would have told me what the investigation involved before I had agreed to take on the assignment. Lieutenant Fujita and the detectives continued to look at Stanley, waiting for a response.

"It's a need-to-know," he finally answered with an insolent shrug.

"And you didn't think she needed to know what she was getting into?" Akeo demanded. Stanley's posture deflated as he sulked.

There was an uncomfortable moment of silence. The IA team shook their heads in disapproval. They looked at me and then at each other with expressions of exasperation and concern.

"So what are we going to do?" They conferred with each other, leaving Stanley out of their discussion. "She has to know what she's getting into!" Lieutenant Fujita said with conviction.

I immediately knew that they, unlike Stanley, would never send an officer into an assignment without letting the officer know what dangers or confrontations he might be facing. I realized too that my safety and well-being were more important than getting me to agree to do the assignment.

"We're cops checking on cops," Detective Akeo said, finally breaking the silence to answer my question. The IA officers asked me to name every police officer I knew, and I struggled to think of the few officers that I knew.

"Do you know anyone by the name of Rivera?"

When I answered that I had never heard of Officer Rivera, they sighed in relief.

"Not yet," Stanley added sarcastically, trying to push his way into the discussion.

"Do you have any problem busting a cop for dealing drugs?" IA asked.

"No," I responded without hesitating. "I busted everyone else, and I had to bust people I knew, too, but he's worse if he wears a badge. That's why everyone I've met in the street says all cops are dirty."

Lieutenant Fujita listened and watched me carefully as I reflected silently on my bad experiences with cops. The IA team voiced their concern about my being unaware of what this investigation would do to me, especially since I had not yet gone through the Police Training Academy. Their concern for my safety touched my soul, and I knew immediately that they were men of truth and honor.

"I'll just do this case like any other case," I stated. "But I'm only going to do this because the chief is asking."

"I don't know about this," Lieutenant Fujita said with a look of doubt. "Maybe we should call this off." In that moment, Lieutenant Fujita, Detective Akeo, and Detective Decaires had displayed the honor, conscience, and integrity that I had never seen in Stanley or Okimoto. I had finally met the kind of police officers that I had always believed in. The IA team had earned the loyalty that I would never give to Stanley

Stanley sat back abruptly and glared at me as if I had just screwed up *his* chance to impress the chief.

Lieutenant Fujita and Detective DeCaires took Stanley outside to talk while Detective Akeo stayed with me at the table. They looked like they were arguing with Stanley, who I could tell was getting defensive by his gestures and expressions. It was obvious that IA was concerned about me, and Stanley looked like he was trying to convince them to use me. He wanted more glory, and again, it didn't matter how he attained it, as long as it was at my expense.

Detective Akeo was staring at me intently from across the table, and I finally asked him if he was looking at my aura.

"You knew what I was doing?" he asked, surprised.

"Yup," I said. Detective Akeo had a very powerful energy and spiritual presence, and I could feel him looking into my soul. He reminded me of a tiger.

Several minutes later, when Lieutenant Fujita and Detective DeCaires returned to the table, I was given a brief history of the investigation. Stanley sat at a table behind us, sulking.

A young female informant who was dating the married officer had initiated several complaints to Internal Affairs. The seasoned patrol officer was dealing drugs, and the informant had already turned in some of the drugs he had given to her. She had volunteered to introduce a UC officer as a friend, and IA needed someone unknown to work the case.

I agreed to be the undercover officer in the case as long as Internal Affairs would be in charge of the investigation and I would not be working with Stanley. Stanley had to be involved, they explained, because he represented the Narcotics Vice Division. After another brief discussion with the IA team, Lieutenant Fujita approved the investigation apprehensively, and Stanley sighed with relief.

I was immediately sent to meet with the informant. Stanley had to do the introductions because it would be unsafe if IA detectives were seen with me. I refused to get into Stanley's car and insisted on driving myself but was denied.

Karin, who seemed to be very familiar with Stanley and delighted to see him, called him by his nickname. She was Japanese and talkative, and she rattled off in police jargon and codes, talking about sectors, beats, and comp time as if she was a police officer.

I had never learned the universal Code-10 series of communication, and the narcs hardly ever talked like that. I couldn't understand what Karin was talking about as she carried on a conversation with Stanley. She was cute, had a sassy personality, and was a few years younger than me. She flashed me a very negative, critical look and rolled her eyes in doubt when Stanley introduced me as the undercover officer.

The meeting was short, and I asked Karin if we could meet later on our own without Stanley, to establish a background for the introduction. I was too uncomfortable with Stanley, and the months that I had not been around him, had not diminished the revulsion I felt.

I was silent on the drive back to my car, but Stanley interrupted and told me to swear an oath of silence, especially with Christy. My anger exploded.

"Why!" I demanded, expecting him to reiterate that Christy was incompetent and that *he* was *the man*.

Instead of insulting her as usual, he explained that the Officer Rivera was her cousin and that Christy would be the one to burn this case if she spoke to anyone. My anger flashed and my stomach turned. He was actually making me physically sick.

Now he was saying that I would be the one to burn this case if I confided in Christy, and my hate for Stanley suddenly grew ten thousand times greater. He was cunning and manipulative, and it seemed to get him what he wanted. If anyone was going to get hurt, it would be me, not him! I jumped out of his car, slammed his door, and left without saying a word.

As always, he was already setting the stage to have someone else to blame if anything went wrong. This time, it would be Christy or me.

I hadn't heard from or talked to Christy for a long time, but I knew if I told her about this case and something went wrong, Stanley would find a way to blame the both of us. I knew too, that it would be harder for her to answer to her family if she knew about the investigation and had failed to warn them.

I met Karin the next day, and we got along fine without the Stanley hovering around. We were both at ease with each other by the end of the day, and I respected Karin for doing what she was doing.

Karin knew a lot of policemen, and she didn't like the dirty ones who made the good ones look bad. She was very well-dressed, wore a police badge pendant, and was very stylish.

I was always in jeans and T-shirts, and Karin laughed when I told her that I didn't own any dresses and was uncomfortable in them. Karin confessed that she was doubtful when she first saw me because I was so small but wasn't anymore because of the sound of my voice and the way I talked.

"Your voice doesn't match your body!" Karin laughed, but she was comfortable about the way I carried myself. "You don't sound helpless and feminine at all!"

I had never heard any of those comments before, and we both laughed and enjoyed the evening of getting to know each other.

We laughed about Stanley, too, and both of us knew that he had to know and control everything and was probably stressing out about what we were doing and saying about him.

Karin had a warm heart and was very expressive with her facial expressions. You could tell what she was thinking just by the way she rolled her eyes, twisted her head, or gestured with her hands. Stanley demanded a debriefing, and I complied by debriefing him on the phone instead of meeting him.

"Don't get close to her. She's just a snitch," he said coldly, but I had already felt protective over Karin and resented the slander of her character. Karin was like a little puppy, trying to find her way and do what was right.

Stanley used people all the time. It was his way to manipulate or intimidate others and then walk away after he had gotten what he wanted from them. This time he was using Karin and me.

I had been wrong to believe that all policemen were alike. By meeting the other officers and detectives, I had begun to see that wearing the badge did not automatically make someone truthful and honest. It was the individual officer behind the badge who made it not only a symbol of power and authority but also a symbol of honor and courage.

The other detectives and officers got to know me, too. One by one, they came up to me on their own and told me that they knew that the stories Stanley had spread about me being in love with him were lies.

"He's always trying to be impressive and tooting his own horn!" they said, and he never cared about who he stepped on to get ahead, not even the members of his own team.

I made a mental note of myself to never take credit for the accomplishments and efforts of others, and to always acknowledge help and support.

I suddenly wished Lolly or Christy was with me, but then I realized that I would only be hurting them.

The Policeman

November 7, 1980. It was 5:00 p.m. and my introduction to Officer Rivera was set for 6:00 p.m. I would meet Karin at the Waikiki Harbor Restaurant, and she would make the introductions.

I recognized the members of the Internal Affairs unit at the debriefing but not the numerous other people in the room who were trying not to stare at me too obviously.

I was introduced to the support team. Captain Gibbs, Lieutenant Nakamura, and Officers Sharon, Mike, Art, and Red of the Criminal Intelligence Unit were busy double-checking their cameras and equipment one last time before they set out to take their surveillance positions.

I had never worked with a surveillance team before and usually just ran around on the streets alone. I was shocked to see so many people.

Stanley did a grand stand performance and announced that everyone should take a good look at *his* UC. It turned my stomach, but I stifled my feelings and erased myself to do the job.

The officers of the Criminal Intelligence Unit instructed me on signals to use and which side of the street to walk on to be in the sight of the surveillance units.

It was 6:15 when I finally walked into the restaurant. Karin was waiting at the door with her arms folded across her chest, pacing back and forth.

"What's wrong?" I asked, and Karin yanked me into the restrooms.

"He's nervous and upset!" Karin said. "He said IA is all over the place and he wants to go somewhere else for cocktails!"

Officer Rivera had gone to the restaurant an hour earlier to check out the area and had apparently seen the IA and CIU units.

"Okay," I said, trying to calm Karin. I went back to my car and parked my Mustang in a position where the surveillance units could see my car as a reference, just in case I never made it back. There were no cell phones, radios, or any way to communicate the change of plans, and I prayed that someone was watching my signal that we would be moving to another location.

I had been given a two-hour window, and I knew if I didn't return to my car, sooner or later, they would know something went wrong and would look for me. At least I hoped they would!

Karin introduced me to Rivera, and he was visibly very upset. He was sitting at the bar with his hands clasped under his chin, watching me approach through the mirrored glass wall behind the bartender's station. He was dressed for an evening out on the town and looked like the kind of cop you see on television, even down to the style of the dark glasses he wore. He immediately got up from his seat at the bar and led us quickly outside, informing us that we were going somewhere else.

"IA is crawling all over the place!" he said nervously, and the matter of leaving was not open for debate.

I tried to stall when we walked through the parking lot, and stood in the middle of street pretending to be adjusting the strap of my sandals, hoping that the surveillance units had picked us up walking to his car.

Rivera had insisted that Karin sit in the middle of the front bench seat and told me to squeeze into the front seat, too.

"That's so that Karin can be closer to me!" he smiled, and Karin rolled her eyes.

Rivera kept looking around and into his rear-view mirror when he was driving. He kept changing lanes and speeding, moving in and out of slower-moving traffic

"Slow down!" I finally said. "You always drive like this?" I was getting smashed into the passenger door at every swerve and lane change he made.

"I'm a cop!" he smiled. "I can do anything I want!"

I pretended to be shocked, and Karin rolled her eyes again in silence.

Rivera eased up a bit and relaxed when he realized that there was no one following us.

"You got anything to smoke?" he asked, still driving in and out of traffic.

"Smoke what?" I asked.

"Grass," he said.

"But you're a cop!" I said with pretend alarm and doubt in my voice.

Rivera assured me that he was a cop "only in uniform" and that he smoked all the time. He went on to explain that he didn't bring his stash because Karin didn't smoke, but I could light up if I had any with me.

I answered that I didn't have any and then told him that I was looking for a good source. The conversation quickly turned to drugs, and Rivera bragged about his stash.

"Anything you want, sweetheart, I can get"

Officer Rivera explained that he did all his deals on duty because nobody checks on a cop on duty, not even IA! He talked continually about his job and about a burglary series he was working on. He occasionally turned on his siren to push his way through traffic that was too slow for his liking.

We had traveled from the Harbor Restaurant at the beginning of Waikiki to the Hawaii Kai shopping center in record time. The conversation continued over cocktails at a lounge in the shopping center, where he talked non-stop about drugs, moneymaking projects, and his job as a cop. Time went by quickly, and I arranged a deal before we returned to my car.

Rivera asked Karin to stay with him and keep him company when we got back to my car. I explained that we had promised to meet some friends for dinner and apologized for our quick departure but we were already late.

Rivera had made it a point to let me see that he was checking out my license plates and wrote the number down. It was obvious that he was going to run a check on my car and find out everything he could. I felt very uneasy about it and was thankful that I didn't use a fake name. No one had given me an undercover car so I knew he would now know my full name and address.

Karin and I drove around in circles for a bit to make sure he wasn't following us and then headed for the debriefing site. We were shocked to find out that no one had seen my signals or seen us returning to my car to leave.

Stanley had failed to tell them what kind of car I had, so my efforts at placing my car as a stationary surveillance point had been useless. The truth was that he didn't know what kind of car I owned or my license plates since he had never really pulled any surveillance on any of my deals. It was too dangerous to run a vehicle registration check at the last minute over the police radio because Rivera had a police radio in his car and might have been monitoring it.

The Heiau

I do whatever and live in my own realm, a sort of different dimension
Nothing means anything to me anymore

Journal entry: November 9,1980

November 8, 1980. Rivera called and said his brother had already sold the half-ounce of marijuana he was planning to sell to me. He referred to it as the "half wizard" instead of using the word "O.Z." or *ounce* when he talked on the phone. Rivera then told me that he was going to pick up some more marijuana, cocaine, and Quaaludes and would call me back to let me know when he was holding.

November 14, 1980. Rivera called and told me to meet him at the Aiea Heiau in the mountains. He had the half-ounce of marijuana for $70, five Quaaludes for $20, and a half-gram of cocaine for $50. We arranged to meet that afternoon at about 4:30 p.m. He started talking about his family and told me that they were all crooks and that he was the black sheep cop of the family.

I had to go to several different debriefing sites before finally heading out to meet Rivera. There was air surveillance, moving surveillance, and stationary surveillance set in place. Everyone except Stanley was worried that I would be alone with Rivera at the isolated location of the Aiea Heiau and that I had no means of communication or protection.

I finally headed up into the mountains and went to look for the Heiau, driving back and forth for a few minutes just to find it. I had never been there before and didn't know the Aiea district at all. *Put me in Waikiki or downtown and I could be anywhere in a flash*, I thought miserably, but I didn't know the west end of the island at all.

The park was quiet and serene. The ancient landmark was canopied by the thick foliage of huge trees and surrounded by flowering plants. It was empty of people except for a couple having something to eat at the picnic bench. I saw the sacred stones of the Heiau site and waited on a bench nearby. Rivera's car was not in the lot, so I wondered if he had decided not to show up.

The sound of the police helicopter hovering around above made me extremely nervous, and I began to panic, wondering if he had spotted the surveillance units again. I was certain that he had heard and noticed the HPD chopper! I waited for about an hour and finally left when he never arrived and it began to get dark. Stanley was in the helicopter, and he had followed me all the way home to Kaneohe and hovered over my house.

What a burn! If Rivera was around, all he had to do was follow the chopper to find me! I thought angrily. My neighbors came out to see what was happening, and I panicked and looked around to see if Rivera was watching my house, too.

I had never been given an undercover car or a fake driver's license like the other undercover officers, and I knew Rivera had run my license plates on the police computers and knew my address. Rivera was sharp enough to be watching me come and go from my house. If he had seen the chopper, I would be burned.

Stanley seemed to love the commotion he was causing and openly signaled to me from the chopper to give him a call. He knew I had gotten home. All he had to do was call me! He didn't have to call attention to me and do the stupid hand gestures! What a total stupid ass!

Frank Perreira, a longtime good neighbor with background in law enforcement, waved discreetly at me as if signaling that he had figured out what was going on and that he would be there if I needed anything.

My mother was panicking in the house and I ran in to tell her everything was all right. The chopper had hovered so low that it seemed like it would touch the telephone wires. The curtains on the kitchen windows blew off, knocking glassware and spices off the dish rack and counters. Stanley's maneuvers were stupid and unnecessary and had put me and my family at risk.

When the chopper left the area, all my neighbors came over to ask what was going on. They had all seen Stanley signaling to me.

"Wrong house," my parents explained, and everyone reluctantly accepted her answer and left it at that.

Frank Perreira was a long-time neighbor. He came over later to tell me and my parents that if we needed anything, he would be there to help. He had been a police officer but was now an investigator with another law enforcement agency. His gesture of friendship had brought an incredible relief to my family. Frank's name would be etched in my heart forever.

Drugs from a Cop

November 17, 1980. Karin called and told me that she was very hurt and angry that I had not taken her with me to the Heiau to do the deal. She had only found out about it because Rivera had yelled at her that I had never shown up at the deal.

Rivera finally called me that evening and talked about the missed meeting. None of us knew that there were two Heiau in that section of the mountains. We were both at different Heiau and we had both believed we were stood up.

Karin called and told me that Stanley had explained to her why she wasn't included in the Heiau deal. He told her that I was nothing but a UC and made none of the decisions, and that he was trying to keep her out of it to keep her safe.

November 19, 1980. Stanley called and ordered me to sever all communication with the Karin. She was irate and insulted that she had not been included in the last deal and had called him to complain that if it weren't for her, there would be no case.

Stanley said that no matter how much he and IA had tried to explain that they were trying to keep her out of the picture to keep her safe, Karin couldn't understand and blamed me for going behind her back and cutting her out of the picture.

November 20, 1980. I was extremely ill with the stomach flu and had a high fever, and the runs. Stanley denied my request to postpone the deal and instructed me to take a bunch of vitamins instead of delaying his precious assignment.

He was anxious to take credit for my success. His great need for glory meant more to him than the safety or well-being of anyone else, especially me. It was another reason to despise and hate him.

This time, I was to wear a body wire and a transmitter. I would meet with the CIU team early in the morning to secure the equipment.

By the time I got to the safe site to be wired, I was burning with fever. Stanley had brought a whole bunch of vitamins and ordered me to take them and clean out my stomach before the wire was taped on.

I was only a hundred pounds, and the tape recorder and transmitter were metal boxes about an inch thick. The tape recorder was about six inches long, and the transmitter was about eight inches. There were wires coming out of the top, and the on/off switch would be left taped in the on position.

The CIU team didn't realize how much the devices would stick out and had to figure out where and how to strap on the equipment. I was reminded several times not to tamper with, erase, or turn off any of the devices. Sharon began to tape the recorder on to the base of my back and became alarmed.

"You're burning up!" she said and hesitated, looking at me sympathetically, but Stanley ordered her to continue.

The team had to shove the tape into my back, and they created a new silhouette by winding the two-inch-wide white surgical tape around my waist several times to smooth out the corners of the box.

The longer transmitter was the size of a police radio and was smashed against the inside of my right calf. The team duplicated the shape of my leg by smashing the calf muscle and smoothed over the metal device, forming a cast. The thick white surgical tape was wrapped around my leg numerous times, cutting off my circulation.

Every step I took was painful as the transmitter dug into my calf muscle, and I had to practice walking without grimacing or limping.

I knew that Rivera would check me for a wire, and luckily, I had worn a blouse with a wrap-around belt that would help disguise my new back and waistline.

"Thank goodness you're so skinny!" Sharon had commented. "Otherwise we would have made you look pregnant!" she joked. I was very thankful that Sharon was there with me, at least for a few minutes.

At 9:15 in the morning, I was told to go to the Kaimuki Restaurant for breakfast and call Police Dispatch and ask Rivera to meet me. He was on duty in Waikiki, and the restaurant was near the perimeter of his sector. I had to order something from the restaurant in order to sit at the table.

I was sick and wasn't hungry, so I picked at the breakfast I had ordered, afraid that I would not be able to keep any food down. My stomach was churning with all the vitamins Stanley had forced me to swallow, and I ended up going to the restroom several times with the tapes and transmitters on.

I used the restaurant pay phone and begged to turn off the tape and transmitters, and Stanley refused my requesting saying that I would screw up the whole case if I tampered with the tape.

It seemed like Stanley was trying to make me suffer and was delighted at my humiliation. The more difficulty I faced in the assignments, the more bows he took when I overcame them.

I was angry but I knew I wouldn't be able to reach the on/off switch even if I wanted to. As I sat at the table waiting for Rivera to arrive, I wondered how many commendations Stanley would get for my suffering this time. I wasn't sure if I believed in the old saying "Every dog has his day."

I hadn't heard from Christy since the roundup and found myself wondering what she was doing at the moment.

Rivera finally arrived at about eleven o'clock and immediately patted me down, looking for wires, running his hand down my back and up my ribs under my arms. I held my breath and was relieved that the team had disguised it well. It had been about two hours, and the machines were hot and burning my skin. I could hardly walk without the use of my calf muscle, and sharp pains shot up and down my leg with every step.

Rivera led me to his car, but this time, he had a blue light on the roof. I was burning up not only with fever but from the devices, too, and Rivera knew I was sick just by looking at me.

"Let's go for a ride," he said, opening the passenger door of his car for me. I could barely lift my left leg to step into the car.

During the drive, Rivera began talking again about the missed meeting at the Aiea Heiau.

"I still have the money," I offered.

"Well I don't have anything right now!" he said with a little sarcasm.

"Okay. I'm getting kicked out of my house," I said, trying to start a light conversation.

"Why?" Rivera asked.

"My parents are upset that I don't have a job and am not doing anything useful with my life, so I was looking to maybe sell this stuff, make some fast money, and find a place." I was using what I had learned from Glenn and Kevin.

"I don't want to talk in the car!" Rivera said suddenly in alarm.

"Okay," I mused. It was, after all, *his* car.

"My friend Sam just came back from working in Guam. It's $4 a Quaalude," Rivera offered.

"Four a piece?"

"It's cheaper than the other guy," Rivera offered.

"Okay. Is it the 714?"

"Yeah, 714 Lemmons!" he answered with confidence.

"Okay, sounds good!" I said easily. I was comfortable talking about drugs but not about police work.

"He sells them in quantities no less than a hundred. For a hundred you get them at $3.50 a piece—that's $350 for a hundred. You can turn around and sell them. In Waikiki they're going for $7," Rivera said helpfully.

"Yes, I know! That's where I can make my money!" I said, trying to sound enthusiastic.

"Well if you want that, the man has to meet you. He doesn't do business with anybody unless he knows them first."

"Is he a cool guy?" I asked upset at the thought that I would have to meet another suspect.

"Very cool. He and I grew up together. All the people I deal with are people I grew up with. That's why I don't get burned. So if I do get burned, it has to be somebody I didn't grow up with. I'm gonna know who it is!" he stated threateningly, staring at me.

"Okay," I agreed calmly.

"If I get burned now, the only person that I'm dealing with who I haven't known for a long time ..."

I finished his statement to let him know I understood his subtle threat. "Is me! Yeah, I get it!"

"If I get burned, you're the one!" Rivera finished his sentence anyway.

"Yeah, okay. I don't like to meet people. What I want to do is test his stuff first. I know I can trust you but I don't know him." I changed the subject.

"Make your test," Rivera said. "That's the way he is. It's going to be up and up! He turns you on to one, you check it out, see how you like it. If it works out fine, we can work out a deal."

"Okay, I have the money with me right now," I said anxious to get the verbal game over with. "I had it from the other day. I was getting really upset at you for not showing up, and then Karin called and told me you were pissed off at me!"

"I felt like I got stood up!" Rivera began to explain just as another uniformed officer drove up.

"Oh God! Who's this?" I asked with genuine anxiety.

"Don't worry about him," Rivera shrugged and continued. "Okay, I have an appointment at three at Lube and Tune. After that, we can go to Waipahu and talk to the man. He's a cook at a restaurant in Waipahu. Can you swing it today?"

"What time?" I asked hesitantly.

"After work. I'll be at the Lube and Tune in Aiea. I just have to leave my car there for about an hour. Just pull in and I'll be waiting for you. From there, we'll leave my car and take a run to Waipahu to talk to the man. I have to leave my car, so we'll have more than adequate time. I'll wait for you and we can go talk to Sam."

I felt the tape recorder beginning to slip on my back, and my stomach was churning with all the stupid vitamins.

Today's activities could have been easily postponed since it was me who had initiated the meeting. It wasn't as if Rivera had called me and it would mean I was putting him off again. But Stanley never told me ahead of time what I would be doing, and I was never involved in the plans, even if it would be me doing the deals. I was furious, realizing that it would be a long and difficult day.

Rivera took me back to the parking lot and drove around a few times.

"That's my car over there," I said, pointing to my Mustang.

"I know. I ran your plates and checked everything from the last time." He smiled.

Rivera stopped behind my car, let me out, and drove around the parking lot again a few times before he left the area.

I made my way back to the meeting place and met with the surveillance team. I was thankful to know that someone was actually watching over me. When I got back into the room, everyone was sitting down, smiling at me.

I suddenly remembered my restroom emergencies and slumped into the chair with humiliation and embarrassment, trying to disappear.

Everyone burst out laughing, and I could feel my face flush red with fever and a whole lot of embarrassment.

"Don't worry," someone said as they all jumped up and started moving hurriedly around the room.

"Nobody's going to hear the tape except the chief!"

Stanley jumped in and added, "And then again when they play it in the courtroom, and for the judge." And someone else added, "And the jury."

"I want to go home. I feel sick. Did everything come out clearly?" I asked.

"Yup!" someone responded, and everybody went hysterical.

The tape holding the devices in place was ripped off quickly and some of my burning skin came off with it. I was allowed to rest for fifteen minutes until they wrapped me up again taping over my raw skin. In a few minutes, the team was on their way, scurrying to set up the surveillance positions for the second half of the day.

I met Rivera that afternoon as planned, and he instructed me to drive him to Waipahu. Rivera was always well dressed and well groomed. He looked like what a cop should look like. Even his dark glasses were "cop" glasses.

"Tiny little car!" he commented, barely fitting into my Mustang and inspecting everything in the interior.

"Try this!" he said as he passed me a marijuana cigarette.

"Not while I'm driving!" I said in shock at his open gesture.

"What! Who's going to bother?" he asked, chuckling. "Just go through the back roads!"

"I don't know any back roads! You have to tell me which way to turn, and I gotta get back to town by four o'clock cause I borrowed the money. Go ahead and take out the money." I rattled everything off nervously while he smoked his marijuana in my car.

"Where's the money?" Rivera asked.

"In my wallet. There's four in there. A little bit over $400, I think."

"You ain't got $400 in here! Just $387," he said, counting the money again out loud.

"Oh yeah, that's right. I filled up some gas!" I had forgotten that I had to fill my car on the way to Aiea and had been short of my own money to pay for it.

Rivera pulled out his issued .38-caliber Smith and Wesson gun and showed it to me while I was driving.

"Tell you what. This ... is as bad as carrying that!" he said and pointed at the nunchaku sticks in my car. "*Nanchaks* are the same as carrying a gun. It's a deadly weapon. Don't ever leave them exposed like that! Hide them under the seat. Otherwise you're going to get your sweet tail arrested! I've arrested people for that!" he scolded.

"Okay, I got it. So how's this guy Sam?" I was worried about meeting Sam for the first time and didn't know what to expect. I didn't really care about the nunchaku sticks in my car.

"Salt of the earth!" Rivera said, and the traffic suddenly came to a stop because of a construction site up ahead. "Take a left and cut right through the cones," Rivera instructed.

"Nobody else is doing it!" I protested.

"Do it!" he commanded, but I refused.

"There's a policeman standing right there!" I complained.

"Well who the hell do you think I am, sweetheart!" Rivera said in an exasperated tone. "Okay, then go down to the next intersection and double back!" he said in frustration.

I stopped and waited for the uniformed police officer to direct me through the intersection, but he seemed preoccupied with traffic flowing in the opposite direction.

"Can I go?"

"I guess so!" Rivera smirked. "The policeman gotta get off the damn road! Just bang him! He got no business walking in the middle of the road!"

"I don't want to bang him!" I protested just as Rivera grabbed my steering wheel.

"Don't touch my steering wheel!" I exclaimed. "Okay, he's letting us go!"

Rivera let go of my steering wheel.

"You're not like Karin. When I let her drive my car and I tell her to hang a left, she just hangs it right there! I don't dare let her drive my car anymore. She's a typical female driver. She's crazy!"

I parked behind the back door of a restaurant in Waipahu, and Rivera got out and showed me his gun again, placing it on the floor of my car.

"Sam wasn't home, so he should already be here," Rivera explained. "He keeps his stash with him in his car. Don't worry!" he said, when I looked worriedly at the revolver lying exposed on the floor of my car. "If anybody hassles you about the gun, just tell them it's mine!" He disappeared into the back door of the restaurant.

A few seconds later, Rivera walked out of the door with a guy in an apron who I guessed had to be his friend Sam.

"Here you go, sweetheart!" Rivera passed me a package through the window and introduced me to Sam.

Sam stared at the gun on the floor of my car when Rivera opened the door to get into the passenger seat.

"That's mine!" Rivera explained.

"Yeah," Sam said. "I was kind of wondering!"

"Get a thousand Quaaludes for the price of $3250," Sam offered.

"Or some toot," Rivera added. "He can get you some of that, too!"

"What about the cocaine? Do you do quarters and stuff?" I asked

"Yeah, I do quarters," Sam replied.

"It's $650." Rivera jumped in. "Very nice quality stuff!"

"Okay," I said.

"All yellow!" Sam said.

"All rocks!" Rivera added.

"He seems like a nice guy," I said when we drove away.

"He's the salt of the earth. I told you, sweetheart!" Rivera paused. "I hope you don't mind that I call you sweetheart. I call all girls sweetheart," Rivera explained and I shrugged indifference. "He's really mellow. Don't worry. You're with me!"

"Yeah, okay," I agreed.

"Anything you want, just come to see me, and, sweetheart, please don't burn me!"

"Okay, already! I know! So where do I turn now?" I was lost.

"Just don't burn me sweetheart!" Rivera wouldn't leave the subject. He looked at me and showed me his gun.

"*You're* the cop!" I said in an irritated voice, and he finally relaxed.

"I'm a cop *only* in uniform," he smirked and then continued, "Take the back roads so that I can smoke a joint and get mellow." Rivera lit a marijuana cigarette.

"I hope Sam didn't mind that I didn't give him my phone number right away!" I commented.

"No. Everything comes through me!" Rivera said reassuringly.

As I drove back around to the front of the restaurant, Rivera pointed out three uniformed police officers eating at a table near the large picture windows. He bragged that he had upset them when he made pig sounds at them from inside the kitchen when he had gone to get Sam.

"The three uniformed officers," he chuckled, very pleased with himself "looked around but couldn't see who was making the obnoxious sounds."

"So what used to happen when you worked in Waipahu? Anything exciting?" I asked, changing the subject.

"All the Filipinos are insane out here. They all carry guns, and they shoot at people. They think they're fucking God or something!" he remarked.

"Some are really nice though!" I offered, thinking about Lolly.

"Well I haven't met a nice one yet!" Rivera said sarcastically. "But it's those immigrant mothers, like those immigrant Koreans, immigrant Chinese, immigrant Japanese. Even my folks!" Rivera continued as he took a drag of the marijuana cigarette and passed it to me.

I panicked, knowing that I couldn't refuse his offer. Instead of inhaling, I blew on the joint instead and it went out. "I'm all stuffed up!" I complained. "I can't smoke it."

Rivera took the joint back. "It's burnt out, anyway," he said and put it away and continued with his racial profiling. "Immigrant Puerto Rican, immigrant Spaniards, immigrant Mexicans. They're all ignorant!" he continued until we reached Tune and Lube.

After dropping him off I sat in my car for a minute and felt the last bit of energy drain from my body. I was exhausted and couldn't think anymore. My mind suddenly went black and couldn't figure out where I was or where I was going. I drove in circles for a while until a surveillance unit pulled up next to me and motioned for me to follow them back to a debriefing site. I had even forgotten where I was supposed to go to debrief.

I didn't remember the debriefing or getting home. I was burning with a fever by the time I got home.

Serpico was that last person I thought of before falling asleep, but that was a long time ago. Everyone would surely realize by now that I was just doing my job.

The Informant

November 26, 1980. It was Thanksgiving Eve and Stanley ordered me to call to Rivera through dispatch again and order more ludes and some cocaine, too.

Rivera didn't want to talk on the phone and told me to meet him at the same place in Kaimuki that he had taken me to the last time. He would be going back and forth between cases, he said, so I was to wait.

There was a backgammon tournament going on with between officers at the covered parking lot meeting place so I shouldn't be alarmed if I saw a bunch of officers arriving, he warned.

I was wired up again and went to the meeting place and waited in my car. Rivera wasn't there, but a few other uniformed officers were hanging around, waiting for the tournament.

One of the uniformed officers told me where to park my car and another called Rivera on the radio.

"He'll be here soon," they told me, and they began to set up the backgammon game table.

A few more uniformed patrol officers drove up and opened the trunks of their patrol vehicles. One officer was showing the others what he had in his trunk as Rivera pulled into the underground parking area.

Rivera asked me to step out of the car, and he made me turn around, sliding his hand down my back and shoulders again. I knew he was checking for wires.

One of the officers had come up to my car and looked inside at my gung fu weapons. He began to joke with Rivera and talk about martial arts. Rivera introduced me to all the officers, and one of them offered me a free carton of cigarettes from his trunk.

"That's okay, not my brand." I was later reprimanded by Stanley for not taking it.

I gave Rivera $400 for another hundred Quaaludes and a half gram of cocaine to test. He held up the money and flashed it around.

"The lady is rich!" he announced, and the other police officers glanced at me without a reaction.

The next day was Thanksgiving Day, so the meeting to pick up the illegal merchandise was set for the following day at a country club. Rivera said he would call me later to lock in the time.

I left quickly when more uniformed officers began to arrive in their police cars. I was the only female and the only one not wearing a uniform, I mused.

Rivera had been in a festive mood that day, smiling and clowning around with the other officers. I wished that I could be the same way, too.

It was Thanksgiving evening, and the hustle and bustle of the holidays was evident everywhere. I was empty, sick, and void of any holiday cheer.

The wires were removed quickly. Everyone had plans for Thanksgiving celebrations that evening and was anxious to go home and get started on the preparations.

Stanley interrogated me at the debriefing about the conduct of the other officers, and when I wouldn't say for certain that they knew why I was there or if they were part of the drug deal, he was outraged. He was furious at me for not making any accusations against the other officers and furious that I didn't remember their names.

"Are all the officers involved?" I was asked.

"I don't think so."

"What were the other guys were talking about?"

"I don't know."

"Did they know what you guys were doing when he flashed the money?"

"I don't know."

"What was in the other officers' trunk besides the cartons of cigarettes? Were they stolen?"

I didn't know the answers to any of the questions at the debriefing, and I didn't want to assume or guess.

Stanley stared at me like I was lying, and I stared back. My hate for him surfaced immediately. I knew he could never do what he was sending me out to do.

"Your phone has been ringing nonstop all day!" my mom said when I walked into the house. It rang again in the evening, and I learned that it was the informant trying to reach me in the middle of a Thanksgiving family dinner.

She was upset and yelling on the phone that I was deliberately not answering her calls. Karin had already been told that she was to call Stanley or IA, and not me directly, because I was just the UC. I shut myself in my room, giving up all hope of a normal evening.

Rivera had called her and bombarded her with questions, she said. He had told Karin that I had bought dope from him twice, and she was highly offended and angry that she had been left out of the deal.

"I only picked up once," I told her honestly, but Karin couldn't accept that she had been left out of the action. She couldn't accept that I couldn't bring her to the deals and was angry that everyone was trying to keep her out of the loop to keep her safe.

"If it wasn't for me, this wouldn't be happening!" she said. "Everyone's lying to me! We'll just see about that!" she threatened.

Karin continued to insist that she be involved with the deal on Friday when I was supposed to pick up my order. If she wasn't included in the transaction, there would be no deal, and he wouldn't deliver the drugs I had already paid for. Karin then told me that the deal was set for eight on Friday night at a country club where he would be working a special duty assignment.

I asked Karin if she had told Stanley about it, and she answered that no one was answering their phones so she called me to let me know what had happened.

When I called Stanley to let him know what Karin had said, he was obviously irritated at the disturbance of *his* personal Thanksgiving night celebration.

"Just stop talking to her!" he demanded.

"Then answer your phone when she calls you!" I snapped back.

"Just don't answer the phone!" he said in an irritated voice.

"And what if it's you or Rivera calling?" I was angry at his stupid, ignorant answer.

"I'll call you back," he finally said, but he never did. He had forced me to go out into the streets when I was sick and didn't care if my family was being hurt. But he was pissed off at a phone call during *his* celebration. He was the detective and should have been taking Karin's calls, not me!

I didn't eat or leave my room after that. I waited anxiously all night for call back from Stanley that never came.

November 28, 1980, 10:30 p.m. Stanley finally did his job and talked to the informant instead of leaving me to deal with her after telling me not to communicate with Karin without him present. Arrangements were made for her participation, as she had insisted.

I was not going to be able to wear a transmitter or recorder this evening because they had learned about the feedback on the police radio if a transmitter was too close.

I had previously escaped detection when I was in Rivera's car only by sheer luck.

Karin was already at the briefing site when I arrived. She was beaming and her eyes sparkled with excitement. She wanted to carry a gun to the deal and was shocked that I never had a gun or a badge. She finally agreed that she didn't have to have one, either.

She talked to the detectives about all the police officers she knew, rattling off in police jargon and codes. Karin wanted to testify against him, she said, and she wanted him to know it that she was the one who had turned him in.

As I drove into the parking lot of the country club with Karin in the front passenger seat of my car, she got scared. It was as if she suddenly realized that it wasn't a game. Rivera was parked at the bottom of the driveway and was watching us drive in. Karin begged me to turn around and leave.

I told her to calm down and act normal, but she began to shake and freeze up. If Rivera saw Karin like this, he would know that something was wrong, and I thought Karin was going to fall apart and tell Rivera who I was.

"This is what you wanted!" I said, baffled at her sudden change. "It's too late to turn back!"

Rivera was in the parking lot, leaning up against the side of his car, watching our arrival and looking off into the distance beyond my car with binoculars.

"What are you looking at?" I asked when I pulled up next to him.

"Did you notice the two guys walking around up there in the dark?" he asked nervously.

"No," I said honestly, and remembered from the briefing that no one was supposed to be pulling surveillance because it would be too obvious.

"You want me to check?" I asked and started my car.

"That's okay," Rivera said and quickly gave me the hundred Quaaludes I had ordered. He was starting to perspire in the coolness of the fall night, and his anxiety was obvious.

Karin's assignment had been to listen and remember everything that I did and said as a corroborating witness. Only a few minutes earlier, she had been bubbling over with excitement that she was going to be a UC. Now she was trembling and looked like she was going to burst out in tears after she demanded to be personally involved.

"Just sit in the car. Watch and listen," I had told her, but she didn't listen and stepped out of the car.

She just stood silently with her arms folded across her chest with her lips pursed. I knew that her actions were alarming him.

"I'm going to lay low for a while," he said, looking at Karin curiously, and explained that IA was following him around.

Rivera gave me Sam's number if I needed anything and told me to go straight to him, and I agreed.

Karin and Rivera talked privately in his car for a few minutes while I waited outside, leaning against my car, trying to look calm while smoking my cigarette. He was extremely upset, and even more so when we left him almost immediately to go to a pretend holiday party.

At the debriefing, I learned that it was Stanley who had been walking the perimeter and that he was not aware that Rivera was watching him with binoculars.

Stanley announced that he wanted to put on a big show when he arrested Officer Rivera and wanted to schedule it Christmas Eve. Everyone decided it was kind of heartless and as usual, I had no say in the matter. He was grandstanding again, and everyone knew it.

December 12, 1980, 2:38 p.m. "You gotta make a deal with Sam," Stanley demanded.

"Why? I thought we were done!" I was sick and tired of hearing his demands. I had wrongfully believed that I was going to be working with IA and not him. I was desperate to separate myself from him.

IA was out of the picture but *he* had to complete the investigation with just one more deal, he begged. He was the detective, and I was just the UC who agreed to do this investigation, he reminded me sarcastically.

Do it yourself! I thought but resigned myself to silence. I reminded myself that this case was for chief and that I had to finish what I started, in spite of my loathing for Stanley.

I wondered if the chief even knew my name, and I didn't put it past the Stanley to try to claim he had done the deals himself.

I called Sam with the number that Rivera had given me. Sam was very down to earth and not flashy or arrogant like Rivera.

"I was expecting your call," Sam said in a gentle voice and told me that he had just picked up a thousand. "Just come down," he invited.

I went down to the restaurant in Waipahu alone that afternoon and picked up a hundred from Sam. He took a quick break and sat in my car for a minute, taking a few whiffs of the last of his cocaine before he went back into the restaurant through the back door.

I promised to call him later if I wanted the last hundred he was trying to sell, but I never called him again.

For the next few days, I tried desperately to deal with the hate and anger I felt for Stanley and the disgust I felt for Lieutenant Okimoto. It ate at my soul day and night like a cancer that couldn't be cured. I wanted to tell everyone the truth, but I knew no one would listen or help me.

I knew too that because I had agreed to work on this investigation for the Chief, I had again given Stanley credibility he didn't deserve. No one would understand that in spite of the intense hate that I felt for Stanley, I had done the assignment only because it was the chief asking. I knew that Stanley was probably telling everyone how much he owned and controlled me or how loyal I was to him.

"Vengeance is mine. It is not for you to do. Only God can judge, and each man shall stand before him in his own time. The truth shall be known. Put away your hate and anger. Take three stones, wrap them in plain brown paper, and tie them with twine. Offer it up and place it on the highest shelf."

I wrote it all down, but it would be years before I finally understood the dream.

I had to learn to erase my hate. I had to learn how to bring my mind, my emotions, and my physical body back together in harmony again. I had been doing what was in total conflict with my mind and my heart. I needed to pull myself together and leave my problems in heaven's hands.

I made a vow to myself that night that I would never let another UC suffer or face what I had alone. I would finish what I started and somehow overcome everything that had happened to me. But I didn't know how.

I sit now, attempting to write again
This writing is an attempt not only to write
But to do something with all I have experienced and learned
But what shall I do now?
I have lost my identity, my ambition, and even my pride
I am waiting for a meaning for everything or just a direction
But all directions are here simultaneously
All I have to do is chose

There is a void, an incredible emptiness
In my search for the enlightenment of Truth
I learned that it is not separate from ourselves, to be sought elsewhere
It is within our own being

Go back to the Source to find your answers. I am my own Source
Nothing is separate anymore, yet I cannot identify with anyone or anything anymore
I cannot identify with being a cop ... I cannot identify with being a crook
Not even with myself

Journal entry: December 13, 1980

Busted on Christmas Eve

December 24, 1980. It was Christmas Eve, and I was given the time off to be with my family. Just as I was about to leave the house to go to a family dinner, the phone rang. I was sick at the sound of Stanley's voice.

"Stand by! Don't leave your house! I'll call you later," he said, all excited. Once again, he refused to tell me why, and I wondered if he was just trying to exert his manipulation and control over me and destroy my Christmas Eve. He had most certainly accomplished the latter.

I stayed home alone and waited for several hours for a call back, and once again, gave up all hope for a chance to find a little reprieve and peace to enjoy the holidays.

IA and CIU were worried and afraid that I would be hurt before I had a chance to testify. Stanley was apparently not.

The officer's arrest had been set for after the holidays, but rumors had circulated that someone had told him about the investigation and he had threatened to kill me before he would let that happen. Stanley immediately accused Karin.

"Don't ever trust a snitch!" Stanley warned me again.

The officer was going to be arrested this evening when he showed up for lineup on the midnight watch. His issued firearm and badge would be confiscated on the spot. Stanley would have his show after all.

I was alone watching the lights of the Christmas tree. An incredible loneliness crept into my soul, but I had learned very well how to cry without tears.

At about midnight, after my family had already gone to and then returned from a traditional family Christmas dinner, I finally received a call.

The officer had been arrested in lineup. The chief and the major had explained to the entire midnight watch, that emergency circumstances had dictated his arrest that evening and not heartless cruelty.

I wondered if Stanley had manipulated his big show and wondered who had leaked the information to Rivera and identified me. He had blamed Karin, but I wondered if he hadn't instigated the story himself to get what he wanted. I knew I would never know the truth.

"Merry Christmas," I said to myself and waited to watch the sun come up in the morning.

The next few days were filled with news about a seasoned police officer being arrested for dealing drugs. No one knew who the undercover officer or the informant was.

A few days later, I received a call from Stanley, who ordered me to report to the Kokohead Firing Range at six o'clock the following morning.

I met Sergeant Burke at the firing range, and for the next several hours, I was taught to shoot a gun and given a permit to carry.

I had never touched a gun before, and the cold metal felt like ice in my hands.

"Why?" I asked Sergeant Burke when Stanley kept playing his secret squirrel mind games and refused to tell me what was happening.

The chief and the support team of IA and CIU were concerned about my safety, he explained. The rumors were flying around that I would be murdered before I could testify. I thought it was kind of amusing that I was finally given a gun, not for protection against the drugs dealers but for protection against cops.

Sergeant Burke smiled at me reassuringly. He saw my uneasiness with the gun and walked me through each step with patience and calm that put me at ease.

"It's not the gun that's evil," he explained, watching me handle the gun. "It's the person who uses it, for good or bad." I was suddenly immediately comfortable with handling the firearm.

⚜

Chapter 15
The Ideals of Justice

Tomorrow is my first day in court
My sword is Truth
My armor is Love
My shield is Justice

Journal entry: January 8, 1981

Breaking the Golden Rule

It was my very first court appearance. I had never even been in the circuit court building before and I didn't know what to expect. The subpoena I received had been stamped in red "Pre-trial Hearing," and Glenn was documented as the defendant in the case. No one knew who I was, but I was already being referred to as Serpico in the ranks of the blue army and the prosecutor's office.

The circuit court building was located at the Hawaii State Judiciary Building on South King Street. The statue of King Kamehameha stood regally in front of the pillared entrance, directly across from the Iolani Palace. My footsteps echoed on the ceramic tiled floors when I walked the corridors of the building.

The halls of the courthouse were empty except for a few people speaking in whispered tones while they waited to testify in their respective trials.

As I turned the corner looking for my assigned courtroom, I saw Christy sitting next to Detective Stanley on a worn wooden bench. I could hear her telling him about being hassled by other officers because of Detective Harrison's suspension. They both saw me approaching and began to laugh and whisper, huddled together like close friends.

I chose to sit alone on a bench against the opposite wall.

Detective Harrison had honorably admitted that he had identified Christy as a Narcotics Vice officer and me as the undercover officer, which resulted in the covert investigation being exposed. It was Christy and I, however, who had been judged the bad guys for identifying him and other off-duty officers as the ones who had put us in jeopardy with the suspects. It didn't matter if we could have been hurt. We had broken the Golden Rule.

When Stanley went to use the restroom, I walked up to Christy, who was refusing to look at me. I hadn't seen her for a while and was hoping to catch up on how she was doing. I had heard that she was going through a divorce and having problems with other officers.

"What's wrong?" I asked softly. "Are you doing okay?"

"You should know!" she yelled, turning red in the face.

The few other people in the hallway turned in our direction, and some stuck their heads around the corner to see what was going on.

"Know what?" I asked, shocked by the outburst and confused by her accusation.

"What? I had to find out from somebody else that you were the undercover officer in the Rivera case!" she yelled, glaring at me. "Did I have the plague or something? You couldn't trust me? And what, so now you're finally talking to me?" she asked with extreme sarcasm in her voice.

"I was ordered not to discuss the case with anyone," I tried to explain calmly. "I was told it was better for you not to know because you were related to Rivera."

"Yeah, so what? You thought I was going to spill the beans?" She was almost hysterical. "I was questioned!" she continued. "And I didn't even know what was going on!"

A small audience had started to gather, watching silently and listening intently, but she didn't seem to care. I didn't know what to say. Confidentiality was critical in the investigation and was standard procedure in undercover investigations. Why should I have to explain what she already knew very well? Involving her would have added stress to her family difficulties.

"Wasn't it easier on you that you didn't know, rather than having to explain why you knew and didn't save your family?" I asked. "Of all people, I thought you would figure it out and understand that you were kept out of the investigation to keep you from getting hurt. Why don't you ask Stanley about it? You two seem to be good friends again. Ask him why he ordered me not to tell you."

I finished explaining what I thought she should have already understood and walked away. Christy was the one person I thought I could count on as an understanding friend. I was wrong.

In that moment, my confusion about the display of friendship between Christy and the detective turned to disrespect and disgust. I realized that everything they had said about each other might very well have been true. She had called Detective Stanley manipulative and controlling; he had described her as unstable and erratic. All I really knew for sure was that I was alone.

By now, a small group of prosecutors and court attendees had come out of the courtrooms to listen. Christy's emotional outburst at being left out of the loop was embarrassing. But instead of asking Stanley, she blamed me. I guess she had forgotten that I was just the UC.

Stanley had come out of the restroom and was standing nearby, listening to the entire confrontation, but hadn't said a word. He stood with his arms folded across his chest and smiled mockingly at me. He was clearly delighted at Christy's attack on me. It was not only a slap in the face for all the times I had showed my preference for Christy over him, it was a rift in our friendship, something he had been trying to achieve all along. He was always dishonorable and cowardly when answering for his conduct, but this time it also suited his purposes very well: to let me take the blame for his orders.

A few seconds later, the bailiff announced my name and led me into a packed courtroom.

The circuit court judge, known for his general disdain for police officers, stopped my approach to the witness stand. He instructed me to stand in the center of the courtroom and face the audience.

I glanced nervously at the prosecuting attorney, who shrugged. He also seemed confused at the judge's order, but he nodded for me to comply.

The judge introduced me to the audience by simply saying, "This is the undercover officer."

He then instructed me to walk back and forth in front of everyone and turn around in a slow circle.

"Let everyone get a good look at you," he announced in a loud voice.

The entire courtroom began mumbling, scribbling notes, and staring at me in what appeared to be dumbfounded disbelief.

"Thank you," the judge said dryly and then pointed to the door. He had called me into the courtroom and put me on display and then callously dismissed me.

My disgust for the two officers who were supposed to be my supervisory team was equaled by the disrespect I now felt for the judge, who was supposed to represent truth, honor, and justice. I had never been in a courtroom before and was confused at what had happened. I felt violated and exposed.

The prosecuting attorney, who was still standing at the prosecutor's table, moved towards me when he saw that I was having trouble opening the huge courtroom doors.

Somehow, I managed to get the doors open, even though I was trembling and felt faint. As soon as I left, the entire courtroom followed me out and disappeared into various rooms lining the corridors. Recess was announced a few seconds later.

The prosecuting attorney walked up to me and asked if I was all right.

"What was that all about?" I asked.

"They were all prosecutors and defense attorneys. They all came to see what you looked like," he answered with a gentle smile. "Are you okay?" he asked again. "I didn't know that you were the undercover officer in the Rivera case, too. What was the argument about outside?" The compassion in his eyes made me want to cry.

"It's a long story," I replied, embarrassed that he had heard Christy's outburst.

I immediately erased all my feelings and emotions. I was very good at that by now. My last bit of hope that at least Christy would understand was dashed to pieces. There would never be support or friendship for anyone who had broken the Golden Rules of the blue army, not even from other narcotics officers.

I had never known about the Golden Rules until I had broken them. They were the unwritten rules of conduct that say you never take down or turn in another cop. No matter what happens, turn away and remain silent when you see something wrong. It's a misguided loyalty issue, I suppose. It is the one lesson I never learned to respect.

Christy left the department a short time later, and Stanley received awards and commendations for the covert investigation we worked on. He was up for promotion, he bragged, and then added that everyone was trying to imitate his success by getting female undercover officers, too. After all, it was *he* who had been highly successful, and *he* had proven that females could do the job.

I saw Christy at a few subsequent trials, and she seemed happier after she left the police force, but I kept my distance. My first day in court was burned in my memory forever.

> *From the Source we came, and through the Source we were born*
> *Life's journey is to expand farther into the Source or diminish within it*
> *All things in between birth and death are but our own illusion*
> *And this is the Source ... I am my own Source!*

Journal entry: February 16, 1981

Maui Vice

One day out of the blue, Lieutenant Okimoto called me into his office and demanded angrily, "Did you go to Maui?"

"No, I've been in court every day and never left the island. I've been here," I answered, confused at his question and demeanor.

"You sure?" he asked accusingly. "What about this weekend?" he asked again.

"What's going on? I told you, I haven't left this island,"" I answered.

"I'll talk to you later!" he said in a patronizing tone and picked up the call he had placed on hold. He slammed the door shut behind him, and I waited in the outer office.

A few minutes later, he walked out of the office to confront me in front of the secretaries, who looked at me as if they knew what was happening. By their expressions, I knew that they believed that I had done something very wrong.

"That was the lieutenant from Maui Vice. They have a girl up there saying she's a Narcotics UC, and she's telling everyone about the Rivera case!"

"Lieutenant, I never left the island. I don't know what you're talking about!"

Again, he looked at me with the same disdain and disbelief I remembered from my first meeting with him.

"You match the description!" he said, and then began lecturing me about truthfulness and discussing the case.

"Look, lieutenant, I never left the island, never went to Maui, and wouldn't dare talk about the Rivera case with anyone." I halted the urge to call him a complete asshole but continued, "I have no one to talk to anyway!"

He looked at me with a smug expression. "And what about this weekend?" he pushed again. "You know any of the Maui Vice guys? Did you go drinking with them?"

"How many times do I have to tell you? I don't know what you talking about! I don't know any Maui Vice guys. What's going on?" I demanded in anger and frustration. Once again, the lieutenant refused to listen to my answer or to hear what I had to say.

Okimoto yelled at me that Maui Vice was very upset and going to call back in a few minutes. I had been accused of drinking with a bunch of the Maui Vice officers, bragging about being undercover with the Honolulu Police Department, and busting bad cops. Apparently, I had also told them that my undercover name was Jo.

The lieutenant was angry and refused to believe anything I had to say. He had already found me guilty and, like before, didn't want to hear or listen to the truth. He stomped back into his office, glaring at me.

"You're going to blow this case!" he yelled, slamming the door in my face while he waited for the phone to ring again.

Howard came out to see if I was all right. Word had already spread through the division that I had "fucked up the Rivera case."

He sat next to me, and I told him what I was being accused of. Meanwhile, Okimoto continued to glare at me through the window of his office, shaking his head in disgust.

I liked Howard. He was honest and blunt and didn't take any shit from anyone. He never bothered with rumors. If he had something to say, he would say it to your face and not behind your back.

"Don't worry about it," Howard smiled gently. "I believe you. It wasn't you," he said in a matter-of-fact tone. He sat next to me quietly waiting for the lieutenant to emerge.

The phone rang again, and after about fifteen minutes, Okimoto emerged again, obviously agitated and stressed out.

"Do you know anybody named Karin?" he demanded loudly.

"Oh, no!" I uttered spontaneously and then sank into my chair.

"What! Is that you friend or something?" he raged.

"That's the informant! You should fuckin' know that!" Howard snapped back, raising his voice and mocking the lieutenant's ignorance.

Okimoto shook his head. "Oh, her!" he muttered to himself.

"Get a hold of her," he then barked. "Tell her to knock this shit off. She's going to blow this case!" he said without looking at me. He walked back into his office and continued on the phone. He never apologized for his false accusations or unwarranted hostility.

Howard looked at me with a reassuring smile. "Don't worry; it's going to be all right. Everybody knows our lieutenant is a useless fuckin' asshole!" he said in voice loud enough for the lieutenant and all the secretaries to hear.

"Okimoto should have known Karin was the snitch," he continued. "He should have found out all the information before he accused you!"

The secretaries gasped at what had just happened. This time they looked at me with sympathy instead of scorn. The lieutenant and the captain were furious at what happened, but instead of asking Detective Stanley to deal with his informant, they yelled at me to find her.

I eventually located Karin and met with her in person. When I told her what had happened to me in the office, she folded her arms across her chest defensively, pressed her lips together, and wouldn't look at me.

"Listen, Karin," I said after a moment of silence, "I'm not angry at you. You just gotta stop talking about the case or I'll keep getting blamed for everything. I'm taking gas from everybody."

Karin relaxed her posture and, with tears glistening in her eyes, she explained that she had indeed gone to Maui and confided in a trusted friend about what had happened. She didn't know that her friend would tell the Maui Vice guys about it.

"Sorry," she apologized softly. "I didn't mean any harm."

"I know that, Karin!" I empathized. "Nobody understands how hard it is."

"Guess you can't trust anybody, huh?" Karin offered.

"Nope. And word gets back really fast!"

"No shit!" Karin rolled her eyes and then added, "I just really needed someone to talk to."

"I know that feeling very well."

Scales of Justice

I am empty . . . I am void
I am without Life, therefore without Death
Co-existence with the Universe, within my own Universe
I am Alone, but I am not lonely
I do not exist, but I Am
Happy Anniversary to me!

Journal entry: February 21, 1981

The prosecuting attorney for Glenn's case was the first trial attorney I met. I still had not gone to the police academy and had no clue what a criminal trial was like.

"Just tell the truth," he had told me, and I never forgot his guidance.

Glenn was the first to be sentenced under the new twenty-year mandatory jail term for class-A felonies.

During his trial, my high school classmates got together and signed a petition on behalf of Glenn. The rumors had circulated again that I had set up a close high school friend, forced him to sell me drugs, and lied about my surgery for the pseudo tumor in my left eye to solicit his sympathy.

No one came to hear the truth at the trials. No one cared to know the truth about what had really happened. No one wanted to see my medical papers. But the rumors flew, and everyone jumped on the bandwagon to say that I was cruel and heartless.

I learned that first day in trial that it was me who would be judged on the stand, for everything I did, everything I said, and even for what I did not do or say. It was not the accused who was interrogated on the witness stand or who would have to answer questions about what he did. The defendants usually sat silently with their attorneys and exercised their rights against self-incrimination.

The defense attorney accused me of heartlessly soliciting Glenn's sympathy, and he eventually who felt sorry for me and only sold me drugs out of compassion. The defense attorney even tried to insinuate that Glenn and I were more than close friends and that we were actually intimate in our relationship and I had used that to entrap him.

Even Glenn looked upset about what his attorney was saying but did nothing to stop his attorney's false accusations that dirtied both of our reputations.

A few months later, after Glenn was found guilty, I asked if I could speak on Glenn's behalf at his hearing for probation instead of the twenty-year mandatory sentence. Stanley heard about my question and was outraged about my inquiry.

"Where's your loyalty! It's against policy and procedure. You're a cop. You better remember that! Cops don't ever ask for leniency for a crook!" Stanley snickered. "You're making me look bad!" He then told everyone in the Narcotics Vice office that I had been "mentally affected."

It was easy for him to play the self-righteous role, especially after he had gotten away with not answering for what he did.

The prosecuting attorney on Glenn's case was the first and only person to ever say thank you and wrote me a commendation. He knew how difficult the trials had been and that I had never had any experience or training. He sensed, too, that I was totally estranged from Stanley and Christy just by observing the conduct of our so-called team.

During the trials, Stanley and Christy took the stand for a few minutes and left me alone while they went out to have breakfast or coffee.

It was the prosecutors and the sheriff's deputies who hung around and made sure the defendants and their friends had not carried out their threats against me.

It was not Stanley, not Christy, and no one else from the police department.

The defendants were allowed to lie on the stand and bring in character witnesses who were never involved in the investigations. It was their right to defend themselves in any way possible. But if an officer made a mistake or confused the facts of the case, he was threatened with perjury.

In order to survive the trials, I learned very quickly, to dissolve any personal feeling and emotions I had felt for my defendants. I had been forced to hang around with them as friends, and my heart was crushed for it.

If I had held on to my prejudices and judgments, I wouldn't have been hurt. But ironically, I was also happy to have lost and overcome the limitations of those misguided beliefs and loyalties. It was a new way of life for me that maybe no one would understand. I did my job without prejudice or favoritism, which was a challenge to my own honor and integrity.

These defendants were now facing prosecution, not because I didn't know them, not because I didn't like them or because they were "the scum of the earth," as Stanley had often described them. It was simply because they had committed a crime.

In these trials it seemed that I was the "bad guy" on trial for doing my job, while the defendants sat quietly with their attorneys. I was questioned and judged for everything I said and did, as well as everything I didn't say and didn't do.

I felt like I was the actual victim of Detective Stanley and the police department, and I knew that no one saw that and only a few would ever understand. I had been used, abused, and then left without recourse or guidance, but I still believed in the ideals of justice.

Chapter 16
Starting Over

After all the discipline
There's is still left
The need for the spirit to be free
And in reality
The greatest challenge we face is within ourselves
Not against the world
But against the fears and limitations
That we alone have created for ourselves
Therefore, we are alone in our search and quests
And in our struggles
Must come forth with our own strength and spirit
To overcome, conquer, succeed
It is extremely hard to accept that I do not belong
My life is different
And that I see what I see

Journal entry: January 30, 1982

The Undercover Stress Analysis

While waiting to begin the training program at the police academy, I was reassigned to the Research and Development Division in order to keep me away from the threats of other police officers. Every time I walked into the police station, uniformed officers with no nametags on their shirts made it obvious they did not want to be near me. I was also informed that I was sent to Research and Development because no one knew what to do with me while I waited to begin my assignment with the police academy.

"That's the one! Stay away from her! She's probably wearing a wire. She's an IA spy, Jap UC cunt. That's Serpico. She better watch out. She's going to get hurt," were the comments I received from the ranks for taking down a dope-dealing cop.

The derogatory remarks and warnings that I would be hurt became a daily routine. Even a few female officers had joined their counterparts with stares of contempt. They too uttered loudly that I had made them all look bad. Comments on my height and size were common, especially from a few of the large, stocky females who appeared to be trying to act and look like men.

My assignment in the Research and Development Division was to shred papers and answer phones. I used the long hours of unoccupied time I had to write a review of my undercover assignment for the Chief of Police.

"You're the first Narcotics undercover female," the Chief had said when we were finally introduced. "There was no one else before you. Write down a few things we can use to help the next female officer. Put down the difficulties so we can see how we can improve, both the good things and the bad things about the assignment."

Instead of a few paragraphs, I wrote a stress analysis thesis of my tour of duty. I outlined and then detailed the transitional steps I had taken to do the assignment, as well as the adverse reactions that resulted from the changes in my lifestyle.

Captain Chester was my supervisor. I liked his gentle, down-to-earth personality and pure heart. He was tall and slim with empathetic eyes. He reminded me of someone who could very well be a priest or pastor.

Captain Chester had read the stress analysis paper I had written on an old pica manual typewriter. Not once did he berate my typing, spelling, or grammatical errors.

He called me into his office a few days later and told me he had never realized how stressful and life-altering undercover work could be. Although I had tried to be as clinical in my stress analysis as possible, he now understood the difficulties that undercover officers faced.

"You're the first!" Captain Chester said. "You're not only the first female undercover officer in Narcotics, you're the first UC to take down a seasoned officer on criminal charges".."

He then explained that it was accepted when a ranking supervisor did the investigation against a subordinate officer, but it would incite outrage if it were a UC who was a tiny female officer and had never even attended the police academy. He shook his head sadly.

"The powers that be should never have asked you to take down a seasoned officer. They should have known how bad this would become."

It was Captain Chester who finally told me that, before this, no one in the police department had ever initiated criminal charges against an officer. The police department usually assigned seasoned ranking supervisors to handle all in-house investigations, and officers were usually given a choice of resigning or being terminated instead of facing criminal charges. It was believed that handling things that way would save the department public embarrassment, he explained.

I never realized that there had never been a "cop against cop" situation. Criminal misconduct had always been handled by administrative procedures or an outside agency.

I was happy that he thought the contents of my paper were good enough to forward to the Chief. I was especially thankful for his honesty and assigning Gene to help with editing the grammar and spelling errors.

"Maybe the Vice Division can use this to help other undercover officers, too," he said. "There are no directives or procedures set for undercover work, especially for females."

In the meantime, Karin took it upon herself to keep me updated on how everyone hated me. She called constantly to tell me that she was worried that I was going to get shot and killed by a cop. She had many cop friends who protected her so she wasn't worried about herself.

"But you don't have any friends!"

Detectives Akeo, DeCaires, and Torco were in the Internal Affairs office next to the Research and Development Division's office. Every day they popped in to see if I was all right.

Detective Stanley, who had sworn that he was the only one that would protect me, never did. I tried every day to erase my hate for him as well as the memory of the incident, but I knew I never would. Lieutenant Okimoto had made it very clear that I could never seek help or talk about it. My disrespect and contempt for him, too, would remain forever.

"You should sue them both!" a few attorneys suggested. They had been contacted by anonymous officers who had told them about the incident and what was happening to me.

"You have an awesome sexual harassment suit against the department and all of your supervisors! We could make millions!"

"It's not about money," I responded to the contingency agreement they offered.

"No! No! It's not about money! It's about what they did to you. Everything they did to you was outrageous! No training, no support—it's unheard of! Look at what you're going through! If you're not going to do it for yourself, do it for the other female officers so that they don't ever have to go through what you're going through!" the attorneys urged.

Even though I had declined offers from attorneys to represent me in what they claimed would be a high-profile civil suit against the department and all of my supervisors, word had circulated that I would be a typical female and file a sexual harassment suit.

"Just take the money and run. There will never be a place for you. You will never be accepted!" a few female officers urged.

It would have been easy to initiate a civil suit but to truly overcome and survive the difficulties, and to make sure others did not go through what I did, I knew I had to persevere against the odds and not give up. I had to prove to myself more than to others, that I could overcome and survive the assignment. No amount of money would ever be compensation enough for what I was going through. I knew too, that as the first undercover female in Narcotics, my decision would affect other females. I chose instead to stand on my own against the slander of the majority, and be around to help others like me to know that they were not alone. I made a vow that I would always step in to help or support a good officer doing his job with honor and integrity, even if it meant being hated and victimized by the blue army.

Detective Akeo would often walk with me to the snack stand on the first floor and glared at anyone who looked at me. He often confronted them, too.

"What? You guys have a problem?" Officers often gathered in the hallway to see what I looked like and to make derogatory or threatening comments when I walked past.

"Nobody's been through this kind of shit before, not even those of us in IA. Nobody knows what to do with you, and it's sad that nobody's backing you up except us! Where are all the Narco guys?" he said in anger. "You're taking all the heat, and nobody's blaming the detective, the informant, or the powers that be that made the decision to go criminal, and now nobody's backing you up! Keep a journal," Detective Akeo advised. "It's good therapy, and one day, you tell your story! Tell everybody how the department treats cops that come up front!"

"One day you publish it!" Akeo urged, when I told him that I had already started one.

I knew I had to learn to continue on my own, even when everyone else stepped back. I drank every day to erase my feelings and the awareness of the reality in which I was living.

If there were cops in the bar next to the police station, they all stood up and left. But I had become used to being alone and preferred it to being lonely in a crowd. I learned the difference between being alone and being lonely.

My stress analysis paper had been forwarded to the Chief. A few weeks later, Detective Stanley found me only to say that I had stepped on toes and broken the chain of command, and that everyone in the Vice Division was pissed off because I was obviously trying to make them all look bad.

I never bothered to tell him or anyone else that the Chief had asked for a review and that I was trying to help other officers not suffer like I did with someone like him as a supervisor. I had learned too well the futility of attempting to tell the truth against the 'man gang" and judgments already passed.

The Police Academy

In June of 1981, I was scheduled to finally begin my training at the Police Academy with the next recruit class. A year and a half had passed and I was still testifying against forty-six suspects in ninety-three felony investigations. I sat silently in a room and listened to Sergeant Miyaki yell at me.

"I didn't want you in my class. Undercovers always cause trouble, and as far as I'm concerned, you already flunked out because you have too much court. But there's nothing I can do about it because they forced me to take you in my class," he said. "I just want to make it clear from the start that you ain't nothing special, you hear? You're on your own!"

Sergeant Miyaki finished his speech with a glare of disgust and contempt. He stomped around in the office, pausing only to glare at me and shake his head.

"What is this department coming to!" he muttered to himself loudly so that I could hear.

"How tall are you!? Cut your hair and don't give me any shit about it!" he barked out the orders. He plopped down at his desk to shuffle papers.

"Well? What the hell you waiting for!" he said, raising his voice. "Beat it! And don't expect me to drive you to Fort Ruger!"

I was stupefied and didn't know anything about Fort Ruger. No one had informed me that the training academy was being held at the old military installation near the Diamond Head Crater.

Sergeant Sasaki had been sitting quietly at his desk in the office they shared, listening to the whole orientation.

"Take it easy!" he finally said to Miyaki. "I'll show her the school."

"Don't do that!" Miyaki warned. "She's going to think she's special!"

"I'm going out there anyway," Sasaki said, excusing himself, and motioned for me to follow.

Sergeant Miyaki shook his head in disgust and disapproval.

Still in shock, I was silent on the way to Fort Ruger; however, I was not really surprised at the introduction to the blue army I had just been through. I was only notified that morning that I was going to join the next recruit class and that I was to find and check in with my new superior officer, Sergeant Miyaki.

"Did anyone tell you where the school was?" Sergeant Sasaki asked in order to break the silence.

"No," I answered.

"Any questions?" he asked.

"What did I do wrong? What did I do to him?" I blurted out without thinking.

Sergeant Sasaki explained that no one in the Training Division liked undercover officers because undercover officers had always proved to be a problem. It was either because of too much court or because they had bad attitudes from having been in a non-conformist environment in Vice. In most cases, undercover officers had already passed their six months probation so they couldn't be terminated without getting the union involved.

"I don't expect special treatment. I don't want anyone to know who I am or that I was undercover. I'm already taking gas for it. Every new officer I meet calls me Serpico or Jap UC cunt".."

Sergeant Sasaki listened quietly.

"I heard about the threats," he said as he pulled into the parking lot of Fort Ruger.

I got out of the car and froze. I had been there before. I suddenly felt very sick and started to shake and fought to maintain my composure. This was the parking lot where the incident took place.

I was surprised to see Karin in the supervisor's office at the Fort Ruger Police Academy. She had told me that she had a lot of policemen friends, but I never expected to see her at the training facility. All of her police friends told her that it was cruel of me to use her as an informant against a cop. No one wanted to hear that I was pulled into the case only after Karin had already turned the officer in to IA or that she had demanded to be involved with the drug deals.

Karin appeared to be delighted in having another opportunity to tell me what all the cops were saying and that her many cop friends hated me. I guessed that Karin and Detective Stanley never took the time to tell anyone how the case had started or to address the rumors that were spreading that Karin had an affair with Officer Rivera.

"The trial is still pending," was the reason everyone was giving me for not disclosing any facts of the case.

A few nights later, I attended a training program orientation class with the other recruits. The other police recruits were told to bring their spouses, a close friend, or a family member to the class. I was only told that I had better show up, so I responded alone.

The first day of recruit class started, and the difficulty began immediately. All the recruits were introduced to each other, and I was introduced as the one who took down a cop. Suzanna and Cetta were undercover for a few months in the Gambling and Morals details, but everyone was okay with that.

Cetta was engaged to a good cop, and Suzanne was dating one. Most of the recruits had friends and family members in the force and had already been warned to stay away from me because I was probably an IA spy. Some had even heard that I had busted police recruits and was looking to bust some more. During the first break, a few of the recruits came up to tell me that I had busted their good friends or family members.

By the end of the first week, I learned that the worse thing that could ever happen to an officer was to be labeled a "cry baby' (those who made complaints to their supervisors or IA), "wimp" (those who were considered useless and could not be depended on), or an "eel" (those who slipped and slivered around making others do their work). I learned too that to be an undercover officer was considered worse than all of that, especially one that had busted another cop!

"I will never work in Vice," some of the recruits snickered as they walked past me. "I hear they're all dirty."

"Yup!" others joined in, "especially Narcotics!" Years later, these same officers all put in requests to work in Vice.

One of the females dating a police officer had complained to her ranking friends about how she was being mistreated in the class. Everyone assumed it was me making the complaint, and I was accused of being a cry baby and running to friends in Vice and IA.

I denied the accusation, but again, no one wanted to hear the truth, and I had already been declared guilty by at least half of my classmates. I was, after all, the Jap UC cunt and the IA spy.

The guilty female recruit finally came up to me secretly to apologize and thank me for not identifying her as the one who had filed the anonymous complaint. She had told her detective boyfriend that she was being picked on, and he had gone to his brass friends.

I had already learned that it was useless to plead innocence when no one wanted to hear the truth. I had known that she had made the complaint, but I had never identified her to my accusers.

Every day the recruits were yelled at, belittled openly in front of everyone, and had their individuality stripped away. Uniformity and unity was the name of the game, and I was constantly being yelled at and called the lone wolf.

I never went to study session because I was studying court cases for trial. I was in court a lot and missed a lot of classes and got yelled at for that, too.

I was yelled at in front of the entire class and accused of trying to circumvent the system, and most of my classmates bought it.

The recruit class was one of the largest and longest in duration. During the eight and a half months of training, the class began to split in half in spite of the class motto, "Lokahi," which means "unity".." Half of the class had learned to hate, despise, and distrust me for breaking the Golden Rules and taking down another cop. It didn't seem to matter that he had sold me drugs. The other half couldn't understand why Sergeant Miyaki hated me so much.

I was subsequently accused of causing the dissension in the class because I must have been chirping and getting people to side with me, even though I had never complained to IA or Vice or told my classmates what I had been through.

Detective Stanley had made it clear that all the Vice officers were pissed off because I had made them all look bad, and I knew that if I talked to IA I would just be validating the rumors that I was an IA spy.

During judo training, I tore my ligaments and had a hairline fracture on my right arm. In spite of the medical documents, I was accused of faking it and wimping out to circumvent the system. I was warned that if I didn't pass this class, I would be terminated. With hate and anger, I learned to do one-arm pushups and barely qualified on the firearms and agility tests.

I still drank every night to fall asleep and to wash away the hurt, anger, and frustration.

Karin was hanging out at the academy almost every day to be with her police friends. It was difficult to see her even if I thought of her more as a friend than an informant. I was then accused by some of the females in my class of inviting Karin to the academy to fix her up in relationships with the class supervisory police officers.

Sergeant Miyaki occasionally announced to the class that he was available for anyone who had problems. He took care of some of the guys, and they often played music together after class.

The rumors that I was the IA spy came up whenever seasoned officers or anyone outside of the class found out what was happening in the class. It had become unbearable. I made the critical mistake of believing what Sergeant Miyaki had said and finally went to see him to discuss the rumors.

"What now!" he complained before I could say anything even though I had never talked to him before. "I told you I didn't want you in my class, so don't come crying to me about anything," he said angrily.

I didn't know that I was excluded from the invitation to talk.

Once again, I had to learn to continue without help or support, but I was still too stubborn to give up. The loneliness and alienation grew with the increased difficulty of testifying and attending the police academy.

My daily prayers began to change. They were not for strength and courage anymore, but rather for peace and deliverance. The dawn of each day no longer brought a new day of challenges. It brought, instead, the regret of having to face another day.

But somehow, through the difficulty, I learned to look beyond the uniformity and conformity that the academy had enforced and found good friends in fellow recruits who encouraged me to not give up and pushed me to continue.

When prayer and even anger didn't work anymore, they came through with friendship and support. God used each one of them as his angels in answer to my prayers.

Cetta and Kuulei were not afraid to be seen talking with me or to be identified as my friends. They made a space for me in the ranks of their class when others made it known that they felt that I didn't belong and wasn't accepted.

Cetta was my closest friend at the academy. She was smart, mature, talented, and athletic. She reminded me of Lolly, especially with her very compassionate heart.

Andrew Tsukano was easy going and had been a Maui County police officer for a year and a half before transferring to Honolulu Police Department. He was mature and easygoing. Nothing seemed to faze him, and he was very knowledgeable about police work.

Derrick "Zip" Kiyotoki was quiet and intense and, like Andrew, had an exceptional knowledge of police work.

Wayne was the most innocent and naive, but his pure heart was always a comfort and strength.

Darryl was stubborn and defiant, while Ray Quon, the youngest of the bunch, had a playful personality. The rest of the class were either part of the silent majority or hated me and made it known.

Everyone was expected to pass the same agility test. No allowances were made for gender or age, and I wouldn't have passed my final run if Derrick and Andrew hadn't dragged me over the finish line in time.

One of the other females never did the qualifying run, but she somehow passed the test, too.

Final Exams

Graduation neared, and the day of the final exam had arrived. I had somehow managed to get through the classes in spite of court and my injured arm. At dawn, the class left for the military compound where we would begin the final and most important exam. It was the first day of mock crime scenes. Everyone stood at attention in perfect formation while the commanders inspected us critically.

Officer Robert "Bobby" Lung came up to me in the front row at the very end of the formation, which is reserved for the shortest person and shook his head.

"Don't get upset," he began, "but I figured I better tell you before you start".."

As I stood at attention, staring straight ahead, Officer Lung told me that Detective Harrison, who had been suspended for identifying me to my suspects, had volunteered to be a final evaluator. He had been assigned to be my personal evaluator throughout the entire week. Still standing at attention, I stood silently staring ahead into space feeling my heart sink.

"Don't they know he burned me?" I asked incredulously, breaking the rule of standing silently in formation.

"They all know!" Lung responded angrily. "I tried to change it, but the mMajor refused! Everyone else is going to have a different evaluator at each scene, but this guy is going to stay with you throughout the whole mock crime scene evaluation!"

Officer Lung had been helping all the recruits to get through the ordeal of training and many times had tried to act as a buffer for me against the harassment of my classmates.

"I turned in my transfer today, Jo," he said. "This is totally unfair. This is way over my limit. I can't take the bullshit that they're dumping on you anymore!"

He was very angry and didn't care if anyone heard what he was saying to me.

Officer Lung had yelled, screamed, and worked the class to the ground, but he was always fair. He had jumped all over us when we failed or had not pushed ourselves to our maximum abilities, but he had always been there to help us, too. He not only barked out orders, he also joined us and did what he expected us to do! He was gruff and rough and demanded the best from each of us, but he cared about us, too. He had earned the respect and loyalty of all of the recruits in the class.

Officer Lung was now standing directly in front of me, staring straight into my eyes. He saw the tears of stress and despair well up in my eyes, and he began to choke up, too. No one had ever seen him choke up before, and the strict formation began to break as he wiped away the tears of anger and shook his head.

"I tried, Jo," he said. "I did everything I could, but they wanted to see how you would handle the stress, and there's nothing I can do about it. The guy is going to be your personal evaluator. You're the only one who's going to have one!"

I looked at the officer's tears of frustration and stress and began to tremble.

"I can't believe this! Why?" I began reliving what had happened at Yoshi's Restaurant.

"He almost got me killed, and he got suspended for it, too! He admitted to burning me!"

"I know," Officer Lung said as his tears of intense anger and helpless frustration began to spill, and he wiped them back again. "Give these guys some shit, Jo!" he half yelled. "You can do it!"

Every ounce of strength I had drained from me as I watched Lung turn and walk away. From behind me, I could hear the voices of the other recruits swearing and talking of walking out with Officer Lung. The perfect ranks of formation at attention began to break.

"Stand fast!" Lung stopped to yell at everyone in my squadron. ""You will complete your training and become commissioned officers!"

Only because it was Officer Lung, the ranks began to pull it together again. Lung came back and stood in front of me one last time, staring at me with fire and intense anger in his eyes.

"Do it, Jo. Show these guys!" he yelled almost threateningly. He turned sharply and walked away.

Sergeant Miyaki had started walking in our direction, calling his name, but Officer Lung ignored him and kept walking. The formation was immediately dismissed for a short break, but I remained frozen in position.

I couldn't move, and it felt like I had failed before I was even allowed start.

What have I done to make them all hate me so much? I began walking toward the parking lot to leave as Andrew and Ray tried talking me out of leaving.

"I give up," I said softly.

"You can't give up now!" Andrew said. "Not after all the shit you took. Just forget about everything else!"

I was reliving the incident at Yoshi's bar and couldn't understand or focus on what anyone else was saying.

"Just do it for Bobby Lung!" Andrew said with a deep sincerity and desperate seriousness I had never seen in him before.

Officer Lung had pushed and worked with all of us to get us this far. I thought of him putting in his transfer because of me, and I heard his voice echo in my mind.

"Do it, Jo!" he had commanded.

Because of Officer Lung's efforts and the words Andrew spoke, I didn't leave, even though I felt I was destined to fail. I knew I had to finish what I had started, even if it meant that I was destined to fail.

Officer Lung returned late in the evening just as the last session ended. He was wearing civilian clothes instead of a uniform. I couldn't remember how I had survived the first day when he asked how I was doing. Everything was a blank spot in my memory, and I couldn't remember what I had done. Instead, I kept remembering and reliving the drug deals I had done and couldn't stop my UC past from flooding back in nonstop memories.

"I think I screwed up royally, Bobby! I can't even remember what scenarios I just went through!" I confessed. "I couldn't think!"

"That's not the point," Lung answered. "Apparently everyone was expecting you to walk out and quit, but you had enough guts to stay, and that's what everyone wanted to see. That was your real test. They just wanted to screw with you to see how you would handle it."

At the end of the week, announcements were made of who had passed and who had failed. I was sure that I had failed because I couldn't remember what I had done. But everyone passed, including me.

Detective Harrison was watching me quietly, waiting to catch my attention. He looked into my eyes, nodded his head silently, and smiled.

I was shocked and confused to see the kindness and compassion in his eyes, and totally bewildered at his nod of approval. I fought the urge to talk to him about what had happened that night at Yoshi's Restaurant. I suddenly had a strange feeling that maybe he didn't hate me like Detective Stanley and Christy had said. Maybe he finally understood what I had been through. I didn't go up to talk to Detective Harrison and resigned myself to knowing that I would never understand what had happened.

I had seen reflections of a pure heart in his eyes when I expected nothing but hostility and disdain. I wept inside of myself without tears. Everyone stayed at the military compound and celebrated with a party. I drank some scotch and left.

Graduation day had finally arrived and I was happy to see a few of the Vice officers and the IA detectives attending the ceremonies. After more than two years, I had finally been issued a badge, a uniform, and a gun. A piercing pain ripped through my soul when my mom pinned the badge on my uniform. My classmates didn't understand how different this day was for me or why I could not share their feelings of camaraderie and happy excitement. They never would.

The Vice officers told me that Detective Stanley wouldn't be showing up. He had been drinking all night and was probably hung over, they explained. And to this day, Detective Stanley never bothered to say Congratulations, Thank you, I'm sorry, or Go to hell.

The next morning, all the brand-new police officers reported to the main police station to receive their Certificates of Training. One by one, we were called into the captain's office in alphabetical order. It was finally my turn, and the captain asked me to step into the office and to close the door behind me instead of leaving it open. He handed me the piece of paper that finally identified me as a real police officer.

"Congratulations," he said, and then he paused to look at me, shaking his head in disbelief. "I have to tell you," he paused as if in reflection, "I have a lot of respect for you. We never gave anybody else as much shit as we gave you. But you surprised all of us. You made it through and didn't quit. I understand you even did one-armed pushups!" The captain smiled genuinely and offered to shake my hand.

"Can I ask you a question?" I asked instead of accepting his hand.

"Sure!" he smiled in surprise. Sergeant Miyaki, standing next to him, shot me a glance that warned me that I was way out of line.

"Why? What did I do?" I asked.

The captain looked at me in shock at what I had asked and was stumped for an answer.

"That's okay," I said when he couldn't answer and walked out of the room, followed by Sergeant Miyaki's piercing glare.

The Contract

Jonathan from the liquor store was now a trustee in the cellblock. I recognized him as he swept up the sidewalks outside of the police station. He didn't look well, and I obviously surprised him when I asked how he was doing.

"I put out a contract on you," he said, looking at me inquisitively.

"I heard," I responded with an offer of a cigarette.

He hesitated a moment and then accepted it. Inhaling deeply, he sat down next to me on the bench.

"I ran out of cigarettes yesterday," he said quietly. "All my friends shafted me. I gave them drugs when they didn't have any money and I never ratted anybody out. Now they can't even bring me one pack of cigarettes." Jonathan stared down at his cigarette, watching it burn a while.

"You're not scared?" he asked, looking at me curiously again.

"Of what?"

"Contracts," he answered. "I've got some really heavy friends."

"I know that, Jonathan," I said observing how pale and broken he looked.

Jonathan searched my eyes. "You're not scared, yeah!" he said in surprise.

"Who said I'm not?"

"You don't act scared. From what I heard, the cops hate you too because you busted a cop. You know they're not going help you out!" he said.

"I know," I answered softly.

Several officers walked by, pausing to stare coldly in our direction.

"You know they're not looking at me!" Jonathan said, and I nodded.

I sat silently, finishing my cigarette, and didn't have anything else to say. Everything he said was true, but for the moment, I was more comfortable sitting with Jonathan than next to anyone else. I trusted his honesty more than any of the cops who were walking around at the station.

"I gotta confess something to you," he said, finally breaking the silence. "I lied in court because I was trying to save my ass, but you got me fair and square. You didn't do all that entrapment shit, but I had to put up a defense. I was pissed off and put a contract out on you even if I knew I got busted because of my own fault." Jonathan paused as if in reflection and then continued.

"I had already heard in prison that you busted a cop. But I didn't believe it until they finally made me a trustee at the station and I heard the cops talking about setting you up."

"Look," he concluded, "I'm not mad at you anymore. I guess maybe I should thank you for setting me straight 'cause I knew I was going to get busted sooner or later. But I kept thinking about you busting a cop, and I started thinking about how fair you were to people like me. Most times, only guys like me get busted because we don't have connections inside. But you even busted one of your own, so I was forced to respect you. So I stopped the contract, and everybody agreed."

In that moment, I felt Jonathan was the only person who really understood how hard it was to do what I did—and maybe the only real friend I had.

"Thank you," I said, overwhelmed at what I just heard. "So which cops are going to set me up?"

Jonathan sat back in alarm. "I'm not like you Jo," he said. "I ain't going finger a cop, no matter what! I'm sorry," he continued. "I'm not a coward, but I can't come up front for that! I just wanted to tell you to watch your back because the hit's going to come from your own guys!"

"I understand," I said, handing him the extra pack of cigarettes I had in my bag.

"Look, Jo,"" he said, "I don't know why, but I trust you and like you. When I get out of here, if you need help, come see me, cause you got nobody!" he said and shook his head sadly. "I don't know anymore. I should hate you, but I respect you. I should be happy if you get hurt, but I'm worried. Stupid yeah? Maybe I'm just going crazy. Nothing makes sense anymore. I don't make sense to myself!"

"Me too, Jonathan. I know what you mean," I said, standing up to leave.

"Take it easy," he said, going back to sweeping the sidewalk.

I walked over to the bar next door. As I entered, all the off-duty officers in the place stood up to leave. Some paused to spit on the floor as they walked past me.

❦

Chapter 17
The Heart of the Badge

The Police Trials

January 30, 1982. Word spread throughout the department that Rivera's trial would begin with a suppression hearing to block the taped evidence from the wire I wore during the investigation. The threats and harassment, which had died down a bit when I disappeared into the police training academy for eight months, were suddenly rekindled.

A crowd of officers, dressed in either blue uniforms or dress suits, packed the hallways and corridors outside my assigned courtroom. They spit on the ground in front of me when I walked through the lobby, and a few officers actually stepped in front of me to block my path. When Officer Rivera arrived, they shook his hand and patted him on the back.

"Don't worry. She's going to get hers!" a few officer announced in loud voices. Others nodded in agreement and added, "She broke the Golden Rule. She better quit before she gets hurt! Even Serpico was smart enough to quit!"

Some of the officers dropped by to see what I looked like and to watch what was going to happen. They stood in various corners of the lobby, staring and whispering among themselves, watching as the other more outspoken officers put on a display of loyalty to the brotherhood in blue. My new names, Serpico, Jap cunt, and IA spy, were being mentioned throughout the courtroom.

Deputy prosecutor Keith Kaneshiro was assigned to the Rivera case. Some of the other prosecutors had shared with me that they didn't want to be the one to have to prosecute a cop. Kaneshiro was not afraid of prosecuting a bad cop even though he knew that he too would also have to face the negative reprisal of those officers who worshipped the Golden Rule.

One police commander had approached me a few months earlier, looked me over, and then shook his head, commenting that the department had never prosecuted their own.

"It should have been left to the commanders," he said. Officer Rivera's patrol commanders were supposed to be the ones assigned to deal with his misconduct, but they had not been notified or involved, which was a breach of the chain of command, he complained. "What you really did was discredit the entire police force!" he finished grimly.

Prosecutor Kaneshiro was waiting for me to arrive, standing like a pillar of marble in the distance. He stood outside the courtroom and witnessed the harassment and threats as I made my way toward him through the thick ranks of animosity. Officer Rivera's entourage of high-priced private attorneys had also just arrived, and a path was cleared for them.

"How're you holding up?" Kaneshiro asked the question that no one, except the prosecutor on Glenn's case, had ever cared enough to ask. It took every ounce of my will power not to sob.

Kaneshiro's face was grim and his eyes were red with fury at what he had seen.

"This is outrageous!" he said, and left to call the police department to notify those in command about the intimidating and threatening conduct of the crowd of officers.

Even the sheriff's deputies, assigned to the security of the courthouse, were watching nervously in anticipation of an outbreak of violence. Emotions were escalating as voices in opposition to Rivera's criminal prosecution grew louder.

I recognized one of the sergeants with the sheriff's department from one of my previous undercover trials. He had stayed inside of the courtroom to make sure I was safe when the defendants brought their families and friends with them to threaten and intimidate me. I watched him slowly making his way towards me through the growing crowd officers.

"Looks really bad," he said calmly when he finally reached me and saw the hateful glares. He had never seen so many officers in the building, he said.

"I'm calling more of our guys in. Our deputies respect what you did. You've got more balls than most of the men in here."

No one responded to Kaneshiro's phone call to the Narcotics Office for assistance. None of the commanders or officers of the Narcotics Vice Division responded to help. Even Detective Stanley, who was my supervisor in the investigation, had failed to appear.

Instead, attorneys from the prosecutor's office and the sheriff's deputies came down to be my protective support as I waited alone on the worn wooden bench for my turn on the witness stand. They were concerned, they confessed, that a zealous follower of the Golden Rule would shoot me before I could testify.

"Kill the witness and the case gets dropped."

As the days went by, the arguments and tension between the attorneys grew inside of the courtroom. Outside in the hallways and lobbies, tension also increased between the police officers and the sheriff's deputies. At one point, a deputy got into a verbal confrontation with several police officers that almost erupted into a war of uniforms.

Kaneshiro had won the preliminary arguments, and the tapes from the body wire would be admitted as evidence in the case. Jury selection was about to begin.

I could see the fear on the faces of the potential jurors as they were led by a bailiff towards the courtroom through the thick crowd of intimidating officers.

The judge's chambers and the prosecutor's office had both received anonymous phone threats to stop the trial.

The media was at the courthouse every day but were banned from bringing their cameras and recorders into the courtroom. They still managed to report details of the events that happened within the courtroom with the help of anonymous sources.

If witness testimonies were discussed outside of the courtroom while trial was in progress, a mistrial would be declared and we would have to start all over again.

When news of the intimidation and threats to the judge reached the Internal Affairs Division, Detectives Wally Akeo, Clarence DeCaires Jr., and Alfredo Torco immediately responded to the courthouse. They had never received prosecutor Kaneshiro's request for assistance.

Akeo walked up to me in front of all the officers and gave me a hug and announced in a loud voice, "Guess we have to bust some more badges!"

Akeo looked around and asked me in an astounded voice, "Nobody's been with you all this time? Where is everyone? Where are the Narco guys? Where is your detective? Where's the ILieutenant?" Akeo's voice had escalated in outrage and was booming through the now silent courtroom lobby.

"I don't know," I shrugged. "Kaneshiro called the Narco office for assistance on the first day but no one came down."

"Nobody told us!" Akeo said angrily. "Where's all your support? Where are all the Vice commanders?"

The IA detectives began walking around the corridors, asking officers to produce their subpoenas. If they were not present for a trial, they were ordered to leave. Each officer took a moment to glare or snicker at me before he reluctantly left. When word got out that my phone was wired, the incoming verbal threats slowly dwindled to a few silent hang-ups.

After each day's session in court, I went to work in uniformed patrol on the evening shift. I was assigned to a foot beat on the training watch, called the 4thfourth w Watch. Everyone whispered when I walked into the station for lineup, and only a few dared to be seen talking to me.

One afternoon as I was putting on my gear in the women's locker room, an Asian female officer approached me.

"You better leave the department," she said. "Those guys are going to get you no matter how long it takes." Other female officers walked in and stomped out after slamming their lockers open and shut.

"It's hard enough to be a female cop," she continued. "You make us all look bad, and now the guys won't back us up either. You better learn that you're not going to survive without the guys backing you up, so just quit."

Most of the female officers needed and counted on the support of the male officers, she continued, and I was apparently making it worse for them. The few possible supporters I thought might understand what I was going through melted into none.

Victor Vierra was my first sergeant in uniformed patrol. He demanded the best effort from each of his officers and was fair in his discipline as well as his guidance. He was not loud and officious but his presence always commanded respect. It was he, who first showed me that the true honor of the badge must be earned by the officer who wears it.

A rumor started that I was going to be held back in the training watch because I was too scared to work the streets and be a real cop. The story circulated like wildfire in a strong wind. One of the guys in my recruit class finally admitted he had started the rumor when Ray called him a liar in front of me for pretending to know nothing about it.

He apologized, explaining that he was angry because I hadn't taken the time to personally tell him why I was being held back, so he started to tell others I was held back by my own choice because I was afraid of the streets.

His apology was too late. My stomach turned to acid and rage burned my heart. I knew it would take years to overcome what he had done. It was bitterly ironic that I was accused of being afraid after going through what I had gone through, after working alone in the streets with the risk of being exposed as a cop, and after standing alone in court against the blue army, who hated me for doing my job.

Jury selection was finally completed. The first day of trial began, and I was the first witness. The defense had a three-man team of attorneys, and Prosecutor Kaneshiro stood alone against them. Although they had the advantage, the defense team still stooped to misconduct, hiding a tape recorder on their desk.

As Kaneshiro questioned me on the stand, he noticed one of the defense attorneys trying to inconspicuously change a tape. Kaneshiro immediately stepped around the table to bring it to the attention of the trial judge and Officer Rivera hastily tried to hide the recorder under a newspaper.

In a flash, Kaneshiro jumped over the partition to grab the recorder, which they then passed over to a friend sitting behind them in the gallery.

Kaneshiro moved like superhero with speed and agility as the defense team scrambled to keep the recorder from his grasp. He ripped off his jacket to answer the taunting challenges and threats of the defense team, as well as the jeering police officers who had lined up against the back of the courtroom in order to glare at me when I had taken the witness stand.

There was complete pandemonium in the courtroom. One of the jurors was screaming and tried to climb over the others to get out. Other spectators began to scramble toward the doors. Sheriff's deputies burst into the courtroom, and the judge hammered his gavel repeatedly, trying to restore order.

The trial judge was livid when the defense denied any knowledge of the tape recorder that he had seen them trying to hide. He slammed down his gavel one last time and declared a mistrial.

Later that evening I was officially notified that I would be held back from moving to the regular watches until the trial was over. The commanders didn't know where to place me and a few of my supervisors were concerned that I might be "accidentally shot" by a fellow officer. They all agreed that I would probably have no backup or support on the beat when and if I needed it.

Internal Affairs investigated the misconduct at the trial. I had not been able to identify the officers who made threatening remarks, spit, or blocked my way, or the officers who called DPA Kaneshiro out to fight in the courtroom. Most of those involved had removed their nametags or wore unmarked jackets over their uniforms.

A clarification was later announced by the Honolulu Police Department's command that the Sheriff's Department was the ruling enforcement agency in the courthouse, not the Honolulu Police Department. Police officers were also notified that nametags were to be clearly visible at all times and that to remove them was a violation. It was also made mandatory that all jackets worn over the uniform had to have names and insignias embroidered on.

The new rules increased the animosity toward me, and no one seemed to care that the officer on trial was selling drugs. I couldn't understand the hate and misguided loyalty of police officers who had sworn to uphold and enforce the law. No one saw that I had been used, abused, and then left without recourse or guidance.

A few months later, a new trial began, but this time a different prosecutor had been assigned to the case instead of Keith Kaneshiro.

The harassment and threatening remarks began all over again, but the great crowd of policemen in the courthouse had dwindled down to only a handful of officers, attending court to testify on their respective cases. The new death threats and harassing phone calls I received were traced back to the police squad room. My family also received threats that our home would be burned down.

The brake lines on my car were cut and the fenders and doors scratched deeply with a sharp object. Someone had stomped on the hood, roof, and trunk of my car, which was parked in the police parking lot on Young Street while I was on duty

During all of my undercover assignments, I had used my own car and was never given any false identification. The only listing in the Honolulu phone book under my last name was my family, and it included my family's address. You didn't have to be a cop to track me down.

Officer Gary, a close friend of Rivera, saw me one day with my four-year-old niece in front of the police station. He smirked at me and said, "I would never be seen with a child. She might get hit with a bullet meant for you!"

"Shoot me now!" I snapped back. "Or tell me where to meet you and I'll be there!" I was sick and tired of the constant barrage of threats and pushed my niece behind me.

"Your time will come!" he said with a smile as he walked away.

"Is that a policeman, Aunty?" my niece Julie asked.

"Yes," I admitted reluctantly, trying to calm down.

I expected threats to myself, but I had never realized that my choice to accept my undercover assignment would end up hurting my family, too. It was cowardly and dishonorable to threaten the ones I loved instead of facing me. I hated Detective Stanley even more for all his lying promises of support and protection if I did my job.

The retrial was granted a closed hearing, which meant the courtroom was closed to the media and all police officers except those who would be testifying on the investigation. The defense had the same three-man team of high-priced attorneys. Officer Rivera was not allowed representation by the attorneys of the police officer's union because he was facing criminal charges. The State of Hawaii Organization of Police Officers Union, I was told, was helping to finance his personal attorney fees instead.

The media followed the trial proceedings from unknown sources in the courtroom. When Stanley showed up to testify, he greeted Officer Rivera by shaking his hand and patting him on the back.

I had been on the stand every day for several weeks during the preliminary hearings and the first trial, and again for the retrial.

Detective Stanley took the stand for a few hours and never showed up again, not even to help his informant, Karin.

When it was time for Karin to testify, I called her and arranged to pick her up and escort her through the courthouse. Stanley suddenly wasn't around and didn't answer her phone calls.

Karin had been watching all the media reports and was now reluctant to testify. She finally understood why everyone had tried to keep her out of the undercover deals, but it was too late. Her excitement about the investigation and persistent demands to participate and testify had turned to fear.

None of Karin's numerous police friends offered to escort her to the trials, including Stanley. I couldn't let her face the difficulties alone, even though I had been finally excused from court.

I stayed with Karin every day during her testimony, even after she told me that her police friends had convinced her that I had set her up and was just using her. I suppose they didn't know she had initiated the complaint against Rivera and had insisted on being a working informant before I had even been assigned to the case.

The media had a ball with all the misinformation reported to them. Someone told them I was actually an informant during the investigation, using the name Karin. In one story, they accused Karin, who many now believed was me, of being a spurned lover who set up Rivera in retaliation. In another article, they reported that I was having sex with him to entrap him into selling drugs. They never mentioned how Rivera made pig noises every time he saw a cop in uniform or how he demeaned their efforts, calling them stupid when they tried to make extra money working at legitimate special duty jobs.

Instead, one of the TV stations aired a short clip of Karin and me walking to the courthouse together. This was after being asked not to broadcast our photos. They also switched our names during the broadcast, identifying me as the informant and Karin as the undercover officer. The courtroom reporter apologized to me the following day, saying she had told the newsroom not to use the photos, but apparently it was too good of an opportunity to pass up.

Because of the media's indiscretion and inaccuracy, I was barraged with insults and called derogatory names, and my family was constantly asked if I had sex with Rivera and if I was just an informant instead of a real undercover officer. Although my family told the truth about the media's inaccuracy, they were often not believed.

Masa, a long-time neighbor, confronted my mother and responded to her explanation sarcastically, "Well, I guess you have to say that. After all, you have to try to protect your daughter's reputation. The media wouldn't make a mistake like that."

I had never met Rivera before Karin introduced me to him during the investigation, and I wore a body wire during the drug deals, but the newspapers never published that. They ran headlines to stir the public's interest, like "Spurned Lover Induced Officer's Ddrug Dealing, Jury Told" and then reported a scandalous story about a sex-for-drugs defense.

The officer was eventually found guilty and sentenced to the twenty-year mandatory sentence for class-A felonies but claimed it was "cruel and unusual punishment." He spent a few months working in the infirmary at the Oahu Community Correctional Facility and was released.

Several months later, Bob Leucci, formerly a detective in the New York City Police Department, addressed the chiefs and commanders of HPD about undercover operations. In his presentation, he noted the serious dangers and possible permanent psychological injuries the commanders were exposing the undercover officers to by putting them on the streets without backup or training, especially when targeting corrupt police officers. He emphasized and discussed issues of "Vicarious Liabilty" and informed the commanders that they too, were responsible for the safety and well-being of their undercover officers and not only the detectives. "I didn't know" was no longer an acceptable excuse for any supervisor regardless of rank when they "should have known."

When Leucci voiced his concern about the Honolulu Police Department's undercover procedures, the commanders responded defensively, claiming, "This island is too small. We have to do things our way. Everybody knows everybody on an island."

At the end of his presentation, Leucci asked me to accompany him to the front of the police station where a car was already waiting for him. I followed him out in spite of the stares or reproach I received from a few of the commanders in the room.

"What have they done to you?" he asked as we hurried down a flight of stairs to the front doors of the building. "I know they didn't like what I said. Do you have anyone to talk to?"

"No," I answered. "All I keep hearing is that I make the department look bad."

Leucci apologized that he had to hurry off to another speaking engagement to which he was already late but said he would try to contact me later through the Narcotics Division to talk more.

As soon as he sped off in a waiting vehicle I was immediately approached by one of the majors who had attended the seminar and counseled about loyalty and speaking to anyone outside of the department. "We don't ever air our dirty laundry outside of the department!" he scowled and stomped away.

I knew that if he tried to reach me through the Narcotics Vice Division, I would never get the message. I never saw or spoke to him again.

The term "vicarious liability" which I first heard at Leucci's presentation eventually became part of mandatory training for supervisors.

The practice of placing untrained officers into undercover assignments and leaving them solely dependent on the presumed honor and integrity of one detective would also be stop. Bob Leucci had unknowingly saved many future undercover officers from hurt and devastation.

Shadows in the Night

One night around midnight, several uniformed officers in unmarked jackets arrived at my parents' home.

This is it! I thought, and for a split second, I reached for the phone to call the police department for help but immediately realized how stupid that was. With a quick glance, I saw the helpless fear and uncertainty in my parents' faces. I decided to go out to the street and face the bullet that I was certain would come. I was not going to wait for them to approach the door for fear that the bullet intended for me might pierce the walls or windows of the house. More than that, I did not want the pending confrontation to spill into the house and harm my family or put them in further jeopardy as witnesses.

"If you're looking for me, I'm right here," I announced quietly, opening my arms in submission to accept whatever was intended for me. "Go ahead and shoot me," I said, hoping that my parents could not hear what I was saying. "I'm right here!"

I did not shout or yell but found my voice to be surprisingly calm and articulate in the quiet stillness of the night. The death threats against me had finally come to this end. I was tired of waiting for the threats to be carried out and ready to accept my fate.

A few shadows moved in the darkness while others leaned up against their vehicles, watching and waiting as others vehicles arrived. I had emptied my mind except for the thought that it was time for me to face my death.

"Come on, just shoot me already! What are you waiting for? I'm right here. Just leave my family alone!" I demanded, but no one responded to my invitation.

It seemed as if I was outside of myself, watching the scene of a movie unfold in slow motion.

"You guys better hurry up and get over here!" one of the officers said over his police radio to other approaching officers.

One police vehicle speeding down the street toward us came to a quick stop on the opposite side of the street from where I stood. A uniformed figure jumped out of his vehicle and hurriedly walked up to me. As he approached, the other officers started walking toward me from their waiting positions.

This is it! I thought. *He must be the shooter.* Facing the approaching officer, I calmly opened my arms, accepting that my imminent death.

"Go ahead; I'm ready," I said quietly.

There are times when you know that you have to do what anyone else would probably not do, even if it means you might not live through the next moment. So I erased my emotions and emptied my mind and focused only on what I believed to be coming. I was ready to die outside on the streets to relieve my family from further pain.

Perhaps a macho guy would have yelled, shouted, and smiled when he uttered the challenge to go ahead and shoot … I don't know. For me, it was a quiet announcement that I was ready to die, but still on my terms, that my family would then be left alone. I guess it's like *hara-kiri*, a resolve that death must be faced.

I didn't want my parents hearing what I was saying and I didn't want them to see me get shot, so I was not going to let anyone get close to the front door. I went out to the street.

"Jojo, it's me!" the officer called out.

Although I was looking at the officer who was now standing right in front of me, I couldn't recognize his face. I could hear that he was talking to me but I couldn't understand a word he was saying. My mind had gone blank, except for the expectation of being shot.

I don't know how long it took to sink in that these were all good cops and that no one was going to hurt me. I suddenly recognized that it was Officer Akiona and Detective Alfredo Torco talking to me, and behind them stood several police officers from District 4 in Kaneohe.

On their own, they had come forward to support me and had organized shifts on their off-duty time to watch over my family. They had heard about the threats that had swept through the ranks that my family's home would be burned down while we were sleeping.

"We're the good cops!" they explained. They had not expected me to come out of the house before they could explain why they were.

I never got to know all the officers who came forward to help me, nor did I get the chance to thank each of them personally. I never had the opportunity to let them know that they had taught me the true meaning of the honor and sacrifice that lives in the hearts of the good officers, shining behind the badge.

A few days later, I moved out of my parents' home and distanced myself from my family for several years. Although the trials had finally ended, I couldn't get back to who I was and I still couldn't bring myself to identify with the other officers.

Whenever the training division discussed my cases with the new police recruits, the instructors would ask, "Would you take down a cop?"

For several years, every new officer who graduated from the police academy knew who I was and what I had done.

Living in silence for so long taught me the true meaning of loneliness. It is not the loss of companionship. It is the loss of one's identity. I learned too that there is a great difference between being alone and being lonely, and I was both.

Every morning I prayed for strength to get through the day, and every night I prayed for eternal peace.

Fort Street Mall:

The sun beat down relentlessly
Baking the hard pavement beneath scant wisps of clouds
The blue woolen uniform seemed soaked through with sweat
Shops began to close and traffic mellowed down
People going home with thoughts on their minds
Of the day, of the evening, of tomorrow

A sense of stillness breezes through the air
The sounds of silence drift down the street
My own footsteps, alone on the stained cement, echo against the quiet
The sun blazes a last brilliant scene across the horizon
Orange, red, pink
And night moves in to quench its fire

Pink shower tree petals float down from branches I pass beneath
Sprinkling me with an uneasy feeling of loneliness
I reflect a moment on the still beauty of the day
And loneliness grows into Peace.

The chapel is closed; I am alone with myself
From the shadows, drunks, vagrants, the mentally challenged
Begin their daily search for a bite of food to eat
Searching garbage almost meticulously, very selectively
As I approach, they halt and stare

In their eyes, a retarded innocence or a hateful glare
But those with the empty eyes, they speak a story of pain, of hopes and dreams lost
Ten thousand roaches scurry beneath my feet
Some even seem to be preparing to attack
Standing by with my mace

The silence is broken by the crackle of the radio
Sending units by their numbered beats to unknown confrontations
The night people are out now
Another night begins
It's time to put myself away

Journal entry: 1982

Chapter 18
Back Under

Yakuza Shabu

In March of 1982, I was assigned to work undercover again with the Criminal Intelligence Unit and Narcotics Vice Division in a liaison investigation of Yakuza activities in Honolulu. The informant I would be working with was a Japanese national who had been a successful businessman. Everything he owned had been seized by law enforcement because of his criminal activities involving prostitution, pornography, and money laundering.

Although he was in his early forties, Nobuo looked like he was still in his early twenties. He was energetic, small-framed, and short, with tailored designer clothes and naturally curly hair. He spoke English quite well in spite of his heavy Japanese accent.

I met him at a small Japanese noodle shop on Uluniu Street in Waikiki. He was comfortable there and enjoyed conversations in Japanese with noodle chefs from Japan who prepared specialty dishes as their customers watched.

Nobuo's business assets had been seized as well, and he had been slowly selling his personal belongings for food. He had severed all ties with his family in Japan and could never return, he said, because of the shame he had brought upon them.

Nobuo was offended at my suggestion that he might consider asking his family or friends for financial assistance. He would never ask them for help, even if he was almost starving and could afford only one bowl of noodles a day.

He had entered into an agreement to work as an informant, not to save himself but to restore the family honor he had lost. How he was supposed to survive and continue his criminal activities for the investigation without his business had not been considered by those who had drawn up his contract.

Nobuo, like me, had to figure out how to accomplish the assignment on his own. Hopefully, he could create a story that would be accepted in his Yakuza-affiliated world.

It was subsequently agreed that he would introduce me to a few young Asian gang members in Honolulu and that I would then negotiate drug deals on my own.

In the weeks that followed, Nobuo introduced me to Sonny, who would later introduce me to Cho. They were two young Korean males in their early twenties who were affiliated with the Korean gangs.

He also introduced me to a few call girls and told me about some of his criminal business associates and the location of their operations, and explained how their businesses were conducted. He described the Korean gangs as "wild and dangerous" and warned me to be very careful.

Nobuo also told me about a few ranking police officers who had been buying cocaine from his friends, and about Japanese nuns being used as couriers to bring in illegal monies from Japan to invest in Hawaii businesses or deposit into our Hawaii banks.

All of Nobuo's information was passed on to my new supervisors, and I was informed that the information would be used for intelligence purposes only and not for prosecution unless I was able to make a drug buy from one of the named suspects.

Susan, a footman in Narcotics, was assigned to work with me in this investigation. Like Christy, she would be working as my cover unit. She was five foot eight, Caucasian-Japanese, busty, and very attractive.

I met with Sonny again and negotiated a cocaine deal. He trusted me because he knew that he could count on what Nobuo had said, that I could move his merchandise if it was good and I could be trusted.

Sonny sold me a packet of Korean Shabu.

"Better than cocaine, but don't do too much. You need more and more too fast," he cautioned in his Korean-accented English. "I will introduce you to Cho later, but he is a very dangerous guy. He doesn't like to meet people."

I agreed to buy crystal Shabu from Sonny instead of cocaine, documenting the first case of the unknown, unidentified drug being introduced on the Honolulu streets.

"You bought shit!" everyone said when I turned in the Shabu as evidence. "It's rock salt or rock candy!" "You were ripped off!" "Typical UC believes everything the crook tells her!" When I tried to explain that it was a new drug on the streets that many chose over cocaine, only a few detectives listened curiously, but the more common response was "You don't know what you're talking about. We would have heard about it if that were true. Don't believe everything the crooks tell you! It's not speed; you just got ripped!" Other officers shook their heads in disdain that I had wasted the buy money.

Despite the ridicule, I submitted the evidence for analysis. The chemical analysis of the Shabu I had bought was completed and returned with a positive result for crystal methamphetamine. A few were surprised but most shrugged it off.

In spite of the positive results of the chemical analysis and the information I relayed that the narcotic I had bought was in high demand on the streets, I was accused of having a "know-it-all UC attitude."

"It's no big deal. It will never catch on. Crystal methamphetamine will never take the place of cocaine," Okimoto snickered, "or the command would have already heard about it." Again I was reminded that I was just an undercover officer and no one wanted to hear what I had to say.

"Don't waste the buy money! Don't buy that shit again. Cocaine will always be the drug of choice in the streets. " "Shabu, cCrystal, ilce, or whatever it's called is unheard of!" "UC's trust crooks more than they trust cops!" were the statements I heard over and over again from many who had never worked in an undercover capacity.

As instructed by my superiors, I turned down offers to be a distributor of the new drug being smuggled into Hawaii by the Korean gangs. Sonny and Cho were confused but they shrugged off my refusal to be part of the huge money-making criminal enterprise.

I knew that my refusal to become a distributor had made Cho suspicious of not only me but also of Nobuo, who had introduced me to their elite circle of friends and vouched for my credibility as a major player in the drug scene.

Even Sonny became nervous. "Don't piss off Cho!" he warned. "He can kill people. No problem!"

I knew very well that declining Cho's offer was a critical error but followed orders and warned Nobuo of what I had been ordered to do. After all, I was just a know-it-all UC and what I thought didn't matter.

Nobuo was upset and worried that his safety would be compromised. After all, it was he who had introduced me to Sonny and Cho, vouching that I could move their product.

"What's wrong with the police department?" he complained. "Cho is a dangerous guy. What do they want us to do?"

Since I couldn't respond to what I didn't understand myself, I stayed away from Sonny and Cho to avoid their doubtful scrutiny. I began to buy groceries for Nobuo out of my own money, which wasn't much, but enough for some fresh vegetables and fruits,

Japanese crackers and canned goods.

At first he refused to accept the groceries out of embarrassment. But I could see that he was slowly starving.

"For me," I explained, "if I come here and I am hungry or thirsty."

Bowing humbly and then turning away with a deflated posture, Nobuo apologized for not having any food to offer me on my visits. He stood quietly in the middle of his living room and began to look around at his apartment.

"I give to you something, too!" he said happily in broken English. A few moments later, Nobuo's brief burst of enthusiasm had ended. He stood silently facing away from me, shaking his head as his shoulder sagged. There was nothing left in his bare, unfurnished apartment. Everything had been seized.

"No problem," I said lightly. "I'll bring my food here. When we get hungry, we'll eat together."

"I will prepare for you now!" Nobuo said, bowing deeply again. "I can cook, too!" he offered excitedly.

"Thank you, Nobuo!" I said, holding back tears. "But I'm not hungry right now. But don't waste it, please. You eat it before it spoils."

He bowed humbly in understanding, and I was thankful that he avoided looking into my eyes.

Nobuo escorted me through Waikiki and introduced me to a few call girls and male exotic dancers who serviced Japanese businessmen. I bought LSD from the girls and Quaaludes from the male dancers.

Ecstasy and Morphine

During the day, I investigated anonymous complaints. I bought the new drug on the street, called ecstasy, from a group of males wearing blue bandanas on their heads, claiming brotherhood and loyalty to the gang known as the Crips. They had been sent by their concerned families living on the mainland, they explained, to relatives in Hawaii in order to force their separation from the mainland gangs.

Instead of severing their gang ties and starting a new life, they had brought with them their colors and their creed, and had banded together, recognizing each other by the colors they wore.

The X was being brought in from Texas, they explained, and had been fronted to their gang to distribute and sell. They had set up drive-through drug deals in the low-income state housing development in Kalihi, and took turns waiting on customers who drove in and out of one of the dead-end parking lots they had set up for business. I documented the first ecstasy case but was ridiculed again for purchasing a bogus unknown drug.

I was sent out one night to buy morphine and guns from Henry, a middle-aged Japanese man who worked as a bartender in one of the numerous cocktail lounges located on Keeaumoku Street in the Honolulu district. It was a strip club, I was told, and the complaint said that the dancers too were selling a variety of drugs.

Greg was a high school classmate, and I knew he recognized me immediately when he walked into the strip club. I pretended I didn't see him and began to panic when he stumbled towards me. He sat a few seat away from me on the bar instead of at the several empty tables on the show room floor. I knew he was drunk.

Greg slumped over on the bar counter, resting his chin on his folded arms, and stared at me, waiting for me to acknowledge him in the middle of negotiations with Henry the bartender.

"What, Jo? You're too good to say hi just cuz you're an undercover cop now?" he slurred angrily when I refused to acknowledge him or to accept his subsequent invitation to join him for a drink at the end of the bar.

Henry stepped back and stared at Greg and then at me.

"I thought your name was Sharon?" Henry asked accusingly.

I made up an excuse that I sometimes give different names to guys I meet in bars, but Greg jumped in to say that I was lying. I immediately excused myself to go to the restroom to escape Henry's further interrogation and noticed that my cover unit, sitting at a table on the show room floor, was watching the dancer and was too far away to hear our conversation above the loud music.

"No need to fuckin' lie!" Greg called out as I walked away from the bar. "Just say you're too fuckin' good to drink with me!" he slurred.

I didn't know that Greg was a regular customer in the club and that Henry knew he worked at the police station as a civilian employee. I didn't know, either, that Henry had slipped something into my drink during my short absence.

"So what's up?" I asked Henry when I returned to the bar, but he glared at me in silence and busied himself washing glasses.

There was a bitter taste when I sipped my drink. My lips tingled with numbness and the walls began to spin.

"Did you put something in my drink?" I asked Henry, who was watching me. During my quick escape and short absence to the restroom, Greg had apparently continued identifying me to Henry as an undercover cop.

"I got nothing to say to you!" he snapped, throwing a towel against the wall behind him. "You come in here to set me up! You wait!" he threatened, stepping back with his arms folded across his chest. "So what did you want? Heroin? Morphine?" he added sarcastically, and I knew he had spiked my drink with one of those drugs.

The last thing I remembered was Greg passed out on the bar as I struggled to stand and then stumbled out of the bar. Everything was spinning as I tried to make it down the flight of stairs to the street until my cover unit finally found me.

Federal agents arrested Henry a few years later, for trafficking in narcotics and firearms.

When I turned in an intelligence report about gang activity, ecstasy, and crystal methamphetamine Shabu becoming the drug of choice over cocaine, Detective Stanley ordered me to stop acting like a know-it-all UC. Although he was no longer in Vice, he had heard that I was making waves again.

A few months later, the Honolulu newspapers published an article quoting one of the Honolulu Police chiefs stating that there was no such thing as gang activity in Honolulu. He also stated that crystal methamphetamine would never take the place of cocaine as the drug of choice, and that both crystal methamphetamine and ecstasy would never be a problem; it was just a fad.

A few years later, a law enforcement speaker at a Narcotics conference gave a presentation on crystal methamphetamine and ecstasy becoming the drug of choice in fast-growing clandestine laboratory enterprises on the mainland. Susan and a few detectives turned to glance at me as I sat in the back of the conference room recalling all the ridicule I had received.

"You were right!" they said during the break, but it was too late. I had been ordered to stop wasting the department's money to buy the drug and stop pursuing the source. Lieutenant Okimoto, of course, ignored me and said nothing.

During this time, I was constantly sent out to bust ex-policemen and often used to open the door on raids and warrants.

"Just knock on the door. When the crook opens it, keep the door open until we rush in. Stick your foot in or your wedge your body in the doorway if you have to," were the typical instructions I received from supervisors. I was often chosen for the assignment because I didn't look like a cop.

"No vest, no gun, no insignias. Just get the door opened."

The Commander

One evening during the investigation, Susan and I walked into a popular bar located at the pier at the beginning of the Waikiki Peninsula. "Buy cocaine from Keoni, an ex-cop who is now the bartender," were the instructions we received.

The room was crowded with a private party. Drugs were everywhere, and no one bothered to be discreet. Susan and I found a small empty booth, and I waited to approach the bartender, who was extremely busy preparing drinks for the demanding crowd.

I finally got up from the table when the drink orders slowed and tried to grab the newly vacated seat at the bar. Just as I started walking up to the bar, a tall man wearing a large Lauhala hat, dark glasses, and an Aloha shirt intercepted my approach.

He leaned over the counter and blocked the empty seat, and I watched him exchange money with Keoni for a matchbook. The man in the Lauhala hat opened the matchbook cover, looked briefly behind the rows of matchsticks, and closed the cover, placing the matchbook into his shirt pocket with a smile.

I glanced back at Susan, who had watched the drug buy, too. Keoni had just poured the man a drink and set it down in front of him.

The man in the Lauhala hat glanced at me standing next to him just as he moved to sit down on the empty barstool. With shock and disbelief, I stared at the man dressed like a tourist in a Lauhala hat. I recognized him immediately as was one of the police commanders Nobuo had told me about. Suddenly feeling sick and nauseated, I turned to look at Susan, who was burying her face in her hands and covering her eyes. She had recognized him, too, and like me, did not want to see what we were seeing.

The commander had recognized me and was visibly stunned as he quickly turned away as if to hide his face. He looked back at me and then at Susan sitting at the table, and then sat motionless, staring at the freshly poured drink in front of him. Keoni continued talking to him, although neither the commander nor I were hearing his words. Time stood still for those few moments.

With concerned confusion, Keoni looked at the commander and then at me.

"What's up?" Keoni asked the commander, in response to his abrupt change of mood and hunched posture. But the commander didn't answer.

"What's going on?" he asked again with an apprehensive tone.

I stood frozen and speechless, expecting the commander to identify me to Keoni, but the commander said nothing. Instead, he shook his head as if trying to wake from the nightmare and realization that I had seen the drug transaction. His shoulders slumped in disgrace, as if he had just gotten busted. The commander sat quietly for a moment and then stood up and walked out of the bar without a word.

Keoni looked at me, and then at Susan, and left the bar to walk outside, too. He never came back into the bar while we were there.

Susan was in shock and was beginning to feel sick. "I heard the rumors about him," she said softly, "but I never believed them!"

I flashed back to my encounters with officers in my prior cases, and I knew that observations without evidence were just allegations.

"At least he didn't burn us," I said, but it didn't help Susan feel any better. The wound in my heart was reopened again. I had heard the rumors and received the information from Nobuo, but I too did not want to believe them.

When the supervisors were notified of what we had observed, Susan was immediately reassigned to another team. I also learned that Keoni never returned to the bar that evening and had quit his job.

Dear God
Truly, in all things I have failed
I put away my belief in miracles
In put away my dreams and false hopes
I lay down my sword
I am tired, I do not belong, I cannot see tomorrow

Journal entry: 1982

Too Many Secrets

One night, my CIU detective informed me that the whole team would be taking an immediate vacation.

"I came to thank you personally," he said, "but nobody expected you to go this far so fast. I can't explain, but I have to leave. You don't know, it but you're knocking on our own back door!"

I had really liked CIU Detective Shiratori, and I sensed that something was very wrong. But no one would talk to me or tell me what was going on. Instead, I was immediately assigned back to a nighttime foot beat in Chinatown, and the investigations were left incomplete.

The city prosecutor had secretly contacted me and asked me to work undercover for the prosecutor's office against a page full of identified police officers, many with rank, who were allegedly involved in illegal gambling and narcotics activities.

It was Nobuo, my Yakuza informant, who finally called me at home to tell me that the feds had taken over our investigation. He had been ordered to tell them everything I had done with him and identify everyone he had introduced me to. Nobuo was then ordered not to talk to any police officers or me.

"Be careful!" he warned.

Nobuo didn't know what was happening or who to trust.

"Nobody working together!" he said in his Japanese-accented English. "They follow you and watch everything you do, too!" he said.

Nobuo explained that every time I left him, Brian from the feds debriefed him on what I was buying and from what source.

"Why doesn't he just ask me?" I asked; after all, we were both law officers.

"I don't know," Nobuo said. "Too many secrets."

Nobuo hadn't seen or heard from CIU Detective Shiratori either. He was now concerned.

"What happened?" he asked.

"I don't know," I answered honestly, and told Nobuo that I was suddenly back in uniform and patrolling a foot beat near the Chinatown fish markets on Kekaulike and Hotel Streets.

"Too dangerous there!" he said in alarm. "Many people know me there. They recognize you, too! I worry for you. Something wrong, I know. Please listen!"

"I have to," I explained. "I know something's wrong, too, but it's my assignment."

I never heard from Nobuo again.

Everyone began trying to debrief me about the cases I had done. Different commanders in the police department and even prosecutors and investigators outside of the police department were constantly calling me about the incomplete investigations, asking who I had investigated or gathered intelligence on.

The questions were focused more upon the dope deals I had observed or done involving police officers and former officers instead of the crooks.

Each caller concluded that I had an obligation to work with his team and warned me not to talk to or trust any other law enforcement agency except theirs. They all said they would protect me if I helped them.

Even Detective Stanley intruded in my life to threaten me again, "Don't burn your own bridges. You better know where your loyalties are!"

He began to tell me about another UC officer who had made the wrong choice by helping the wrong team. Apparently, that officer had helped the prosecutor's office on an investigation and had to leave the island before he got hurt. I turned and walked away before Stanley could finish his story.

After all, I had no bridges of support to burn with him, and he had no right to counsel me on loyalty. His concept of loyalty was politics, and I would never be part of his game. He had no right to even be near me, let alone talk to me, but he wouldn't leave me alone.

A circuit court judge with an honorable reputation found me late one night as I walked my Chinatown foot beat alone and without an assigned partner. It took me a while before I recognized him in the shadows without his judge's robes.

"I know what's happening," he said. "You're all alone in a political mess and everyone's trying to use you but no one's helping you!" "I'm here if you need me." He then handed me his business card with his private home number written on the back.

"Anytime!" he said. "Call me!"

Although many of the supervisors seemed to know what was going on, only the judge known as Togo had offered his help without an ulterior motive or a hidden agenda.

Another officer in CIU constantly told me, "You knew the job was dangerous when you took it," repeating the *Super Chicken* cartoon slogan. It reminded me that I was alone, on my own, and that there was no one to show me the way back to home to myself.

But the young officer was wrong. No one told me that everything I believed in would be destroyed, that my family would get hurt, or how to readjust and become and identify with what I had been brain washed not to be..."a cop".

Most of all, no one told me that when the assignment was done, undercover officers would be left alone to face life's difficulties alone.

Chapter 19
Choices

Trigger

I give up the futility of the struggle for help
And the hope that somehow others will see the truth
I give up trying to forget ... I give up trying to erase the feelings of hurt and betrayal
There's nothing left. I want to come home God

Journal entry: May 24,1982

May 24,1982. Tonight was different. The loneliness and desperation for a friend stabbed painfully at my soul. I had no one to talk to. I was not allowed to talk about my cases, and no one wanted to hear the truth. Even I didn't know what the truth was or who to trust anymore.

Sometimes the rain was warm, sometimes cold, but it had always been cleansing. Tonight the heavens cried the tears that I could not.

This time the scotch did not dissolve me into the escape of slumber. The silent security of my studio apartment did nothing to protect me from the hurt. It could not protect me from my thoughts, my memories or myself. It felt as if my apartment was a cell and the walls were slowly closing in on me instead of keeping the reality of the world outside from crashing in.

The streets had often provided solace; they had become my home and my comfort, but not tonight. I walked in dimly lit alleys and side streets that smelled of urine and garbage. I walked on the main streets and watched others caught up in their own worlds, moving hurriedly through life towards their intended destinations and their dreams. I had none.

"Get an apartment close to the station," my new detectives instructed. It was a good idea to be separated from my family. Distance would keep them safe, and anyone who wanted to find me would not have to search for me at my family's home. I did not want to hurt or jeopardize my family anymore. My one-room apartment on Young Street was just two blocks from the police station in the McCully District and easy to find if anyone wanted to seek me out.

Sleep brought nightmares, and waking only continued them. I was used, violated, and left to suffer alone in silence. I had nothing left, nothing I wanted to do. I had learned the lesson very well, that it was futile to appeal to the judgment of the masses in blue. I realized too that I could never forget and never go back to who I had been.

Every role I played was in conflict with the others. When I tried to be an honest cop, I was hated and distrusted by other cops because I had broken the Golden Rule by taking down a dirty police officer.

In trying to bring honor to my family, I had hurt them and put them in danger. The uniform and badge I had finally been issued represented everything that hurt. The constant struggle to keep the different identities separate was lost; they had begun to merge. There was no threshold to cross between identities, no door to close. Which one was the real me?

To do the undercover assignment, I was forced me to become everything I did not want to be and everything I knew was wrong. Stanley forced me to stay in my undercover identity day and night, with no guidance or supervision. I learned to live in isolation and to forfeit everything I believed in. Nothing mattered except that he was highly successful through my efforts. And by example, he had taught me the lesson of the ultimate betrayal truth, honor, and loyalty.

I was wrong to believe that my nightmares would end and that I would be okay when it was over.

Tonight I was drawn back into the night, into the darkness, into the streets and the rain. I made my way to Central Union Church to pray and find peace, to feel closer to God, to sit in his sight. Maybe he would see me and let me sleep in the comfort of his pocket. But the doors of the church were locked, and I was shut out.

I slipped out into the darkness and wandered around, lost in the shadows. I had forgotten where I lived, what day it was, where I was going, and who I was. Tonight the rain was cold and heartless and drenched my soul.

Neither identity emerged to help me through the difficulty. Both the real me and my street identity had given up and stepped back. There was only a void as they both watched me in silence.

I finally found my way back to my apartment, but the emptiness was unbearable. I called the suicide hotline, but the phone was busy.

Outside my window, a light mist of rain fell and the heavens seemed to call me home. A full moon lit the dark skies through wispy shreds of clouds. It seemed to be guiding me home, lighting my way among the stars. Vast dimensions of time and space, eons of lifetimes past, stood in this moment … still.

There was a moment of indescribable peace and calm.

I am one with the universe. I have no ambition, no determination, and no will to live. I have already died. I finally know the meaning of relief. It is peace. I will close my journal … I am done. All my identities have merged. Everything I am is what I chose to be, but I am too tired to fight.

Warmth that emanated from the center of my back enveloped me. I had a choice, and I chose to die—not at the hands of cowards who would sneak up behind me, but by my own hands. I would release my family from the worry and danger I had unforgivably put them through. I would take back my life and give it back to God. And then I would be free ... then I would set my family free …

I lay on my bed, looking beyond the ceiling into the universe and then I reached out for my Smith and Wesson 38-caliber Chief's Special. I placed the gun to my right temple and pulled the trigger.

Back in Time

It was near noon when I finally woke with the sound of traffic and sunlight filtering through the room. I glanced around, and my surroundings slowly came into focus.

Why am I still here? I thought, dazed and confused, remembering pulling the trigger. My gun was right next to me, lying on the bed.

The hammer had hit the empty chamber. The cylinder had moved forward, past the empty chamber, to the loaded one. The rule of most old school cops is that you leave the first chamber of your gun empty for safety. If the bad guy takes your gun away and fires at you, you still have a split second to react, which may save your life. The rule had indeed saved my life.

A new day had dawned and I forcibly with it. The sun was brilliant in a spotless sky painted cornflower blue. The rain from the night before had washed the streets clean, and everything seemed to be exceptionally bright with a new freshness. My head was clear and my soul felt light. I felt different but didn't know how or why. I found myself standing at the threshold of the past and future, and I didn't know what to do.

As I searched for answers, I realized that if I was willing to die to end the pain and protect my family, I should be willing to live and endure the difficulty to accomplish the same. My decision to end it all would only have made it easier for those who wished me and my family harm. There would be no one left to protect my family from the choices I had made, including this one if I had succeeded. The choice was simple: live or die, give up or continue. I had been given a second chance to choose my own destiny.

The world stood still as I gazed back into my past.

I was born at Kapiolani Hospital in Honolulu. I remember growing up as a child in the Kalihi Valley District at the base of the Koolau Mountain Range on the island of Oahu. I cherished the iridescent blue-and-orange-spotted ladybugs and the colorful dragonflies that hovered around the mango, mountain apple, and tangerine trees that lined the property.

My mother, Jean Kimiko (Kakazu) Takasato, was born in Honolulu to parents who arrived from the Uroku Prefecture in Okinawa. She grew up on a vegetable farm with six brothers and six sisters in the Waikane Valley District.

My father, Roland Takasato Sr., was born in Papaaloa on the island of Hawaii, known as the Big Island. My father's parents came from Goeku, Okinawa, in 1902, and worked on the sugar plantations until his mother died carrying stillborn twins. My dad was only seven years old when he and his two siblings were taken back to Okinawa to live with his grandmother until his father could care for them again.

Not much is known about my family history beyond my parents, except that their parents came from Okinawa. There are things they have never spoken to me about, but the life lessons they taught could have only come from difficulty and strife.

As a child, I eavesdropped on my parents sharing memories of their childhood. Through their reminiscing, I learned the essence of perseverance to attain a goal, honor in truthfulness, and *makoto*, acting with sincerity from the heart.

Both parents came from humble beginnings as *Nisei*, working with the earth in their hands as farmers.

"Make the best of what you have; don't dwell on what you don't have" was my mom's philosophy;

"Don't give up no matter how hard things are" was my dad's.

Difficulties were always dealt with in silence, and whining and blaming others was never accepted. Overcoming difficulties on your own was a way to build strength of character. It was improper to put on emotional displays.

My parents rarely discussed the past, but when they did, I would listen. They had grown up in the generation that had survived the time of the bubonic plague at the harbors, war with Japan, and the years of depression.

I listened intently as they described the explosions they heard, the smoke-filled skies, and the dread they felt when they realized that war with Japan had begun. But as did all Japanese-Americans born in that time of war, they endured any hate and prejudice they experienced against them as *Issei* (first generation to arrive) and *Nisei* (first generation born in the USA).

My father reflected once about the morning of December 7, 1941, and I listened intently to the story he told. It was just before 8:00 a.m., when he at sixteen years of age. He had just left a restaurant in the Pearl Harbor area and was on his way home. The restaurant suddenly exploded behind him, and he ran back through the smoke and dust.

In a moment, a friend he had just talked to lay dead with his head partially blown off, and another friend who had been standing nearby was alive but missing two legs. People were walking around dazed and confused, and some lay dying in the streets. In the days that followed, he scraped flesh off the walls while helping in the cleanup efforts in the Pearl Harbor area.

A few weeks later, FBI agents with military escorts barged into his house and ransacked his home while searching for unknown evidence. They only found a small homemade flag of Japan used for traditional new years' celebrations in an old trunk filled with keepsakes. There was nothing else to seize.

My grandfather, Seiki Takasato, a tiny-framed man who spoke no English, was dragged out of the house without a word of explanation.

My father was only sixteen years old, but he still tried to fight the assemblage of government men until my grandfather looked directly into his eyes and shook his head no.

I saw the silent tears of rage and desperation in my father's eyes when he recalled the incident.

The Constitution and laws of the United States had failed to protect the innocent. My grandfather, Seiki Takasato, was interned from 1942–1946 in Santa Fe, New Mexico.

In spite of what happened to my grandfather, my dad left McKinley High School and enlisted in the army to serve his country. He was assigned to the 25th Division and sent to Osaka, Japan, while my grandfather was still interned. He became an interpreter and was in charge of the Foreign National Dormitory and helped people in Japan, displaced by war to get food, clothing, shelter, and placement. He had learned to speak Okinawan and Japanese from his parents.

In Japan, he saw adults and children eating rats, some too weak to move. He was thankful that he had learned the language of his ancestors from his parents, which enabled him to help the victims of war.

He spoke no further of the devastation and human suffering he saw. Some who he helped wrote him letters for a while when he returned home, but communication eventually stopped. He returned to finish high school in 1948 and made the McKinley High School swim team, but he was disqualified from the Olympic team tryouts because he was too old. He is still today like a dolphin in the water.

My father, his brother, and all six of my mother's brothers served their country in either the army or the air force. Two fought in World War II with the legendary 442nd Regimental combat team, and two received Purple Hearts. The others served in both Korea and Vietnam, and one uncle was a Green Beret. They had been willing to sacrifice their lives for others in service of their country.

From my parents, I learned that truth, honesty, and a sincere heart were traits of an honorable person. To take credit for the efforts of others or to victimize others to get ahead was the conduct of a dishonorable man. I learned to honor my ancestors and to perpetuate the lessons they taught about truth, honor, and perseverance.

"Never be afraid to work hard and always finish what you start" were the words of wisdom passed down through the generations.

Mom always said, "Be honest and kind to others, and learn to forgive." I got the first two lessons down by the time I graduated from high school, but I never got the forgiveness part. I preferred justice.

Dad taught me to face and deal with my fears. "Don't be afraid to stand up and fight for what's right," he said, "but you have to learn when to dodge and duck."

My childhood was always an adventure. I played army instead of dolls, and samurai instead of Jacks. My sisters, Faith and Cheryl, older and younger, were well behaved, clean and neat, and always gentle. I was not.

My brother, Roland Jr., was born eleven years after me and he too would eventually swear an oath of service as an officer in the Honolulu Police Department. He too would perpetuate the lessons of honor and integrity passed down through the generations.

I loved to do ladybug races, placing two ladybugs on a flat surface to see which one ran the farthest on the ground before flying away. Grasshoppers and crickets were everywhere, butterflies and dragonflies, too. I used to pretend to be an insect and see things through their eyes. I knew I was a giant to them while the small weed was their tree.

Dad taught me how to catch and carry big praying mantises by the spine. One day, I brought a praying mantis nest into the house and hid it in the bedroom even after being told a hundred times to leave my captive insects out in the yard. The nest hatched while we slept, and my sisters woke the next morning screaming hysterically. Hundreds of tiny baby praying mantises were crawling everywhere! I wasn't slapped or spanked, but the silent treatment that followed was worse as I watched my mom clean out the room.

I always took risks and loved walking on makeshift gangplanks, climbing trees, and balancing on top of high rock walls. Instead of pretending to be a fairy princess, I was always pretending to be a samurai, ninja, or adventurer. I tried to make a tree house by watching my dad build things out of pieces of wood that had no meaning until he put them together. The tree house I built all by myself was a piece of wood to sit on with imaginary walls and a roof.

Our usual evening family outings were to go to the nearby Toho and Toyo Japanese theatres to watch samurai movies. Although he suffered injuries and usually had no food, the samurai remained true to his cause of honor for the lord he served. He never went home until the mission was complete. The good samurai was always ready to die for honor, and the samurai's wife was always at home, suffering in silence, unable to do anything but wait. She was always pictured standing alone and looking in the direction of the sunrise and sunset of each day, waiting to see her husband's silhouette returning home to her.

Watching samurai movies taught me the lessons of undying loyalty and commitment to a cause and the honor of self-sacrifice for those you love. I knew right away that I wanted to be the samurai and not the subservient female waiting at home, wondering what her destiny would be.

Mom took us on monarch butterfly caterpillar food excursions, catching the bus to pick leaves from crown flower trees growing wild along the streets. She was always sewing with tireless patience and love, creating different garments for us to wear, and beautiful blankets out of different materials.

I also remember our walks through the Chinatown market place, seeing the different people shopping for things that were unfamiliar to me. Headless, featherless chickens and hairless baby pigs were hanging upside down by their feet. Live lobsters, crabs, and fishes moved and swam nervously in large tanks, waiting to be bought for someone's dinner. The different smells of different shops selling herbs and teas. There was always the smell of mothballs in each of the dry goods stores.

Above all, there were ethnic foods everywhere! Vegetables and fruits, herbs and spices, steamed buns, sweet breads, and sauces. Some of the items for sale smelled bad but were not spoiled. Some goods were fermented but not smelly.

One day after school, while in the kindergarten class at Kalihi Elementary School, I decided not to go straight home from school. I decided instead to start a quest for honor and explore the world on my own.

Just before dark, I noticed my mom running up the steep street toward the school, hysterically calling my name. When she finally saw me, she ran up to me, gasping for breath. I did not understand the desperate fear I saw in her eyes, which melted into sobbing tears of relief.

"Don't you ever do that again!" she scolded. She had been searching for me for hours. It was the first time I had made her cry, and it would not be the last.

At five years old, I already knew I wanted to fight against the evils of the world, but I knew too that there was no such thing as a female cop, and the samurai no longer existed. In fact, there was really no female anything, except a teacher or a nurse, so I thought I might be one, too.

For me, my journey into the Honolulu Police Department was a spiritual journey.

The Vow

Solitude my safety
Silence my defense
Loneliness my companion forever

Journal entry: August 10, 1983

I made a choice that day *to live,* even if it meant my journey would be difficult and I would be alone.

I made a promise to myself to always help new officers who came after me. Even if I didn't know all the answers, I could at least be there for the others, and they would know that they were not alone and abandoned. I was the first female Narcotics undercover officer, and I would not leave the department until a line of support was established to assist other undercover officers, especially the females. I had to survive my assignment.

I made a vow that day to never give up again, and then perhaps maybe one day, I would bring honor to my mother, my father, and my family, instead of tears.

I had heard about police officer suicides but never knew I was falling until I had almost become another statistic. I had to figure out how I had lost myself and my hope in tomorrow. I needed to be sure that I would never get to that crossroads again.

"A Time for Change"

We are the Sentinels
We are the Guardians
We are the Peace-Keepers for all to turn to
We cannot show fear
We cannot be weak
We cannot have faults
We represent the strength and the Honor and the Integrity of our society
Crucify us, judge us, condemn us
For every action we take and every decision we make
And when we need help, when we have lost all hope
When we have nowhere to turn
Then we seek to go home ... to GOD ... to peace
We take back control of our lives and give it back to GOD
This is who we are ... That is what we do

Journal entry: February 4, 2002

Kerry

I believe in Truth, Honor, and Justice
I am a Cop
But before that, I am a person
With Rights, with emotions, with Feelings
My badge makes me nothing more than me
It does not give me strength, wisdom, or courage
It does not turn me into a Sentinel or a guardian
It is merely a symbol of the position I represent
It is I who makes it shine
Creates its meaning, earns its respect

Journal entry: 1983

I had changed that day, but I wasn't sure how. I started looking around for other undercover officers to talk to but found none who had shared the same experiences. No one had ever broken the Golden Rule, and they all confessed that they would never take down another cop.

"It's your fault," was the usual condescending response from most of the officers who had seen the challenges I faced and who themselves had never been assigned to the Narcotics Vice Division or worked in an undercover capacity. I had already learned by experience not to try to justify my decision.

There were a few other Narcotics officers who had bragged that they had it all together and under control. But these officers had not really completed the same assignments, taken down another police officer, or gone into the streets without training.

They had done mostly surveillance and support work, which was totally different.

I had learned that several undercover officers before me had resigned bitterly after their assignments or crossed over the line to the criminal side. A few had taken their own lives, and a few were still in the department but, like me, had learned the code of silence too well.

Several months later, my CIU detective and several other supervisors were arrested for various federal offenses. I never knew why.

About a year later, I learned about the status of my interrupted CIU investigation by reading about it in a newspaper article. My suspects had all been arrested in a federal investigation, and Nobuo's life was in jeopardy because he was publicly identified as a Yakuza informant who was now being forced to testify.

One day after my shift, I walked into the tiny bar next door to the police station and, as usual, several of the officers stood up and left after I entered. I sat at the bar and noticed that one of the cops remained seated a few seats away from me, drinking by himself.

"You're not leaving too?" I asked sarcastically.

"Nope," he shrugged. "I'm not leaving," he said in a matter-of-fact tone.

I fully expected that in a few seconds he would tell me to get out but he remained quiet.

"You must not know who I am," I prodded curiously, still feeling irritated that everyone else had walked out. I was convinced that if he knew who I was, he would walk out, too.

"I know who *you* are. The *real* question is whether or not you know who *I* am," he replied calmly.

I paused to study the tall Caucasian cop and failed to recognize him. More than that, I couldn't understand why he didn't leave like the others. By his demeanor, he didn't seem to be anyone I had ever had a confrontation with, and for some unknown reason, I didn't feel any hostility from him.

"Do you remember me from the Point After disco?" he asked.

I began to frantically search my memory of all the undercover assignments I had done at the popular Waikiki nightclub, but I still couldn't remember him.

"I was the other undercover officer working in the place," he smiled calmly.

Trying to recall the drugs deals I made at the Waikiki discotheque was like rewinding and watching clips of an old movie in vivid detail. I began to relive the drug deals as if I had traveled back in time. The blaring music, swirling lights, and the voice of the disc jockey flooded back like an overwhelming wave of melancholy. I suddenly remembered that

Stanley had cautioned me about another undercover officer working in the discotheque.

"Stay away from the back bar," Stanley had warned, but he refused to identify or describe who I was supposed to stay away from. I was only told that the other undercover officer could cook up some awesome beer hot dogs.

Kerry Finuff and I spent several hours sharing stories about our undercover assignments. We had both been assigned to Detective Stanley, and I had begun my investigations just as Kerry was ending his. It didn't bother Kerry that the other officers who came into the bar were staring at him with contempt in their eyes for talking to me.

There was no malice in Kerry's eyes. I saw instead compassion, understanding, and a quiet wisdom I had never seen in the eyes of another officer. It was incredible to learn that we had shared some of the same insights and feelings about our undercover tour of duty even though we had worked separately. The issues of not having backup and support, as well as being excluded from any operational planning, were shared difficulties.

"It's not about being male or female. It's about being a good cop," Kerry said in parting.

My struggle to find my old identity had been futile, and I had finally realized that the person I used to be had been forever destroyed. I could not identify with the officers I had met, and my street identity, although no longer in existence, had become a permanent part of me. I was stuck between two worlds, and the shattered pieces my two adverse lifestyles could not fit back together as one.

Like Kerry Finuff and Terry Bledsoe, I was used and abused and then abandoned. There was no avenue of help to heal the wounds of betrayal or readjust to a normal life.

In my struggle to find a way to live my life, I had overlooked this simple and basic truth. With those few words, Kerry given me a new path to follow and ended my conflict. His words became my inspiration and helped me to stay focused through the years of difficulties and confrontations that lay ahead. I had learned a way to live my life as a police officer and still continue with my search for truth and honor.

"It's about being a good cop!"

It's time to stop looking for acceptance!
Life is so interesting when we finally realize
That the Happiness we strived for was all simply an illusion
And we are left alone again
To contend with ourselves
In the shadow of loneliness

Journal entry: January 6, 1983

ॐ

Chapter 20
A New Direction

The Healing Begins

In the years that followed, it became obvious that I should never expect support or understanding from the department's psychologist or the majority of the department's personnel and supervisors. Most never understood or wanted to hear the truth about the stress factors and safety issues in the undercover assignments. Most supervisors would become very defensive or offended if stress and safety issues were brought to their attention, and the words "vicarious liability" became more important to them than focusing upon the problems.

"If you don't know about it, you're not responsible" and "What you don't know can't hurt you" became the excuse for not addressing problems and taking responsibility as supervisors.

"Who do you think you are?" "Undercovers always cause trouble." "You're just trying to make us look bad!" were their usual responses. It was quite some time before I finally realized that those who spoke those words felt ignorant and insecure about facing the truth.

A few attorneys had advised me to sue both my supervisors and the police department. "I heard what happened to you; you can make millions!" they had coaxed. Furthermore, you can set the precedence for how the department should supervise undercover officers and female officers!" Those same attorneys later admitted their relief that I had refused to file sexual harassment or a hostile work environment suit.

"We didn't know what this involved," they confessed. "We have to work with the police department. We have to live and work in this state. If you ever decide to sue the department, you would have to find someone from another state." In the end, it was all about their percentage, and they stepped back quickly when they realized there would be difficulties.

It was never about hurting the department or making big bucks, as many had tried to persuade me to do. It was simply about helping undercover officers.

As time passed, a few screenplay writers approached me to tell my story. While some hated police officers, others represented the female rights platform. Some even wanted to create a whole new *Hawaii Five-0* series, and others wanted to write a Hawaii *Charlie's Angels* movie. Each writer saw big money to be made, making demands and judgments, without understanding the undercover issues.

None of these people really cared about the undercover officer's sacrifice or stressors. No one saw the unquestioned loyalties they held for their respective police departments or the deep commitment each had for their assigned missions. For them, it was all about their percentage or royalties.

Very slowly, other undercover officers and former undercover officers contacted me to let me know that they had shared the same difficulties—isolation, loneliness, and negative judgments—and had no one to turn to. Many still felt betrayed and had even left their families, unable to change back to normalcy. When an officer showed signs of weaknesses or flashbacks, he found out very quickly that there was always no help or support.

"You better see a psychiatrist or just quit!" was the general response, which always came in a patronizing or defensive tone.

It wasn't long before I realized that the negative experiences and difficulties that undercover officers shared were not personal failures or gender based. They were the normal response to the adversities of the job and were still haunting many undercover officers years after the assignment.

Flashbacks, isolation, guilt, and loneliness were more severe depending upon how deep the officer infiltrated the criminal world, how long he stayed in an undercover role, and how controversial the undercover assignment was.

It became apparent that virtually all of us had hidden our difficulties for fear of being labeled "emotionally and mentally affected." If these officers sought help with their emotions or had difficulties with feelings of guilt, they would be ridiculed or embarrassed and judged inept.

A few officers were even removed from their assignments and declared unstable and then abandoned to contend alone with feelings of alienation and guilt for having emotions.

As soon as undercover officers showed any emotional reactions to their assignment, the immediate response would be, "Go see a shrink! I'm just telling you that as a friend."

Undercover officers were not allowed to be human or to display any sensitivity to the difficulties we faced.

"Just forget the past!" too many "friends" had told me in patronizing tones.

Much like a friend who returned from Vietnam with Post Traumatic Stress Disorder, I knew that I could not forget a trauma that had not yet been faced, accepted, or understood.

No one bothered to listen to the undercover officers' experiences. Supervisors were only concerned with stats. If they did listen, it was easier to respond with quick judgments and callous remarks than to try to understand what they had not experienced. Like many other undercover officers, it was easier for me to be alone.

As the years went by, there was still no psychological help for readjusting from the undercover identity change. None of the supervisors understood the negative effects of the transitions or seemed to care enough to look at undercover trauma. All too often, undercover officers were pulled from assignments and thrown back into uniformed patrol on the following working day. Most supervisors and commanders were oblivious to the stress they caused the officer, especially if investigations were still incomplete and suspects had not yet been arrested.

"If you have a problem, it's an undercover problem. If you can't handle being a real cop, just quit" was the usual response when undercover officers displayed difficulties with immediately adjusting to uniformed patrol.

Undercover officers were crucified if they felt any guilt or remorse resulting from creating friendships only to betray them with arrest and prosecution. If they were depressed, they were condemned. If they asked for help, they were openly humiliated. If they shared their trauma with the wrong person, they were told they needed psychiatric help.

I began to understand that experiencing flashbacks is a healing process. It is the mind's way of slowly and intermittently bringing back the memory of the traumatic incidents by reliving the trauma a little at a time, to eventually face, understand, and finally accept what had happened. With each flashback, a little healing occurred and lessened the traumatic reactions to the incident.

Politics

"Cops are always competing with each other. You guys don't work together and help each other out," too many informants had said through the years. In the investigative and covert fields, it was often true.

> *Aloha Chief Keala*
> *Filled with sadness, I watched a Great Lord*
> *Lay down his sword*
> *Were I his warrior, I would do battle*
> *Were I his sage, I would comfort*
> *Were I his vassal, I would follow*
> *Alas, I am but a simple farmer*
> *Tending his fields the best I can*

Journal entry: February 25, 1983

During the selection process for a new Honolulu police chief in 1983, members of the Police Commission and a few commanders who sought the vacant position brought up my undercover tour of duty. Each person sought to drudge up the difficulties and incidents of questionable ethics, but none of them were interested in helping undercover officers. Instead, they were only interested in obtaining negative information against other commanders to use as a political hammer against their opponents. Two factions fought for the top position, and both called me for interviews to learn any information that could malign the reputations of their opponents.

One faction counseled me on loyalty and being part of the winning team.

"Who's approaching you?" they asked, and, "What are they asking you to do?"

Even Stanley had searched me out again and found me in front of the police station. He tried to lecture me about loyalty.

"You better make the right choice and get on the winning team," he warned. I walked away when he went on to say that he was on the winning team, that he would take care of me.

"Don't pull a Johnson!" he warned as I walked away. I didn't want to hear what Stanley had to say, and it repulsed me to see him. All I knew was that whatever team he was on, I wanted no part of.

Officer Johnson was police officer acting in an undercover capacity. All I knew was that he suddenly quit and moved out of state to escape either reprimand or retaliation from the police department for working with an outside agency.

The other faction counseled me on my duty to stop the political favoritism of the winning team and force the commanding officers on that team to take responsibility for their actions and their failures.

"Make complaints!" they pushed. "You can make a Prosecutorial Misconduct complaint. What they did to you and put you through was wrong! Just keep it internal and we'll take it from there and take care of you!"

But I did not want to be a pawn in their political rivalry. I refused to make IA complaints against the commander Susan and I had observed buying cocaine or share information I had gathered about other officers and a few politicians involved in illegal gambling and narcotics activities. I knew that without evidence, the intelligence information would be deemed hearsay and I could be found guilty of malicious statements against a member of the Honolulu Police Department.

It's all in the Records Division, I would answer. I had turned in all my investigative reports and intelligence information to my supervisors, but then later found that many of my reports were missing. Everyone seemed to know that I had kept copies of my investigations and a journal. I subsequently received a written reprimand for loyalty and truthfulness.

Soon thereafter, rumors that I was going to take down commanders began to circulate again. For the next several years during my assignment to uniformed patrol, rumors continued about the undercover investigative assignments I had worked on with the Narcotics Vice Division and the Criminal Intelligence Unit. But as always, I found good officers who would become my lifelong friends in spite of the talk.

In every new assignment, I was greeted with the comment, "I heard about you!" usually followed by insults or subtle threats from officers I had never met before.

Every assignment in the Patrol Division came with the challenge of proving myself. During the first few months, I never had any backup. The other officers watched to see if I could handle a patrol beat on my own or whether I would be a crybaby and make complaints to IA or be a wimp and refuse to go on cases alone.

Officers routinely called off on issuing parking violations to avoid being sent to back me up when I was dispatched to affrays or domestic disputes. On one occasion, an HPD dispatcher was audibly choking back tears on the police radio when she tried to send me help and backup and could find none. Every time I tried to use my police radio, unknown officers would key their microphones to block out my transmissions.

There were never enough portable radios available when I tried to check one out from the arsenal. If and when one was finally available, it didn't work. But the quality of the radio was insignificant without a good dispatcher at the console. The dispatcher was the true lifeline to safety in patrol. One dispatcher actually waited for me to finish my shift in order to tell me that she was a friend and couldn't take it anymore.

Delphine was a seasoned dispatcher and had too often witnessed what was happening to me in the streets. Although I had never met her, she told me how she had many times cried in frustration behind the radio, and finally waited to meet me in person to say she felt helpless and outraged at what was happening.

Delphine was the dispatcher who had sent me on an affray that night, with numerous reports of multiple suspects, unknown weapons, and glass beer bottles flying into the streets. She had made several calls for officers to assist, but no officer responded to back me up on the case.

Delphine had yelled over the air, "Knock this shit off," at the anonymous officers who blocked her transmission when she tried to find a second unit. Her voice cracked when she told me to wait until she could find help from units from another district.

"That's okay," I had said, and responded to the assignment alone. I knew that no one would answer the call.

> *Blue horizons . . . wispy clouds . . . sunset*
> *The shadows play with leaves in the wind . . . Loneliness*
> *Alone again . . . Emptiness . . .. My soul in silence waits.*

Journal entry: June 28,1984

Like many other officers, I ended up buying my own portable police radio in order to make it a little safer for myself on the streets. I eventually proved myself to my beat partners by handling cases alone and not making any Internal Affairs complaints.

Instead of relying on the support of my beat partners, I learned to count on the residents living on my beat. I learned the identities of the good citizens in the community and worked with their anonymous information and support. However, when I tried to establish a community support group and an anonymous information hotline, I was called "UC affected" and a "wannabe social worker."

My proposal for a community support group was refused and returned with an explanation that once the department opened its doors to work with citizens, it would lose its control, power, and authority.

Jim was a TV reporter I had met on the beat at numerous cases in the Makiki area, and I had learned to trust him as an honorable and ethical news reporter. We had talked about possibly broadcasting information on wanted suspects on the six o'clock news. When I turned in my proposal, it was suggested that I should quit the department and look for a job with the Department of Social Services.

Years later, *Community Relations* and *Crimestoppers* programs were initiated with the same agenda and basic procedures I initially outlined and was ridiculed for.

But it was during my twelve years of patrol as a beat officer that I found the friendship of outstanding officers, male and female, who put their lives on the line every day. I would finally come to know the true courage of the uniformed patrol officer: first to approach, first to confront, and the first line of defense for the innocent victims.

Every case was a loss or a tragedy, an injury or death, a confrontation or an arrest. There was no time for preparation, no forewarning of difficulties and dangers, and usually no thanks from the community for any job well done. But criticism and judgment would always come too quickly, for everything we did and for everything we didn't do.

It was during these years that I came to know the great hearts of the dispatchers. Unseen and unnoticed except for their voices, they were the lifelines for officers out on the beat. Like guardian angels, the good dispatchers kept watch over us from afar, sending help or providing as much information as they could to help us with our unknown confrontations. Many held their breath until they heard our voices again, after having to send us to cases with reports of weapons and violence. The experienced dispatchers would remain calm in a critical incident and know what we needed before we asked.

Secret Support

"You should forget," they say
"What the Code of Silence had forbid revealed"
But I cannot forget what I have not yet faced
Shattered dreams, fading realities
Emptiness, lost illusions, incredible loneliness
Haunting memories driving my soul to an unknown destiny
To what end . . . to what tomorrow?
Slipping back into the void
The unfinished nightmares incessantly lingering
Like shadows of the night . . . like shadows of the past
Ever close yet far away
Intangible and heartless
I shall leave the UC s a legacy, unending and proud
Of debts we paid that were never owed. One day I shall tell their story

Journal entry: October 10,1986

It wasn't long before a secret support system began to develop, and through the years, even during my patrol assignment, a number of undercover officers secretly sought me out to discuss their difficulties or just to find a friend who would understand their doubts and fears without the patronizing negative judgments.

Each undercover officer's experiences and the intensity of his stressors differed, but all the undercover officers who found me knew that I would never betray their confidence, judge them for their tears, fears, and doubts or their failed attempts at drinking away the depression. They knew I would never walk away when they were in trouble.

A few undercover officers would call in the twilight hours of the morning; a few would find me on the beat in the middle of a busy day to vent their anger, frustrations, and tears.

Although I had no answers to end their difficulties, they knew they had at least found a friend who would never cut them off and suggest that they see a psychiatrist. I, at least, would allow them to be human.

In February of 1985, I married a young police officer who seemed unafraid to be an individual in a department that stressed conformity and identified officers only by identification numbers, badge numbers, and beat numbers. No one was allowed to be an individual, but he dared to be one, and more important, he made me laugh again.

He too had known who I was and what I had done, but he was unaffected by the warnings to stay away from me. We soon became great beat partners and friends.

As soon as we were married, the department separated us and enforced the mandatory rule that married officers could not work on the same shift or in the same district. We complied, even though a few couples were exempt from the rules and regulations that we were subjected to.

We rarely spent time together or did anything together, and even the laughter eventually stopped when the old controversies of my undercover career began to surface again after I received a new assignment to the Alpha Detail.

In 1986, during my uniformed patrol assignment, I was the first female officer to receive the Hawaii State Law Enforcement's Officer of the Year award, and also the Loyalty award from the Veterans of Foreign Wars. Plain-clothes details to support the uniformed patrol division were being formed, and though I did not submit the customary request to transfer to a new assignment, I was assigned to the Alpha Detail.

The Alpha Detail initiated undercover narcotics investigations without experienced supervisors or safeguards for the undercover officer and his family. It was all about competing for statistics, and for the most part, no one worked together or helped each other out.

While assigned to the detail, I learned from confidential informants on the streets that one of the police officers working in an undercover capacity had been bragging to everyone in discos and bars about his assignment, and openly identifying his gang member suspects. Everyone in the streets knew that to escape prosecution, the witness had to be killed.

My attempts to inform supervisors that the undercover officer, as well as the other UCs in the detail, needed help and guidance were met with disdain. Instead, the undercover officer's sergeant and the lieutenant were annoyed at my intrusion into their "secret" investigation.

Highly offended, they refused to listen to the information and warnings I tried to relay about the identity of the officer being compromised and that the identity of the suspects in the covert investigation were already common knowledge in the streets. I was told that I was acting like a know-it-all, trying to make them look bad, and that I was unbalanced and stressed out because I had no babies.

"Don't be a social worker. It's none of your business. Why don't you quit and be a counselor. Stop trying to embarrass the department. You should be making babies to balance your life."

Expect from each man only what he chooses to be
Judgments predetermined, words unheard
No justifications can overcome
The barriers of arrogant attitudes and prejudices learned
It is rather for us to understand instead the mirror in each man's soul
To be content with the knowing, to observe the learning
To silently extend the experience
No words can confront a judgment passed

Journal entry: April 8, 1987

Instead of helping the undercover officers, I was ordered to participate in a psychological review by a police psychologist, who informed me that his detailed evaluation would be sent back to commanders and that I had no confidentiality rights. "They pay my salary," he said.

Since the psychologist had no experience as a police officer and was incapable of understanding undercover stressors, I gave him a copy of my stress analysis. The police psychologist read my stress analysis and promptly had it published as his own research after verifying my analysis with surveys he created to test my findings.

Police officers attending a University of Hawaii psychology class immediately recognized my stress analysis information and reported him to the commanders of the police department. The officers knew too that the police psychologist had failed in his attempt to be a reserve police officer and could not have achieved any in-depth understanding of undercover stressors on his own.

When word finally reached me about what had happened, he responded to my confrontation by saying, "It's too late; I already published."

Months later I was informed that he was reprimanded. I was also told to forget about filing a plagiarism suit since everything I did as a police officer was owned by the Honolulu Police Department. Instead of helping undercover officers, the police psychologist, like Stanley, had gained recognition and profited from my efforts, difficulty, and suffering.

Tragically, the undercover officer I was concerned about was murdered by his suspects. The Narcotics Vice Division made it very clear in a media statement that the murdered officer was not under their supervision or attached to their division.

Meanwhile, the other undercover officers in the detail fought to remain loyal to their commitment to behave like good soldiers. They were forced to remain on the streets and hang out with their suspects with no guidance or instructions except "Don't get too close."

They were left in extreme distress, trying on their own to hang on to their personal lives and relationships with their families the best they could.

My assignment with the Alpha Detail ended, and so did my marriage. Eventually, the detail was dissolved.

As long as I live I shall never conform, never give in, never concede
If conforming, giving in, conceding
Means the interruption and forfeiture of ideals
To embody an attitude of prejudice, favoritism, and spiritual weakness
I would prefer to live in Silence, dwell in my dreams
And escape to the solitude of the mountains and the seas
These things I have made my priorities
Therefore my shadow follows me beyond the judgments, beyond the prejudice, beyond the slander
of the majority
For I have learned that my shadow is not a hindrance
But just another me . . . when I walk in the light
And when I am tired, I slip into God's pocket and cry

Journal entry: April 15,1987

Even through the years that followed, UCs were never recognized, thanked, or honored in successful undercover operations. Only their respective supervisors and commanders received recognition for the job well done. The efforts and sacrifices of the undercover officers were never credited or validated.

Someone has to make it through and overcome the difficulties. Someone has to be there for the officers and let them know that it's okay to be truthful, honest, and just, and that it's also normal to have trauma from an undercover assignment. It's okay to believe in God and take guidance from spiritual faith, but most of all, it's okay to be human.

Let me live on the wings of my dreams
Soar to the Heavens like birds in flight
A tree is but a tree
For these things, we accept as they are
The trees, the sky, the birds in flight
Thus let my soul be free from judgment
I am what I am, in spite of your perceptions

Journal entry: June 15,1987

The cool, crisp air floated through the silent night
Breaking into dawn
And with the rising of the sun
Came the stark clarity of reality
The scent of cleansing, the sounds of life
The sight of brilliance, the taste of tears
The beating of my heart, relentless repetition
My Soul flies free among shreds of clouds
Against sky blues
Truth and reality . . . the sword at my side

Journal entry: June 1987

The changes came slowly, both within the department and within myself. Each day brought new learning and a deeper understanding. I prayed every morning for guidance and protection, and every night I said a prayer of thanks that I was returning home safely.

In 1987, I was the first female police officer to be nominated for the Outstanding Young Persons of Hawaii. Although selected as one the finalists, I had failed to participate in the final interview because of my assignments.

A light shower of rain fell
Leaving a soft blanket of dew
on blades of grass
The coolness of the night
Comforted the fire in my heart
Burning tears melted
into the silence of Solitude

Journal entry: October 28, 1987

In 1990, I became a single parent of a baby girl who would not only fill the void in my life but would also become the true essence of my love and joy. I had finally found my happiness. I named her Michele after

Saint Michael, God's right-hand warrior of light, who was known as the patron saint of police officers and firefighters. Her middle name, Takeko, meant "warrior" or "strong and versatile like the bamboo," and was inspired by one of my closest friend and beat partner, Gene Kalua.

I raised Michele on my own with no child support from a cop who expected me to be loyal to him, despite his denial of who we were to him. He thought nothing of his deception and lies, often calling me weird for my constant strife for truth and honor.

"Nobody thinks like you. No one will accept you," he said. He didn't care who he lied to or who he withheld the truth from as long as he retained his honorable macho façade.

"I made you no promises," he said, "and no one wants to be with a female who already has a child." I worked as a part-time security officer for several years, not only to pay for medical bills but also to make ends meet, but I never asked him for financial assistance. If his support didn't come from his heart, I didn't want anything from a court order or a forced obligation.

From him I learned to despise the words "I would have … was planning to … was going to," which I realized were always excuses when someone failed at their commitments and responsibilities. Again I had to learn to continue on my own when others stepped back.

In 1995, I was finally promoted to detective. In previous exams, I had lost "time and experience" credits for the time I had spent in the undercover assignment before entering the police academy. It had been a constant battle to correct the city and county records. My ranking had suffered.

"If you make waves about this, it will affect all the other promotions and it will be time for the next test anyway."

As a detective, I was constantly placed on special assignments, working back and forth between two divisions, Vice and CID. All too often, when a controversial assignment came up, especially if it possibly involved police officers, the assignment was given to me.

"I know you can handle it. You should be glad. It's a compliment," my supervisors explained. It didn't matter if I would suffer again. As always, when the difficult investigation was completed, no one bothered to say thank you after taking their bows, and no one would approve my overtime for those assignments.

When bulletproof vests became mandatory equipment, I was told I'd have to buy one on my own or I'd be banned from the road.

The vest cost $825 with a police discount. As a single parent with no child support, I couldn't afford it, except with a credit card. I was being reassigned to the Narcotics Vice Division on the following day for another special assignment, and both the Criminal Investigation Division and the Vice Division had left me out of their personnel order list. Each command had insisted that I belonged to the other division, who should have included me in the request for issued equipment. For several years, I shared a desk in CID with a detective on the midnight watch. I was never given a desk or a computer since I was never expected to remain in one assignment for too long.

April 1999. Nineteen years had gone by, and the loneliness, nightmares, and hurt from my undercover assignment had lessened but still not ended. It was time for me to stop hoping for understanding and healing and do what I had to: finish my journals.

It was time for me to accept that I would never really belong and that no one would understand or ever know the truth of what had happened in 1980.

I had always felt compelled to go back in time, to do the investigation right and to finish the lines in the link chart. I believed that if I could do everything over, I would come back unhurt and maybe complete. Then maybe I could put everything away and finally accept and understand what had happened to me.

The trauma of my memories would then stop, the silence would no longer be threatening, and the nightmares would finally end. I knew I needed to finish the journals, and maybe then the trauma of my undercover life would end.

Did you ever have your life controlled by those who care
Only about what you can do for them?
Expect you to accept less, cover their deceit
And dwell in the silence of their mistreatment
Have you ever seen the Truth, twisted and bent?
Have you ever had a nightmare and then woke to find it wasn't a dream?
Have you ever tried your best and then been called stupid for trying?
Have you ever been honest and been called a fool?
Have you ever believed in Truth and watched the liars win?
Have you ever been afraid to be violated in your sleep?
These things I have seen ... these things I have come to know

Journal entry: February 9, 2000

Once again, I was stuck between the Narcotics Vice Division and the Criminal Investigation Division, working under two different commands. I was constantly placed on numerous special assignments at the whim of the respective commanders. I was given no adjustment time, nor was I left in one place long enough to establish a link of companionship or be a part of the camaraderie within the units. Once again, I was the different one, bouncing between different divisions, even units within the divisions, leaving me no sense of belonging or even where I would be on the following day.

Most of all, there would again be no support in times of difficulty. I never wanted to be "the lone wolf," as many described me. The command had forced me to be what I had become.

But through those years, I had found the friendships of the innumerable county, state, and federal law officers who, like me, believed in truth, honor, and justice. They were law officers from the Honolulu Police Department and the various state and federal agencies who would never be swayed by favoritism, prejudice, or politics. They would never hide behind the abuse of power and authority or blame others for their errors and mistakes. They never wore their badges with an attitude of arrogance and power. For those exceptional law officers, their badges were symbols of the ideals of justice and the oaths they had sworn to the service of those ideals.

They too believed that politics and favoritism were not synonymous with law enforcement and justice. Honesty, integrity, and accountability were not just words on a mission statement; they were a way of life. Some of those good officers were my beat partners in the uniformed patrol divisions while others were officers and federal special agents I worked with in multi-jurisdictional plain-clothes units and undercover operations.

We had always stood by each other during critical incidents and hostile confrontations, good times and bad, laughter and tears. We shared happiness at weddings and supported each other through divorces. We celebrated the blessings of the birth of our children and shared tears of sorrow at funerals of family, friends, and fallen comrades. In the hearts of these exceptional law officers I found manifest the true essence of honor and integrity. We shared a bond of eternal friendship in a lifestyle that only law officers could truly understand.

I learned that for every law officer who had tainted his badge, there are hundreds of unrecognized officers who wear their badges with honor, dignity, and integrity, living lives of thankless sacrifice.

Although I had learned, overcome, and accomplished much and had finally found true friendship, the wounds of my undercover assignment had still not healed and remained a hidden burden that I could not share. Perhaps the hurt, anger, and isolation I still felt would be with me forever

Nothing stays the same
Lose your self-importance and dissolve the hurt of judgment
Lose arrogance and anger disappears
Expect nothing . . . mistreatment no longer matters
Stand alone . . . manipulation cannot touch you
Listen to the music . . . gossip cannot affect you
Stand back, be silent, and learn

Journal entry: September 9, 2000

Finding Chief Band

In February of 2001, I was again placed on a special assignment to the Narcotics Vice Division as a detective in the Criminal Asset Forfeiture Unit.

One morning, my new supervisor, Lieutenant Kimura, handed me a copy of an article contained in a recent issue of the *FBI Law Enforcement Bulletin*. The article was entitled "Managing Undercover Stress: The Supervisor's Role," coauthored by Stephen H Band, PhD, which was a reprinted article originally published in February of 1999.

"It's exactly what you've been trying to say," Lieutenant Kimura commented.

The article focused upon a newly established Undercover Safeguard Unit within the FBI. I was overwhelmed. It was advocating what I had essentially written twenty-one years earlier in my undercover stress analysis papers.

I suddenly felt compelled to write a letter to Dr. Band, who was a supervisory special agent and the chief of the FBI Behavioral Science Unit. Again, I broke one of the Golden Rules: never talk to an outside agency … especially the FBI."

At long last, I had not only found someone who understood what I had undergone but who was also trying to assist *all* undercover officers.

Although the number and severity of flashbacks and nightmares had diminished through the years, I had still never figured out why I was experiencing them. They were triggered by a similar assignment, returning to the same location of the trauma, or discussing it. Each time I relived a traumatic incident, it lessened the emotional reaction of the incident. Every flashback and every nightmare was, in a way, a healing process, helping me to gradually face and accept what had happened.

"You will never forget," Chief Band counseled during our first conversation on the phone, "but you are not alone. "There are others like you out there."

Although we never met he had touched my soul. I immediately knew that he not only understood but had also walked the same path. With those few words, he set me free, releasing me from my feelings of isolation and loneliness. He had set me free from the futile struggle of trying to forget what I knew I could never forget. I had a newfound hope that I could one day end the piercing loneliness.

"You have got to meet Special Agent Rayfield," he said enthusiastically.

I never met Rayfield in person, but through our phone conversations we found an immediate understanding of each other's experience. We not only shared a parallel journey, but we had both also found a lifelong friend and mentor in FBI Chief Stephen Band.

Before reading that article, I had been struggling to erase and forget the past as everyone had insisted I do. But it had been impossible to put the unhealed wounds behind me.

The hurt and anger began to slowly dissolve only after I finally allowed myself to *remember* and *confront* the trauma of the incidents I had desperately tried to forget. I would later understand that the scars of the wounds in my soul would remain forever and permanently affect my life, but the eternal friendships I found in new friends would heal my soul.

Raychelle

March 23, 2001. Early, very early in the morning, on a spring day in the first year of the new millennium, we gathered quietly in the darkness of the crispy chill of the dawning of the new day.

From the different law enforcement agencies operating in the Aloha state, the hit teams began to arrive. Each member was identified by the large bold acronyms printed on their blue and yellow Spam shirts and vests, which would serve in part to identify us to each other, distinguish us from the bad guys, and protect us from death. Teams assembled, and introductions began.

"Jeff, FBI. Bill, ATF. Raychelle, HPD."

Raychelle Dungca was Filipino in ancestry and had a pretty face and a warm smile. She was not only an outstanding police officer; she was like a younger sister and had already become my lifelong friend. We had both been assigned to Team 2.

Most of us were meeting the law officers of the other federal agencies for the first time. Trust in each other's knowledge and abilities, though not yet developed, was given blindly in order to accomplish the mission we knew nothing about before this day. Anxieties and doubts were quelled by jokes, small pranks, and stories we shared to kill the silence of waiting.

"Llet's rock and roll!" the mission had commenced, and the teams moved out to their assigned targets.

After a six-month-long investigation involving the illegal trafficking of narcotics and firearms in the Ewa districts of the island of Oahu, eighteen federal warrants would be simultaneously executed in a coordinated effort between the FBI, ATF, and HPD.

Each of the seven teams began heading out for our destinations. What lay ahead remained unknown.

We put away our stories, we put away our jokes, we put away our personal lives and thoughts of our families safe at home. Our lifeline to each other was dependant on the transmissions of our radios, the monitoring ears of the FBI command post, and the watchful eyes of Alan and Jimmy in the HPD chopper that hovered above us like a blue dragonfly.

Dogs barked, cars stopped, and the neighborhood watched the execution of the search warrant as the members of the elite Specialized Services Division's strike force hit the house at our first assigned location.

When the perimeter was breached, a small, old, black and white poi dog named Sushi walked casually under the picnic table in the garage and watched us calmly. A monster-sized purebred Rottweiler watchdog yelped and scrambled between the wooden slats supporting the house. He urinated in fear when he got stuck between the slats as he was trying to escape to the underside of the structure.

The entry had been executed with excellent precision, timing, and professionalism, with no injuries and no incidents. The suspects had been identified and secured, along with more than ten purebred Rottweiler dogs and one mixed-breed dog named Sushi all living in the household.

Large rats scurried about in the main section of the house as we entered, obviously upset at our intrusion into their comfortable home. After releasing control of the scene and the suspects to our team, the SSD officers began washing off dog excrement stuck on the bottom of their shoes from inside of the house.

"The Power of Pakalolo" signs in large bold green letters had been painted on the windshield of a vehicle in the garage and on the outer walls of the front side of the house, clearly visible from the street. It seemed to advertise and announce that drugs were for sale. We knew we were at the right place.

Grandmothers and grandfathers in their forties, mothers and fathers in their twenties, and children—lots and lots of kids ranging from newborn to high school age—all lived together in the confines of the two-story single-family dwelling that had been divided into separate living areas.

The suspect was known as son, grandson, great-grandson, father, brother, and uncle to the different members of the household. He was sleeping in a small room behind the garage with his girlfriend, who was the mother of his six children, when the warrant was executed. His six children lay like sardines on a blanket on the bare concrete floor between his girlfriend's handicapped father and mother, while he and his girlfriend slept on a double bed behind the partition in the room.

When all the members of the household except the suspect and his girlfriend had been released, most of the adult females approached the uniformed law officers and engaged in light conversations, some smiling and carrying infants. Others warned the young ones not to tell anyone about the cops raiding their house.

No one in the entire household was gainfully employed except one adult male who had left for work before the warrant was executed. The suspect admitted that he didn't want to marry the mother of his six children, as he did not want to accept financial responsibility for them and lose the welfare money from the state.

FBI agents documented the evidence with expert efficiency, seizing large quantities of methamphetamine, marijuana, paraphernalia, and cash. Numerous pieces of beautiful Hawaiian jewelry worth thousands of dollars also lay sparkling on the dresser with the drugs in the suspect's room.

"No take my jewelry!" the suspect's girlfriend shrieked after seeming unmoved by the investigation. "It's mine! I'm on welfare and that's all I have!"

Raychelle and I glanced at each other, knowing we shared the same thought. Even with the countless hours we worked, we could not afford what she had.

The young men in the household began to edge their way outside of the house into the front yard, gathering at the chain link fence that enclosed the perimeter of the yard to peep at us from a distance. Numerous cars were passing by slowly, honking their horns and waving, some at the young men and some at us.

The large males humbly shaking and trembling just minutes before began to puff up their bodies and make snickering sounds when a few carloads of their friends pulled over to watch. They began to berate the law officers, speaking cockily in front of their friends, who seemed delighted at their boldness. Crossing their arms across their chests and spitting on the ground became the stance of the day. The circus had come to town, and the once terrified young men now fearlessly identified us as fuckin' clowns.

The loud audience of the circus became silent when I began to explain the warnings of possible seizure of their home, property, and assets for the illegal use of their property to traffic in narcotics.

"Do you understand the seizure of the narcotics and profits of your drug sales?" I asked after finishing my routine explanation of the forfeiture laws.

The suspect nodded silently.

"Do you understand the warnings of the seizure of your home and property should you continue your illegal activities?" I asked.

The suspect nodded with regret.

The rowdy circus was now a silent wake as the suspect hung on to a fluffy Rottweiler puppy for support.

The impudent members of the crowd, who had moved a few steps closer to me to listen to what I was saying, suddenly stepped back, and their once puffed-up bodies began to deflate and sag in a moment of enlightened awareness.

Raychelle and I watched as the *true* clowns of the day stopped their act of arrogance and began yelling at their large crowd of friends to leave immediately. A sudden silence filled the humid air of the hot Waianae morning, mingled with the stench of vaporizing dog urine and excrement.

Regrouping for the second hit of the day in a vacant lot, Raychelle and I stood under the small bits of shade provided by a large thorny Kiawe tree. Dust swirls added a little bit of softness to the harsh desertlike scenery. We took a few minutes to rehydrate and relax with our teammates before we continued on to the next target.

The exhausting day would finally come to an end with a successful mission. We would not only find new bonds of trust and friendship with the law officers from the other agencies, we would all go home to our families.

I received a call on the following morning from the first suspect's grandmother.

"We gathered in prayer as soon as all of you left," she said. "We are a Christian family, and my daughter was severely traumatized by the raid and what HPD and the FBI did to us! This has never ever happened before, but we knew you guys were watching us ever since my grandson was arrested before for the same thing. I want you to know that my daughter's ex-husband is FBI, and his sister is HPD, so I already called them!"

"Wasn't your daughter talking with the officers and smiling?" I asked, remembering her daughter's very friendly demeanor with the SSD officers.

"Okay, yes … but she was severely traumatized after you guys left! Listen," she paused, "I just want the money back!"

◈

Chapter 21
Aloha and Farewell

Happy Holidays 2002

Thanksgiving: a time to put our self-importance away
And take a moment to be thankful
For the things we have
For the lessons we've learned
For the time we shared in tears and laughter

A time to reflect on the beauty of the sunrise
On the peaceful tranquility of a sunset
A time to appreciate our moment in history
And those who shared that moment with us

Tomorrow is promised to no one
Tomorrow might be too late to say thank you
Tomorrow might be too late to say I'm sorry
Tomorrow might be too late to say I love you
I have never given in to the odds
And I will always believe in miracles
And the strength of the mind and a true spirit

But I will never be ready to say good-bye
I love you, Dad

Journal entry: November 2002

The holiday season had arrived, but instead of excitement and joy, there was a sense of foreboding. Too many of our relatives had passed away on Christmas Eve, and my father had just been diagnosed with throat cancer. His father too had been diagnosed with the same disease at about the same age.

Our customary dinner of thanks was scheduled a few days earlier, since his cancer surgery was scheduled on Thanksgiving Day.

During dinner preparations, my younger sister Cheryl pulled me over to the corner of the kitchen to talk quietly. We had both sensed that someone in our family was going to leave us during this holiday season.

"I'm going to go first," she said seriously. ""I have no regrets. I have lived my life fully but can't bear to see dad or anyone else in the family go first! If someone has to leave, it's going to be me first. Then I'll help everyone else come through. Remember your promise!" she added.

"What promise?" I asked, hearing the seriousness and conviction in my baby sister's voice.

"You promised to be there with me when the time came," she answered quietly.

Cheryl reminded me of the pact we had made as kids, a pact we upheld through the years.

"I'll always be wherever you need me!" I answered, adding, "But if anyone has to go, I'll go." I knew that something was coming, too.

"You can't!" Cheryl answered in alarm. "Michele is too young, and my kids don't need me anymore. And besides, only the *good* die young!" she said, trying to bring a little levity to our heart-to-heart talk.

"Sometimes you have to fight for what's right, but you have to learn when to duck and run." I remembered what Dad had told me. "Sometimes, it's not worth the fight, but if you're going to fight, then fight with everything you've got!"

If there was anyone who could beat the odds, it was our dad. My father's surgery a few days later was not entirely successful.

For Cheryl

On December 6, 2002, at two o'clock in the afternoon, while assigned to the Narcotics Vice Division and preparing to assist on a search warrant, I heard that inner voice loud and clear: *Go home!*

"I have to leave, captain. I have to go home," I said to Captain Kevin Lima.

Captain Lima nodded, adding, "Let me know if you need anything." He had sensed that something was very wrong if I had asked to leave in the middle of preparations for a raid, but I couldn't explain what I myself did not understand.

I immediately left for home, still confused about why I was doing what I was doing. I had never left work so early before and had never walked out of a pending raid.

When assigned to Vice, I usually returned home around midnight. Captain Kevin Lima had been the commander who had argued on my behalf against the assistant chiefs who had refused to allow me to accept Chief Band's invitation to attend a seminar at the FBI Academy in Quantico, Virginia.

One of the assistant chiefs had been offended that I, instead of one of them, had received a special invitation.

I attended the Behavioral Science Unit seminar on my vacation time in order to avoid further controversy.

At 2:30 p.m., I unlocked my front door and stepped over the threshold into the house. Suddenly, I heard an explosive sound.

Turning towards the sound, I saw my old German shepherd, Casey, looking at me through the glass patio doors and heard her whimpering. I went outside to see what was wrong.

Casey ran towards the hedge outside of my bedroom window, and I followed. She glanced back to see if I was following her and stopped at the hedge, whimpering softly and looking anxiously out towards the street below.

I stood between the Christmas angels sitting on the top of my hedge and peered down into the street just below. I immediately recognized my father's truck, smashed up against the gigantic city and county tree I had so often asked to be removed. I shook my head in disbelief and looked again.

It was not my father slumped over behind the steering wheel; it was my sister Cheryl lying motionless in the driver's seat.

In disbelief and panic, I ran out to the truck and realized at once that my sister was dying. I had seen too many fatalities and recognized the signs. I immediately understood the urgency in the voice I had heard and realized that it had sent me home for this reason.

"I'm here, Pips," I said to my sister, calling her by the nickname that only I had used, but knew that there was nothing I could do. I had helped so many victims involved in motor vehicle accidents and assaults, but I could do nothing for my own sister. I was outraged and desperate at being so helpless.

Don't let her suffer, God! I demanded, screaming silently in my heart.

Cheryl was still breathing on her own but was lapsing in and out of consciousness.

The steering wheel had been bent forward by the impact of her chest against it. My sister already had a bad heart and was being considered for a pacemaker. On top of all of this, she was deaf in one ear and was losing the last of her hearing in the other.

I knew that she had massive internal injuries and that there was virtually nothing I could do to help her as I listened to her labored breathing.

A witness who passed Cheryl in the opposite direction a moment before the accident returned to help. Cheryl was not speeding, she said, totally confused at what had happened.

Mom and Dad ran up to my house, and a few days later, I learned that I had called them on the phone and told them to hurry to my house and that my sister wasn't going to make it. I couldn't remember calling them.

I gently held Cheryl's hand and whispered, "Mom and Dad are here."

I was suddenly sent back in time and relived every significant moment in her life that we had shared together. I glanced behind me and saw her as a little toddler following me around. She was next to me catching ladybugs for races, and then I went through every trauma and drama of our high school years. I was standing next to her as a witness to her marriage and then witnessing her great joy and happiness at the birth of each of her children.

All the significant incidents in her life we shared together came flooding back, up to our last heart-to-heart Thanksgiving pact.

"I love you, Pips," I said softly, and Cheryl opened her eyes for the last time.

"I love you, too," she said with a silent gaze into my eyes, and then she closed her eyes forever.

A later autopsy would reveal that she had suffered a massive heart attack just half a block away from her home, where she lived with my parents.

I saw a little person follow me around
I saw a little person on the road of life walk down.
I think she said, "I love you," and then she made me know
That I had kept my promise made oh so long ago
That I would come to find her, wherever she should be
That I would be there at her side and bring her home with me
She made me keep my promise, and I thank GOD for this
That I could be a witness to her last Good-bye and Kiss
All her pain had melted . . . all her sorrows drowned,
But I keep looking back to see if she's around

Journal entry: December 18, 2002

My Last Undercover Investigation

In 2004, I was assigned to assist a covert investigation that had been initiated by another division and had grown on its own to encompass numerous felony offenses.

This time, I was the detective and assigned to be the investigation's coordinator and case agent instead of the undercover officer. My involvement in the investigation, however, remained secret and known to only the commanders of the divisions involved.

Several suspects had not bothered to hide their connections to family and friends in the Honolulu Police Department on this island that often seemed, for covert law enforcement investigations, to be too small for comfort. Extra confidentiality precautions were taken to keep the undercover officers safe and the investigation uncompromised.

I had come to know those investigators assigned to other divisions and federal agencies who worked well in teams and had earned credibility for their knowledge and experience in their respective fields. None were arrogant, loose-mouthed, glory-seekers. Each of these investigators were carefully selected and asked to assist in the investigation as the need for their expertise had arisen.

"What can I do to help?" was always the response to requests for their assistance. They never made demands for credit, recognition, or overtime before the task was done or as a condition of their participation. I knew I could count on them to fulfill their commitments and their integrity.

A few HPD supervisors, as well as investigators in other federal agencies, had heard about the covert operation and began to make inquires.

"Who's in charge? What's going on?"

Rumors circulated, bringing unwanted attention to the investigation that almost compromised the safety of the undercover officers and the confidentiality of the operation. Each had subsequently approached members of investigative team with demands to participate.

"I should be involved. I should be in charge. I will help you if you make sure you give me recognition, credit, and overtime for my help."

They had made demands and presented ultimatums for their assistance without contribution or even knowing what the investigation involved.

I was denied a Special Assignment status and had to work on the covert investigation on my own time. Overtime was denied by my lieutenant in spite of captain's orders to properly credit me for my work. His refusal to properly document the hours that I worked for over a year would severely impact my retirement income.

"You're not working for me. I'm not involved in this," the lieutenant had said too often, especially when I assisted detectives in other units with their investigations and warrants. I worked a double assignment, while others in my unit were awarded a Special Assignment status and relieved of their assignments for "personal reasons."

He had called me into his office and accused me of starting a task force without authority or permission. More than that, he was obviously offended and unable to understand why *he* was not assigned as the supervisor in the investigation, even after informing me that he didn't get along with almost every investigator involved in the investigation.

The investigation was one of the most successful multifaceted investigations of the department, primarily because each investigator worked in support of each other instead of competing with each other for recognition.

Together, we worked through difficulties and adversities and made a major impact in the fight against property crimes and the sale and distribution of narcotics and firearms. These law officers were not only outstanding investigators in their respective fields, but I had come to know them as my brothers.

Sergeant Teddy Chun and Officer Jeff "Keahi" Omai from the Kalihi Crime Reduction Unit, and officer Victorino Tolentino Jr. from the Narcotics Vice Division were the undercover officers in the yearlong covert investigation.

Detective Gordon Gomes from the Narcotics Vice Division and Detective Brian Johnson from the Criminal Investigation Division's Robbery Detail were the supervisors in charge of their respective investigations and evidence.

Special Agent Joseph Lau from the Bureau of Alcohol, Tobacco, Firearms, and Explosives and Special Agent Ray Yuen from the Federal Bureau of Investigations supervised their respective federal investigations.

Special Agents Leroy Fujishige and Jonathan Dela Vega, two retired Honolulu Police Department detectives, represented the National Insurance Crime Bureau and assisted with the recovery of the brand-new stolen vehicles we purchased, and coordinated the insurance aspects of the auto theft investigations.

Thirty-five suspects were subsequently arrested for narcotics, firearms, robbery, auto thefts, and money laundering—federal and state offenses.

Members of the Specialized Services Division, more commonly known as SWAT, and units from the Kalihi, Waikiki, Pearl City, and Waianae Crime Reduction Units assisted in a successful arrest and asset seizure silent raid that was accomplished without injury or incident.

The yearlong investigation was ended prematurely when a newspaper reporter refused to hold the story. In callous disregard of the safety of the undercover officers still active in the investigation, news of the successful raid hit the front page, circumventing all of our efforts to continue. The reporter had refused to identify from whom he obtained a copy of my arrest warrants and affidavits.

Lost Harmony/Transitions

I saw many changes in the department through my tour of duty. Most were good changes, but some had gone too far. It seemed that some of the good ideals of the old school had been forgotten, and a new school attitude was born. The true mission of our oath to serve had somehow been lost in the transition, although some still fought to perpetuate it.

…TRANSITIONS…

OLD SCHOOL	NEW SCHOOL
Be truthful---	*but don't stick your neck out*
Honorable conduct-	*Kiss ass, PR and bullshit to get ahead*
Justice for all---	*Depends on who you know*
Spiritual Faith	*Politically incorrect*
Ethics, do what is right---	*only if you don't make waves*
Effort, give 100%---	*just do the minimum required*
Commitment/Dedication---	*"trying to save the world?"*
Constitutional Rights---	*Rights of suspects, not victims*
Integrity---	*Just go with the flow*
Accountability	*Depends who you are*
Sacrifice---	*as long as it's someone else's*
Morale: The responsibility of every person---	*Blaming only the Chiefs*
Wearing the Badge Is a privilege---	*is a right because they passed the test*
Loyalty/Respect: Works both ways	*destroyed without support, fairness*
Whining, Cry Baby---	*Hostile work environment victims*
(Inept, unable to perform under the standards)	*(It's always someone else's fault)*

The higher the Rank---   *The higher the Rank*
The more responsible you are to guide   *More personal privileges, take And*
support your subordinates   *care of friends; responsible to public*
and politics

The needs of the Many---   *The needs of the One*
Outweigh the needs of the One   *outweigh the needs of the Many*
(move or discipline the inept Officer)   *(take care of the inept Officer)*

It's not who you favor; it's who can do a good job and get the job done. To disregard this rule is to negate the efforts of good workers. The best way to destroy morale is to be unfair. Time to stop the whining, the selfishness, the pettiness, and the arrogance of power. Find the balance, find the peace.

Journal entry: December, 2004

It became a tradition that every Christmas, I would decorate whatever division I was assigned to with a silvery blue Christmas garland attached to the ceiling that linked each detail together as a family.

A huge mural depicting every person assigned to the division was also created. Many of the officers and civilian personnel would add a personal touch of artistry or a message in a dialogue bubble to the shared holiday project.

It brought the detectives and the civilian staff together with one agenda, showing we were all connected to each other, and cops deserve a happy holiday, too!

In December of 2004, I did my annual Christmas poster for the Criminal Investigation Division, but this year's New Year message was different.

On the New Year's mural, I posted my journal entry "Transitions." I also posted the old Oath of Office my friends and I had sworn to, next to the new politically correct oath, which read like a contract.

The old Oath of Office had been deemed politically incorrect and changed because it ended with the phrase "So help me God."

I was warned to remove the "Transitions" poster, because it was too controversial, as well as the old Oath of Office, which would possibly be deemed too offensive and politically incorrect.

When the detectives of the division learned about the warning I received, they began to sign the "Lost Harmony/Transitions" poster in support of its contents and message.

They too were tired of the favoritism afforded to a few who had befriended the commanders and the unfair distribution of investigations that overwhelmed the hard workers and favored those who whined and complained with a minimum caseload.

I have the right to say "Merry Christmas," and I have the right to believe in God, I thought sadly.

"They can't stand the truth, Jo. Leave the poster up, and we'll back you up!" the seasoned detectives encouraged as the list of signatures grew. But I removed everything a week later before it became a protest for Internal Affairs to investigate against all the detectives who signed the poster.

TRUTH is universal. It remains constant and transcends time.
But a clever man can manipulate true facts and perpetuate a lie by words not spoken and half-truths told.

IDEALS OF JUSTICE: judgment without prejudice, politics, or favoritism.
Justice is a reflection of time and place. Its meaning is measured and identified by those who sit in judgment of man's decided laws. Therefore, it is inconsistent; it is not universal; it is not blind. What is justice today may not be deemed so tomorrow.

HONOR: true honor, is being accountable and responsible for our own actions or the choices we made, regardless of whether that conduct appears to be worthy of honor.
I have learned that the true essence of these words is not always manifested in those who represent the law. It is not always a priority of those in power in business or government, or in the souls of those who justify wars between the different churches of the world. It dwells in the depths of each man's heart and soul … or it does not.

We have always been free to create our own destinies, in spite of our fate. Therefore, I have lost my concerns about judgment and being judged and have learned the futility of argument and debate.

We alone can set ourselves free by accepting responsibility for our own conduct and choices. We will be free by letting go of expectations and our dependencies on others, and the false promise that there will always be a tomorrow.

Therefore, I no longer stay where I do not belong. I do not take or accept what is not rightfully mine. I do not pretend or try to be what I will never be.

In these ways, I have set myself free.

Journal entry: 2004

Time to Leave

In November of 2005, the Honolulu Police Department was finally given approval to introduce the only program that openly addressed undercover stressors and helped to train law officers from all law enforcement agencies for the covert assignment.

Chief Steve Band of the FBI's Behavioral Science Unit and members of the FBI's Safeguard Unit flew to Hawaii to introduce their program to the various Vice Divisions in the State of Hawaii, through the sponsorship of Hawaii HIDTA, High Intensity Drug Trafficking Areas, and the successful efforts of Officers Patrick Fo and Stan Sales of Honolulu Police Department's Narcotics Vice Division.

Law officers from different agencies in different states gathered to offer their experience and expertise, support and friendship, to Hawaii's undercover officers. It was the lifeline I had vowed to see in place before I left the force.

Each instructor represented the honor and integrity of the badges they had earned through loyalty and sacrifice. Eddie, Steve, Epi, Mike, Mike, Vince, Beau, and Sonny were the instructors of the program, and the recently retired Chief Steve Band was an honored guest speaker.

Even in the brief period of time that we spent together, I found an immediate kinship and understanding with the instructors that I had never found before. We had all made the same journey.

I was given the honor of introducing the program and addressing issues unique to female undercover operatives.

"It's time to go," the familiar voice said one night in a dream, "time to do what you're supposed to do. Write down your journey and what you have learned."

I retired eight months later.

One month after I retired, I learned that the Hawaii State retirement system had taken me off the active duty list and failed to keep me listed as a retiree. I had lost all my retirement benefits, and once again, I did not exist.

The Oath of Office

I solemnly swear to faithfully support the Constitution and Laws of the United States of America, and the Constitution and laws of the State of Hawaii. And that I will conscientiously and impartially discharge my duties as a police officer in the Police Department of the City and County of Honolulu, State of Hawaii, and any and all other duties devolving upon me in connection with such office ... so help me God.

Honolulu Police Department Oath of Office, 1980

The completion of a promise of Service
The fulfillment of a solemn Oath
The end of a lifestyle unique
Dedicated to the pursuit of Peace, Truth, and Justice

A fond Aloha to all
With memories of shared trials and tribulations
I bequeath to you my love and friendship
As I leave to continue on my journey through life

But there is a universal bond
Understood by all Law Officers
That the badge of the Sentinel of Justice
Can never be retired
It will remain forever in your heart

As my new adventure begins
I will take with me the memories
The tears and laughter from the past
And I will remember always
The strength of the Brotherhood
The shield of the Ohana
And friendship everlasting

Journal entry: July 1, 2006

CONCLUSION

By the time I retired in July of 2006, I had completed almost twenty-seven years of service. Twelve of those years were served in uniformed patrol and fifteen years were served in the investigative divisions. The changes in the department during my tour of duty were indeed great and impressive, and a few women had already attained the ranks of commander and assistant chief.

Sexual Harassment and hostile work environment laws had not only been established but were now enforced within all ranks of the police department. Yet like with the Bill of Rights, there were those who manipulated the laws and abused them to protect themselves from being accountable for their misconduct.

In the eighties, men and women, regardless of height or age, were required to pass the same physical agility tests. In time, the physical tests were changed to accommodate age and gender, and women were not forced to cut their hair.

From handwritten reports and manual typewriters that were too often broken or missing keys, we stepped into the new age of computers. We went from carbon paper and Wite-Out to scanners and printers and onward to a paperless environment of digital imaging,

From the call boxes of yesterday to portable radios, and from payphones to cell phones, our communication abilities became almost instantaneous and enhanced officer safety.

From 38-caliber revolvers to 9-mm semi-automatic pistols and less lethal weapons, we advanced in our weaponry and are now community oriented. Most of all, officer safety became the priority and replaced the competition for stats.

Technology had indeed thrust us into a new age. But no matter how specialized we had become, we still needed to work together to accomplish our tasks, and the age-old lessons of truth, honor, and integrity, passed down by from generation to generation, could never be replaced by advanced technology. It could only be promoted and perpetuated by those who led, taught, and supervised us.

In my twelve years of service in the Patrol Division, I found a special kinship with my uniformed beat partners. We spent each day together confronting those who chose to embody what was worst in our human nature.

Through difficulties, tragedies, violence, and death, my patrol partners taught me the true courage of the uniformed patrol officer. We were first to respond, first to confront, and the first line of defense for the innocent victims. It was a rare blessing that we might arrive in time to circumvent injury, damage, loss, or death. It was devastating when one of us fell in the line of duty.

I came to know the hearts behind the voices of the dispatchers, who were truly worthy of deepest respect. They vicariously experienced the stress and difficulties we faced in the streets, and like guardian angels, they often became our lifeline as we dealt with uncertainty and chaos.

As a detective in the Criminal Investigation Division and the Narcotics Vice Division, I learned the meaning of commitment. It was an honor to work with those exceptional investigators who spent endless and exhausting hours completing an investigation, even without the promise of overtime or compensation. There was no consideration for much-needed sleep or time to see our families in the forty-eight-hour rule. If we failed in our commitment to finish our investigation in that designated time, then we failed the victims who trusted us, and the suspect would be set free.

The prosecuting attorneys, who scrutinized every fact and detail of our work, also screened the honesty and integrity of our words. They would continue our efforts in the courts and represent us when we testified. Some saw the demands of the prosecutors as unyielding obstacles; some saw them as team players. But every prosecutor shared one steadfast rule: never falsify your reports or lie in your testimony. A few would become my lifelong friends, and without them, my efforts would have been lost.

Instead of having the smallest, most unassuming officer, attired in plain clothes, breaching the threshold to gain entry at search warrants, it eventually became mandatory that all raids were executed by the officers of the elite Specialized Services Division, highly trained in tactical operations. They were first to enter, making the scene safe for the investigative units. They are the police officers' sentinels.

The Honolulu Police Department has indeed changed and continues to evolve; yet perhaps in some way, we have lost the heart and honor of the old school traditions.

The basic needs of the people all over the world are the same: food, clothing, shelter, and the right to live without fear of being victimized for what we have or who we are.

Law officers all over the world share the same challenges and difficulties. We pray for courage and strength to do our jobs well and that we survive the day to return home to our loved ones.

May our commanders and supervisors, in heaven and on earth, continue to guide our steadfast pursuit of the ideals of justice, and inspire our abilities to act with truth and honor.

Every living entity has an inner voice
Bears, bees, flowers, and trees pay heed to it
And live in harmony with the earth
Only Man has lost the capacity to hear it

Some talk too much, some yell too loud
Some choose not to listen
Some distort the message to fit their own agenda

The message is simple; it is a universal truth
We are all connected to each other
In spite of our differences

Only Man has been given the gift of choice
To choose his own path and his own destiny
To destroy one another, to disrupt the balance
To live contrary to the natural order of things
Is to destroy ourselves and the future of our children

The artists of the world have already begun to bridge the world with rainbows, by sharing the
wonderful diversity of cultures through music, paints, dance, and sonnets

Journal entry: October 1, 2006

My career in the Honolulu Police Department was a spiritual journey of learning and awakening. Almost thirty years have now passed since I ventured forth to seek the true meaning of truth and honor in the field of justice. I found it in the hearts of those exemplary law officers, male and female, who brought honor to their respective badges.

It was truly my honor to serve with them.

❦

EPILOGUE

All the suspects in my undercover investigations plead or were found guilty by trial.

Undercover Officer Terry Bledsoe continues his career with the Honolulu Police Department, as a Detective in the Criminal Investigation Division.

Undercover Officer Kerry Finuff retired as a Lieutenant in 2004 after twenty-six years of dedicated service. He is now a disaster assistance employee with the Department of Homeland Defense, Federal Emergency Management Agency.

Richard Fujita retired as a Major in 1987, after twenty-six years of dedicated service. He continued his career in federal law enforcement as an agent with U.S. Customs and Border Protection until he retired in 2002.

Wallace Jennings Akeo retired as a Lieutenant in 1991, after thirty years of dedicated service. He has since passionately pursued the perpetuation of Polynesian arts, music, and culture.

Clarence DeCaires Jr. retired as a Detective in 1994, after twenty-seven years of dedicated service. He was ordained as a Roman Catholic deacon on June 15, 1987, while still a police officer in the Narcotics Vice Division, and commissioned as a Honolulu Police Department Chaplain on August 30, 2008, a day after his daughter's graduation from the Honolulu Police Department's police academy.

Alfredo Torco retired as a Lieutenant in 2001, after thirty-five years of dedicated service. He became a substitute teacher, assistant varsity coach, and historian at Farrington High School, where he mentors students to help prepare them for their futures. His sons, Ty and Travis, continue their careers in law enforcement as federal agents, and Terrence works in the airline industry for Hawaiian Airlines.

Robert Lung retired as a Sergeant in 2008, after thirty-six years and nine months of dedicated service. He is now a highway safety coordinator and consultant with the State of Hawaii Department of Transportation.

Victor V. Vierra left the Honolulu Police Department at the rank of Captain in 1988 after 19 years of dedicated service. He continued his career in law enforcement as the Chief of Police with the Hawaii County Police Department until he retired in 1994. He is now a private investigator in a partnership with Russell Botelho Sr. doing business as Victor Vierra and Associates.

Keith M. Kaneshiro left the Honolulu City Prosecutor's Office in 1996 after eight years of dedicated service of unwavering integrity. He is now in private practice.

Kevin Lima continues his career with the Honolulu Police Department and is now the Assistant Chief of the Investigative Bureau.

Gordon Gomes and Raymond Quon continue their careers as lieutenants with the Honolulu Police Department in the Criminal Investigation Division.

Brian Johnson, Derrick Kiyotoki, Gordon Makishima, Michael Ogawa, and Victorino C.Tolentino Jr. continue their careers with the Honolulu Police Department as Detectives in the Criminal Investigation Division.

James Nobriga and Andrew Tsukano continue their careers with the Honolulu Police Department as sergeants in the Patrol Division, and Roland Takasato Jr. continues his career as a sergeant in the Waikiki Crime Reduction Unit.

Raychelle Dungca, Jeffrey Keahi Omai, Stan Sales, and Patrick Fo continue their careers as Officers in different investigative divisions in the Honolulu Police Department.

Theodore Chun retired as a Sergeant in December of 2008 after thirty-seven years of dedicated service.

Ray Yuen continues his career as a Special Agent with the Federal Bureau of Investigation.

Senior Special Agent Joseph Lau continues his career with the United States Department of Justice, Bureau of Alcohol, Tobacco, Firearms, and Explosives as the resident agent in charge of the District of Hawaii.

Dr. Stephen R. Band, a former Elizabeth, New Jersey, police officer and FBI Special Agent, was Chief of the FBI's Undercover Safeguard Unit and the FBI's famous Behavioral Science Unit prior to his retirement from the Bureau in 2005. He now resides in Virginia and serves as a consultant to the Intelligence and Law Enforcement Communities.

AFTERWORD

IN SEARCH OF TRUTH AND HONOR

Every belief I had was challenged
Every prejudice I had was confronted
Until I was left with nothing
Until I had lost my identity and myself

I had learned with much difficulty
That the true identity of man
Cannot be known by what he looks like
The origin of his ancestry or his gender

The true worth of man cannot be judged
By the clothes he wears, his badge, his religion
Or symbols of his allegiance

The true essence of man can only be measured
By the clarity of his vision
The lessons of Truth and Honor he perpetuates
And the unselfish and universal love he holds in his heart

True success is then perhaps achieved
When we are finally recognized and respected
Not for what we are or our origins
But what we stand for

As long as there are those who represent evil and bring darkness into this world
There will be those who represent goodness and light to confront it
And the hope of a better tomorrow shall never be lost
A world of universal peace and harmony
Is therefore one day attainable

PHOTO GALLERY
The Undercover Officers

Joanne Takasato
1980   1981

_____

Kerry Finuff
1979   1980

_____

Terry Bledsoe
1980   1979

_____

Internal Affairs

Wally Akeo
2001   1993

Clarence DeCaires Jr.
1981   2008

Alfredo Torco
1975   1995

Richard Fujita
2009   1986

Police Academy

Andrew Tsukano
2002

Robert Lung
2001

Aloha Photos

Joseph Lau
ATF Senior Special Agent Joseph Lau
1981   1993

Criminal Investigation Division
Robbery Detail
June 30, 2006

Detectives: James Nobriga, Raymond Quon Jr., Brian Johnson,
Taro Nakamura, Derrick Kiyotoki, Michael Ogawa,
Gordon Makishima, Joanne Takasato